The Upper Room
Disciplines
2007

UPPER
ROOM BOOKS®
NASHVILLE

AN OUTLINE FOR SMALL-GROUP USE OF *DISCIPLINES*

Here is a simple plan for a one-hour, weekly group meeting based on reading *Disciplines*. One person may act as convener every week, or the role can rotate among group members. You may want to light a white Christ candle each week to signal the beginning of your time together.

OPENING

Convener: Let us come into the presence of God.

Others: Lord Jesus Christ, thank you for being with us. Let us hear your word to us as we speak to one another.

SCRIPTURE

Convener reads the scripture suggested for that day in *Disciplines*. After a one- or two-minute silence, convener asks: What did you hear God saying to you in this passage? What response does this call for? (*Group members respond in turn or as led.*)

REFLECTION

- What scripture passage(s) and meditation(s) from this week was (were) particularly meaningful for you? Why? (*Group members respond in turn or as led.*)
- What actions were you nudged to take in response to the week's meditations? (*Group members respond in turn or as led.*)
- Where were you challenged in your discipleship this week? How did you respond to the challenge? (*Group members respond in turn or as led.*)

PRAYING TOGETHER

Convener says: Based on today's discussion, what people and situations do you want us to pray for now and in the coming week?

Convener or other volunteer then prays about the concerns named.

DEPARTING

Convener says: Let us go in peace to serve God and our neighbors in all that we do.

Adapted from *The Upper Room Daily Devotional Guide*, January–February 2001. © 2000 The Upper Room. Used by permission.

Cover design: Ed Maksimowicz
Cover photographer: Jeff Wiles
First Printing: 2006

Lectionary texts from *The Revised Common Lectionary* copyright © 1992 by The Consultation on Common Texts (CCT), P. O. Box 340003, Room 381, Nashville, TN 37203-0003 USA. All rights reserved. Reprinted with permission.

Scripture quotations not otherwise identified are from the *New Revised Standard Version Bible* © 1989, Division of Christian Education of the National Council of the Churches of Christ in the United States of America. Used by permission. All rights reserved.

Scripture quotations designated RSV are from the *Revised Standard Version Bible*, copyright 1952 (2nd edition, 1971) by the Division of Christian Education of the National Council of the Churches of Christ in the United States of America. Used by permission. All rights reserved.

Scripture quotations designated THE MESSAGE are taken from *The Message* by Eugene H. Peterson, Copyright © 1993, 1994, 1995, 1996, 2000. Used by permission of Nav-Press Publishing Group. All rights reserved.

Scripture quotations designated NIV are from the *Holy Bible, New International Version*. NIV. Copyright © 1973, 1978, 1984 by the International Bible Society. Used by permission of Zondervan Publishing House. All rights reserved.

Scripture quotations designated REB are taken from the Revised English Bible, copyright © Oxford University Press and Cambridge University Press 1989. All rights reserved.

Scripture quotations designated KJV are from the King James Version of the Bible.

ISBN–13: 978-0-8358-9820-1
ISBN–10: 0-8358-9820-2

Printed in the United States of America

Contents

Foreword

I like reading the Bible in unlikely places—in traffic court, a busy hotel lobby, a long bank line, and on a beach in a 40 mph wind.

Windy or not, the words arrive with jarring impact in such unexpected corners of life. I've read the Christmas story in a newsroom, psalms at the Grand Canyon, Ecclesiastes at thirty-six thousand feet. I recommend it.

These aren't stunts. They're memorable exercises, for two reasons. First, Bible reading in familiar confines can become routine. The words can get dulled by habits of place.

A second reason: Reading scripture in far-flung places reveals the Bible's reach. Perusing Ecclesiastes on a night flight at 550 miles an hour, you are visited by words like "for God is in heaven and you upon earth; therefore let your words be few" (5:2).

At such gravity-defying heights, it's a startling reminder that the human predicament is never quite out of range of the strange pull of the Bible. Even in this still-new century of religious pluralism and laments about biblical illiteracy, scripture summons a person to amazement, consolation, decision, and spiritual realism.

Sometimes it whispers, sometimes shouts. Falteringly I seek it out. Or unfalteringly it finds me.

Not long ago in the car, creeping along in a driving rain, I noticed one of those outdoor church marquee signs: "Believe in the good news," quoting Jesus in the Gospel of Mark. The traffic was thick and tense, and I was preoccupied just trying to get through an afternoon of heavy weather.

It was one of those moments symbolic of the vexations of life. In a world where everybody's navigating through the daily news of our lives, figuring out what's authentic and what's bogus, hoping to fill the hole of dread and ignorance, here was a plain-spoken announcement about good news: the kingdom of God is at hand.

Miserably waiting there in traffic, I had to shake my head, smiling. Funny that a word like *news*, with its anxiously modern, secular associations would show up in the ancient message of

Jesus nearly two thousand years before Web sites, cable, and the *New York Times*. The daily news is furiously revised every half-hour, always correcting or contradicting itself. The Good News stands opposite, serene; the same yesterday, today, tomorrow. The words of Jesus patiently wait for me to catch up to their truth.

I feel that way about the Bible every time I open it: It stands ready to resume the conversation, the argument, the sheer over-whelming story line of failure and redemption and human des-tiny. This bundle of Gospels and epistles, thunderous histories and wisdom was somehow gathered and preserved all those centuries ago and sits nearby even now, as if in safekeeping, until the next person arrives to come to grips with its world-bending speech.

Every edition of *Disciplines* makes this point: It provides a daily record of encounters with scripture and an invitation to readers to seek what news awaits them.

Days later, still thinking about that marquee sign, I pulled into a used bookstore in search of a replacement copy for an old study Bible. I found a nice RSV edition, unmarred by any scribbles. Or so I thought. When I got home with it I noticed a single passage on page 802 marked in yellow. The defacement dismayed me until I read the highlighted passage: "Two things I ask of thee; deny them not to me before I die: Remove far from me false-hood and lying; give me neither poverty nor riches; feed me with the food that is needful for me, lest I be full, and deny thee, and say, 'Who is the Lord?' or lest I be poor, and steal, and pro-fane the name of God" (Prov. 30:8-9).

What a credo. I had not remembered it. It spoke to every-thing—my private temptations and lapses, our national politics and fear. This latest sudden encounter only reminded me that scripture keeps breaking out, making a straight line from its ancient setting to this morning's very need. It hears the question of every generation, "Who is the LORD?" and answers with secret power for every reader.

—RAY WADDLE

Columnist and author, living in Nashville, Tennessee; his latest book is *Against the Grain: Unconventional Wisdom from Ecclesiastes* (Upper Room Books).

The Peace of Israel, the Hope of Creation

January 1–7, 2007 • Amy Laura Hall[‡]

MONDAY, JANUARY 1 • Read Psalm 8:3-4; Ecclesiastes 3:9-13

We have awaited the arrival of a weary young woman, a strong donkey, and a patient father to the stable. We have anticipated the birth of the son through whom the world was created, born now, wrapped in strips of cloth, surrounded by livestock. And we have celebrated the joy to the world that is Emmanuel. With tree and lights and neighbors and family, some of us have spent a week set apart, a week of holy holidays. Even for those who work outside the home during the time between Christmas and New Year's Day, the interim week has a different rhythm, time not fully within the normal everyday.

Now we anticipate the new year and a return to the real world. For most people, New Year's Day marks the impending return to the regular work week. For many people in retail, New Year's Day marks the impending return to a work week full of grouchy returns—a rather abrupt end to holiday cheer. What is January 2 that God is mindful of it? What have we gained from spending Advent in anticipation and Christmas in celebration? What is our toil that comes tomorrow that God cares for it? What gain have we for our Christmas sabbath from ordinary toil?

The scripture readings for today and tomorrow offer a particular hope. The same one whose fingers stitched together the fragments of the universe, setting moon and stars in the heavens, has also come to be mindful of us.

PRAYER: Lord, make me mindful of you—you, who are always mindful of me. I cannot know what you have done from the beginning to the end. But I can ask for the gift of knowing you are with me tomorrow. Amen.

[‡]Professor of theological ethics, Duke Divinity School, Durham, North Carolina.

TUESDAY, JANUARY 2 • Read Matthew 25:37-39

In Matthew's Gospel, the ones called righteous seem quite surprised by the revelation that they have, in their daily work, given sustenance, solace, welcome, and clothing to Jesus himself. Lord, when was it that we encountered you in our daily lives? When were you there with us? If Jesus Christ is God with us, does this mean that he goes with us into the day after New Year's Day? Does he come down to earth and enter ordinary, mortal time?

Reading Matthew's story with yesterday's readings echoing in our imaginations, we may be given eyes to see the return to our New Year's work in a new way. *We* are ones cared for by the incarnate Lord, who came to be with us in the business of our toil. The Wise One who wrote Ecclesiastes has seen the busyness that God has given to everyone and knows it can be seen as either nothing or everything—as either one darned task after another or as mortal time and mortal work redeemed. Christ came to define our daily work as God's gift—that we might eat and drink and take pleasure in all our toil—even the work that comes tomorrow and the day after that.

In the midst of this gracious gift, we may become gracious. Our work may come through care for others in our home, through patience with coworkers who seem anything but righteous. For some, the work of patience outside the home must be combined with a second shift of patience within the families to which we return. Will there be forgiveness and grace sufficient for this day, and the next? The daily work of such care and patience can seem to be a burden that cannot possibly be rendered righteous. But God is mindful. God is with us, giving hope sufficient for the toil of righteousness. When I cannot see it as such, God may be present in Christ, redeeming my efforts in spite of my lack.

PRAYER: Lord, give us eyes to see. Make us gracious and redeem our feeble efforts. Amen.

In the time of waiting that is Advent, Christians read the prophets. We mark the time forward, forward into the birth of the Messiah through whom the nations will be saved. Words from Israel's prophets about a time when all will be made new often sound discordant—not quite in tune with the "most wonderful time of the year." They break into the daily domestic and marketed preparation for Christmas with a somewhat rude reminder. The birth of Jesus Christ is not primarily about us.

What do I mean by this? By anticipating the birth of Christ with the prophets, Christians mark time forward with the people of Israel. We find ourselves marking time as those adopted into a story of God's first beloved. God creates Jacob, marks him as his own. As Jacob limps away from God's wrestling match, he limps away as one marked—created, called forth, and reformed as God's own. Jacob becomes Israel, and the scriptures attest that God's first beloved is Israel. Some people have called this the scandal of God's particularity. God chose to make God's own a particular people living on a particular scrap of land. The redemption brought through Christ is thus one that has abiding import for the people first beloved by God.

By Paul's interpretation, Christians are adopted into this love, and this adoption by God in Christ spreads unpredictably. The apostles send Peter and John quite literally running to Samaria, trying to catch up with the word of God—a word that is catching people up into the promise of God for all of the nations. Those of us who have been so caught up with the word and those of us who try to run to catch up have been called to pray at least two prayers daily: for Israel and for the nations.

PRAYER: Lord, bring peace to your first beloved, to Israel. Bring peace to the nations. Let your redemption spread to the ends of the earth. Amen.

Thursday, January 4 • Read Luke 3:15-17, 21-22

With a call to "repent!" John the Baptist quite notably attracts to himself two groups of people despised among the Israelites. Both tax collectors and soldiers did the bidding of Rome for the sake of the likes of Herod the ruler, and both tax collectors and soldiers hear the call of John the Baptist. "What should we do," they ask, "to repent?" What does repentance entail? In each case, John gives a simple answer: "Do not use your position of power to exploit others. Do the ruler's bidding only to the extent that you must. Do not seek profit as a by-product of Roman rule."

John the Baptist speaks likewise to the people at the heart of righteous Israel. To those who would take their salvation for granted, John has a word. To those who might say, "We have Abraham as our ancestor," John gives the following reply: "Your power is granted or withheld as a matter of God's sheer, gracious desire. If God wished, God could raise up children from silent rocks strewn on the ground at our feet."

What is the response proper to God's gracious favor? What is the repentance proper to God's grace? Generosity. The fruits worthy of repentance, according to John the Baptist, involve giving away half of what we have. As those whose power comes from divine rule, God's people have more than enough.

The story's logic makes Herod, the ruler, seem like the worst of tax collectors and the worst of soldiers—a man of Israel who has exploited his people. Herod hears John's call to repentance as a threat to his privilege. Yet John continues his ministry, preparing the way, facing evil writ small and large. In John's imprisonment, we may read the dangerous clash of true righteousness with false, worldly power. How may we have courage also to prepare the way? Another is coming. Another is coming whose power is God's own in bodily form, born incarnate for us—God's Beloved, pleasing to God.

PRAYER: Lord, may your love for your son embolden me. May I repent, speak the truth, and give freely what I have. Amen.

The psalmist cries out to the heavens themselves. To the angels, the psalmist summons praise due to God. May the heavenly throng sing out of God's glory and strength!

To experience the power of God's creation can be terrifying. To know the strength of God's providence can render one speechless. The psalmist may well have been writing in a land of precarious splendor, dependent on the whims of land and grace. When rain falls hard in the desert, water soon courses through the tributaries. A strong thunderstorm over parched earth may result in a flash flood that sweeps away much in its path. In the midst of a drought, a dry landscape in a strong wind can carry a spark of fire. A lost ember may fly wildly across the yellowing grass and shrubs, across homes and villages of people praying for rain. When such a fire has stripped the land bare, how can one shout "Glory"? How can anyone who sees the mighty force of wind and rain say with the psalmist, "The LORD sits enthroned over the flood; the LORD sits enthroned as king forever"?

There are those few for whom the forces of nature inspire praise. Many of us find ourselves speechless instead. Growing up in West Texas, we could pray for rain for months. We could watch the cracks in the earth deepen, see the mesquite trees give up their already minimal green. Then, standing outside on the porch, we could watch the storm clouds rolling in, knowing that they could bring flash flooding or even a deadly twister. Such fragility may make us grateful for the angels, who can ascribe to God glory.

PRAYER: Lord, when I am speechless, may the angels ascribe you glory. Amen.

EPIPHANY

Matthew opens his story of Jesus' birth with a sixteen-verse genealogy. We may be tempted to skip these lines, but they are crucial to Matthew's perspective on the good news of God with us. Jesus is the Messiah, the son of David and the son of Abraham. He is also the grandson of a few lesser-known players in the economy of God's salvation. Matthew reminds his listeners that God's salvation for the people has moved through some unlikely channels, through Tamar and Rahab and Ruth and the wife of Uriah. What Luke conveys through manger and shepherds, Matthew conveys in the opening genealogy. God's promises to Israel are being fulfilled in unexpected ways.

God's promises to the nations through Israel are also key for Matthew's account of Jesus' birth. A strand running through God's abiding love for Israel is the promise that God will bless all of the nations through Israel. One of God's first promises to Abram is that all of the peoples of the earth will be blessed through his descendants. The genealogy with which Matthew opens the Gospel narrates a lineage of blessing upon Israel—the descendants of God's covenant with Abram. It is a blessing so brilliant, so compelling, that the nations will come searching for the source of the light.

In the story of the magi, or wise ones, Matthew echoes the promise prophesied by the prophet Isaiah. In the midst of darkness, the light will shine; and the peoples of the earth will converge from every direction, eager to discover the brightness dawning through Israel.

To be continued . . .

PRAYER: God of unexpected surprises, may we walk in the light of your promises this day. Amen.

In the story of the magi, Matthew echoes the promise prophesied by the prophet Isaiah. But with the birth of Christ, the light is a distant star, not the blinding sun itself. It is a glimmering light, one that shines in the darkness without completely overcoming it . . . yet. The source of the light is not the expected king who will reign as during the days of King Solomon. The light shining in the darkness will not summon the Queen of Sheba, for example, who would be sorely disappointed in the royal scene played out in Bethlehem. Here, in the unremarkable town whose name means "House of Bread," a baby has been born. God has brought divine promise to fruition. Here, through a betrothed young woman otherwise shamed and a courageous, faithful man otherwise wronged, God-with-us is born—the long desired light to the nations is small, surprising.

The magi may have already known that the light seen in the darkness was due a different kind of homage than King Solomon. Perhaps King Herod, steeped in the power of a particularly arrogant nation, does indeed suspect that his kind of gig is up. There are at least two possible readings here. By one, Herod hears the magi's words and, misunderstanding, fears that the infant will grow up to usurp his power. By another reading, Herod understands precisely what is occurring. Herod fears that the infant prophesied to undermine all worldly power has now been born. Indeed, the star in the East on Christmas morn beckons the nations to a different sort of power altogether. The star beckons the peoples of all the earth to a Prince of Peace.

The magi come to pay homage and receive a vision. Finding the baby with his mother, they can perceive that this little one marked by a star is a light that will challenge the empire and all who are privy to that sort of power. They receive a vision sufficient to eschew Herod and his death-dealing power. They go home to their countries by a different way.

PRAYER: Lord, we pay homage. As we leave this place of Christ's birth, may we go home by a different way. Amen.

Divine Comedy in Seven Acts

January 8–14, 2007 • Laura Huff Hileman[‡]

MONDAY, JANUARY 8 • Read Psalm 36:5-10

Classically speaking, a comedy isn't necessarily funny. What makes a story or situation comic rather than tragic is its perspective on human nature and destiny. Remember Dante's *Divine Comedy*? I bet many of us never made it out of Part I: Hell. But we know that after Hell comes Part II: Purgatory and finally Part III: Paradise. That final arrival makes the whole thing, ultimately, a comedy.

How does comedy differ from tragedy? The tragic view emphasizes our disastrous pride, greed, and ambition with their resulting terrors—war, injustice, destruction, and the ubiquitous suffering that has no apparent redemptive value. Comedy points to human finitude—foolishness, humiliation, weakness—and it smiles wryly, ironically, at the deep-down goodness of creation manifest despite us, and even through us.

While we know tragedy is true because it shapes our world, comedy is even truer because it says to tragedy, "Yes, but. . . ." This "Yes, but. . . . " helps us know that we are not the measure of all things and that however strange God's movements may seem, we are engaged in a life that is both blessed and blessing.

This week's passages all point to the comic vision—the "yes, but" of a life lived in the confidence of God's steadfast love and abundant grace: fountain of life in whose light we see light. We acknowledge that God is here, however awful or uninspiring here may be.

PRAYER: Lord of life, grant us the conviction that your love steadies us in all tragedy and draws us through it, transforming us through the events into people who can follow the light of your star. Amen.

[‡]Teacher of dream work as a spiritual discipline, author; member, Second Presbyterian Church, Nashville, Tennessee.

We could read Psalm 36 in its entirety with an eye to the comic vision. In the first four verses, the psalmist laments the ascendancy of evil and evildoers, and, at the end of the psalm, he prays that God may not only spare him from their influence but also envisions them lying in the dust, unable to rise.

Verses 5-10 describe God's steadfast love. Clearly, God's goodness is much more inspiring than the wicked's badness. All of creation comes within the scope of God's love and justice—not only the people and possibly not only the righteous. I am not a Bible scholar, but I don't think the psalmist ever intended that "all people" of verse 7 would include the wicked—not in that vision of life-giving abundance and radiance that suffuses the psalm through verse 9. This psalm clearly pits the good, law-abiding, God-fearing "blessed" against the wicked, unjust, self-serving godless. And we're with the psalmist. We know who the wicked are, and we can name names.

The psalmist speaks of two entities—the wicked and the blessed—but are they not both aspects of himself? And aren't all of us in the same situation, all the time? Is this not part of the real tragedy that challenges us—our blindness to our own wrongdoing? Another part of the tragedy is the reliable irony of seeing the speck in another's eye instead of the log in our own.

According to the Bible, God takes all people into the shadow of God's wing, not just the good and not just our "good" selves. God loves every bit of us, even our shadow selves. In God's blessings, we encounter life and light that transforms the shadows. The wicked, be they someone other than us or the wicked within us, may, in God's light, turn out to be wiser or more compassionate than we thought or in some way necessary to the harmonious conclusion. God help the blessed to allow such mystery!

PRAYER: Forgive us, Lord, for our judgment against those who differ from ourselves and our indulgence of those who are much like us. Remind us that in Christ each person is whole and all of us are one people. Amen.

Over and over in comedy, the plot and the laughs hinge on mistaken identities. The foe is the friend; the fool is the sage; the beast is really the prince; and the wild confusion finally brings the true lovers into harmonious union. The disguise enables the true personality to shine, or the alias names one's true essence.

Over and over in scripture, people touched by the power of God's presence receive new names of God's choosing. The new name—Abraham, Sarah, Israel, Peter—suggests what God sees in the person: Father of multitudes, Princess, One who strives with God, Rock. In today's passage, we see this renaming at work in the metaphor of marriage. After long trials in exile, tragic for both nation and individuals, God's people are given a new name that signifies that the time of trial is over. The Israelites will return to Jerusalem, and God and the people will begin their relationship anew.

What have these exiles been calling themselves? Piteously, they have known themselves as Forsaken and their land Desolate. Now. As they hear the call to return, they are given love names: My Delight Is in Her, and the land shall be called Married to God. The struggle of life in exile, during which time the Israelites came to remember who and whose they were, culminates in a return as joyous as a wedding as God and Israel renew their vows.

The new names, here and anywhere, offer a glimpse into the divine imagination. They help us know what Love sees in us. And like guides in the wilderness, lights in the dusk, or a long-forgotten scent in the air, they help lead us back to our best and truest selves.

PRAYER: **What name, loving God, do you wish to call me? to call your church? to call this nation? Open our ears, our hearts, and our imaginations so that we may hear our new names and revive our covenant with you. Amen.**

The wedding day is here for Jerusalem, for the Israelites, for us. But this doesn't look like such a brilliant match: Jerusalem is an impoverished bride, dressed in rags, her face streaked with dust and tears. Certainly we've all had times like this, when God has called us, and we are not fit to be seen, much less look the part of the radiant bride. And what about the dowry? Love match or not, aren't we supposed to bring something to this marriage? It feels uncomfortable to be empty-handed.

But ironically at this renewal of vows we're here because we belong to God, and our "nothing" is the very best thing we have to give. The relief of putting ourselves into God's hands to be loved into strength and wholeness—the humility not to be "self-made souls"—this "nothing" is the greatest thing we could possibly bring to the relationship.

It's a lovely comic touch. The irony is that this "holy nothing" that we offer is fuller and richer than any cynical, limited, human-only version of nothing. Given our humble nothing, God can do anything.

The Corinthians passage opens up some of the spiritual gifts that God might include in "anything." I like Eugene Peterson's paraphrase here from *The Message*: "Each person is given something to do that shows who God is." Notice, it does not say, "We are all given something to do that reveals our personal magnificence." Although God blesses us with talents to appreciate and develop, God lacks interest in our becoming stars. We try, by the grace of God, to accept the "holy nothing" that we bring to the marriage, give ourselves over to Love's vision, and allow ourselves to be surprised by what we see God doing through us, even if we never completely get it.

PRAYER: Lord and Lover of our souls, help us lighten up and enjoy the irony that our "nothing" is the source of your greatest promise. Amen.

The wedding at Cana is a classic one-act comedy. On one level, it contains several comic elements: the wedding itself, a common setting for comedy; the minor calamity in which the wine runs out to the disappointment of the guests and the embarrassment of the host; the stereotypical pushy Jewish mother; the reluctant hero who saves the party; the servants who play the straight guys; the totally unforeseeable transformation of water into wine; and the stupefaction of the chief steward and the bridegroom.

On another level, the wedding crisis brings to the forefront knowledge present from the opening of John's Gospel: Jesus is the Son of God, the Word made flesh. His ministry must begin; he must become a public figure. He says this wedding is not his time, not yet. But he gets involved anyway, so it becomes his time. It's the kairotic moment—that right and holy moment when time opens up beyond the hours and minutes and days that mark its surface, and we behold the intersection of time and eternity. He shows who God is by turning the water into wine, transforming the wedding and transforming the spiritual presence that has been in him into something physical, miraculous, timely, celebratory, relational, and generous.

Jesus pours himself out like wine for us. As the wine at the wedding gurgles forth from the jars, we hear the echoes of his future: "I am the true vine. . . . This is my blood of the covenant, which is poured out for many. . . . Let this cup pass from me." Jesus is the living water, the cup of salvation. The real feast, the real table, the real bread, the real Story are all about to happen. Thanks be to God that we are able to celebrate the ultimate comedy, the ultimate goodness of this tragedy-laced story.

PRAYER: Thanks, God, that like the wedding guests, we don't have to be aware of the miracles in the Story the moment they occur. But even more, thank you that as guests at your marriage feast, we can. Help us know what we're celebrating, and help us respond with reverence and revelry. Amen.

Once again it helps to quote from *The Message*, Eugene Peterson's translation of the Bible. In today's passage on spiritual gifts, he writes, "What I want to talk about now is the various ways God's Spirit gets worked into our lives. . . . I want you to be informed and knowledgeable. . . . God's gifts are handed out everywhere; but they all originate in God's Spirit."

Be informed. Be knowledgeable. Be forewarned. God is alive and moving in and through all of us, and no one is immune to the mystery of the Spirit. I wonder about those "various ways [that] God's Spirit gets worked into our lives." The image that comes to my mind is one Jesus uses: he says the kingdom of heaven is like yeast mixed into flour (Matthew 13:33). When the Spirit works that yeast into us, there's going to be pounding and kneading, scraping and turning. We're mixed and shaped and left alone in a warm, dark place for a long time and then stuck in a hot oven until the time is right.

Maybe the Spirit tends us carefully and bakes us into a tender, fragrant loaf; bread for the feast. But most of us are half-risen or half-baked or burned to a cinder. We can take the tragic view here: the loaf is ruined—it fell short of its glorious ideal—woe and despair. Or we can take the comic view: so this loaf isn't perfect. And, as we come to the table and look around, it's clear all have fallen short of the glorious ideal. Finally, we get it: the product may not be so much the point as the process. Holiness isn't so much about grasping spiritual truths as being grasped by that Spirit of truth who makes us and shapes us according to a purpose we can't always guess.

Be informed. Be knowledgeable. Be forewarned about that final comic stroke: like water into wine, all these loaves are, at the marriage feast, transformed by the divine presence into something miraculous, celebratory, and nourishing.

Suggestion for meditation: Give yourself some "rising time" today to feel the Spirit moving like yeast in you. How do you try to stay attuned to your own spiritual process?

The river of God's delight flows from this affirmation: "With you is the fountain of life; in your light we see light." A fascinating image, this lively, liquid light of God. What is it? The language of faith gives us some names for this light of God that enlightens us: inspiration, hope, the indwelling of the Holy Spirit, imagination, revelation, spiritual intuition. These emotions, processes, and attitudes illumine the soul and help us stretch enough to begin to see the possibilities of God's love, power, and grace.

But for many people the understanding of light begins with an experience of darkness. The absence of light deepens the darkness and heightens their longing.

What about that *deep* darkness? What about those times when we desperately need light but can barely long for it? If the divine comedy is only an ecstatic vision that satisfies our longings and that converts conflict into happily ever after, then the premise is a lie. Darkness truly exists; we don't just wave the magic wand of faith and watch it disappear. If God is ultimately God, then the darkness must somehow be of God too—and it is. The divine comedy includes this divine irony: our longing itself is of God. Maybe we could even say that our truest, most terrible longing, the kind born of real suffering is actually a form of God's presence. So while that painful longing certainly deepens the darkness, it also paradoxically summons and opens us to God's indwelling presence.

Think of those wise men trekking across the wilderness, risking their lives in the crazy, dangerous conviction that the star isn't just a ball of flaming gas. Whatever it is, it symbolizes the crucial, beautiful, irresistible truth. Whatever it is, we see it most clearly in the dark. Whatever it is, it is God's light in which we see light.

PRAYER: Thanks be to you, O God, that nothing can separate us from your love in Christ Jesus our Lord. Grant us the faith, the imagination, the heart, and the hope to follow the light of your life within us. Amen.

God, Bible, and Community

January 15–21, 2007 • *Eric H. F. Law[‡]*

MONDAY, JANUARY 15 • Read Psalm 19:1-6

While walking in the desert one night, far from the city lights, I stared at the sky layered with bright, twinkling stars. I realized how amazing and great this creation is, while recognizing my own smallness. Against the breadth and depth of God's limitless sky, I acknowledged how little I understand about this universe, how many voices I cannot hear!

God does not limit community to humankind and the things we build and gather around ourselves. God's vision of creation includes and encompasses the heavens and the whole earth. God's realm has language that we humans cannot hear, contains knowledge that we cannot know. To God the sun is like an athlete running the track across the sky. And like the sun's heat that warms everything on earth, nothing is hidden from God.

Recognizing the vastness of divine creation helps us perceive our smallness. And yet God pays attention to us. God sent Jesus to demonstrate God's yearning for us, in spite of our smallness. The Creator does not abandon us to our own smallness. In the greatness of God's creation, God touches each one of us.

SUGGESTION FOR MEDITATION: Find a place where you can see for a distance—like looking out at the ocean or a great lake, at the sky or distant mountains. Contemplate how small you are in the greatness of God's creation. Reflect on how God is working in your life.

[‡]Internationally known trainer and consultant for building inclusive community; author of five books; priest of the Episcopal Church; playwright, composer, and photographer; living in Palm Desert, California.

TUESDAY, JANUARY 16 • Read Nehemiah 8:1-3, 5-6, 8-10

Nehemiah 8 tells of the people's gathering around the book of the Law of Moses after the rebuilding of the walls of Jerusalem. Ezra the scribe reads aloud in Hebrew all morning and then a group of people help interpret the reading; they "gave the sense, so that the people understood the reading." The people needed interpretation because they spoke Aramaic.

In Christian community, we gather around the word of God—our Bible. We listen to the text, but that is not enough. Many times, we do not understand the text because the setting differs from our own. Therefore, interpretation is always part of our tradition as we read the sacred text in community.

In a diverse community of people from different backgrounds and traditions, the matter of interpretation can become an issue. Many available resources and tools for interpreting scripture came from the European branches of the church. So do Europeans have more power and right to interpret scriptures for others? No, no more power and right than other persons of faith.

Asian and African Christians have been exploring how to read scripture without European influence. Many are discovering that the culture of biblical times closely resembles the cultures of Africa and Asia. This approach recovers insights that might be lost if scriptures are interpreted solely from a European perspective. Native cultures are rediscovering the richness of their own traditions as the Bible is interpreted within the framework of their understanding.

SUGGESTION FOR MEDITATION: As a Christian, in what ways is the Bible part of your life? How often do you read it? How often do you read it with others in community? When do you serve as an interpreter for others? In what settings do you become the one who listens for others' interpretation?

In the human society of our own creation, we live with many rules. Rules control people's behavior so we can feel safe. If I fear that someone will rob me, society establishes a law that punishes robbery. If I am afraid that another car might crash into mine as I drive down the road, motor vehicle departments develop traffic rules that drivers must know and abide by. Furthermore, drivers are tested to make sure they know these rules before driving. Violation of the rules results in fines.

Most rules in our society started out as ways to support our communal life. But for some reason, humankind often turns rules into something oppressive in which the powerful control the powerless. I have a student who shared his experience with the "Respectful Communication Guidelines" on campus. The guidelines were being enforced in such a way that they became oppressive and exclusive, though their original intent was to ensure the safety of individuals who chose to engage in dialogue.

The psalmist makes a qualitative distinction between rules that oppress and God's covenant with us. The covenant of God consists of ground rules that revive the soul, make the wise simple, rejoice the heart, and enlighten the eyes. Following God's unambiguous commandments brings great reward—greater than gold and sweeter than honey.

God's covenant with us is not about oppression or control; it is about upholding the well-being of each person in God's community. When we follow these rules, we enrich ourselves and others.

SUGGESTION FOR MEDITATION: List the rules that you follow each day. Which ones oppress, and which ones support and enrich? How do you challenge the rules that oppress you and others? How do you help your community uphold those ground rules that support and nurture the people in the community?

THURSDAY, JANUARY 18 • Read Psalm 19:11-14

In spite of our earnest desire to keep God's commandments, we sometimes are blinded by our own limitations: hidden faults that we do not even know exist in us. Sometimes we act to bring about good and yet come to realize that our actions harmed others. What do we do about that harm? Do the words "I didn't mean to" repair the damage? People often say, "I didn't mean to hurt you," implying that they are not at fault and that those who are hurt should forgive them or at least not be so "sensitive."

Those who have been hurt focus not on intent but on the actual result. Their response might be, "It doesn't matter whether you intended to hurt me or not. The result is that I *am* hurt, and someone needs to take responsibility."

The psalmist recognizes our human folly and offers a prayer before speaking and acting: "Let the words of my mouth and the meditation of my heart be acceptable to you, O LORD." How often might we refrain from speech or action that is not acceptable to God?

Not only that, but in meditating we ask God to guide us and to help us discover our hidden faults—*before* we act. It is no accident that the image of God evoked here is of "rock" and "redeemer." Knowing that we stand on God, the rock, provides the foundation of our communication. God supports us as we engage in truthful dialogue. When we make mistakes and discover our faults, intended or not, God can redeem us and our relationships.

"Let the words of my mouth and the meditation of my heart be acceptable to you, O LORD, my rock and my redeemer."

SUGGESTION FOR MEDITATION: Reflect on an event in your life when you acted with good intention but with hurtful results for another. How might you approach that hurt one with hope of reconciliation? Before approaching the person, pray the prayer: "Let the words of my mouth and the meditation of my heart be acceptable to you, O LORD, my rock and my redeemer."

Listening to the word of God has its consequences. When we truly understand God's yearning for us, we might be confronted by the fact that we have not followed God's call. Our initial reaction might be that of weeping. We weep because we have not loved our neighbors as ourselves. We weep because we have not loved God by working for justice in our community and the world. We weep because we have not been good stewards of God's creation. We weep because we have chosen death again and again, instead of choosing life.

Our recognition of our waywardness emphasizes the importance of reading scripture in the midst of a loving community. The community stands ready to support us as we realize that we have not followed God's commandments. In community, in the midst of our weeping, someone will respond, "Go your way, eat the fat and drink sweet wine and send portions of them to those for whom nothing is prepared, for this day is holy to our LORD; and do not be grieved, for the joy of the LORD is your strength."

Yes, go ahead and weep, for we have sinned; but do not stop there. Celebrate the fact that we are returning to God in repentance. In the midst of the celebration we waste no time. We move directly toward God's command to feed the poor and hungry, to "send portions of them to those for whom nothing is prepared."

SUGGESTION FOR MEDITATION: As you listen to Holy Scripture being read in your own heart or in community, consider what God is inviting you to do or to change. Allow God to confront you. When confronted, how do you move from weeping to celebration? How does your celebration move immediately toward sharing your resources and serving others?

Five blind persons encounter an elephant. In their usual manner, they use their hands to touch and feel this unknown creature in order to learn what it is like. One says, "I know what an elephant is like. It is like a great big barrel suspended in the air." Another person says, "No, you're wrong; the elephant is like a big tree trunk." "No," the third person argues, "the elephant is like a fan made with leather." "No, the elephant is nothing like that. It's like a rope," says a fourth person. And the fifth person states, "You are all wrong. The elephant is like a snake."

If these five persons continue to argue over who is right, they will never discover what an elephant is like in its entirety. Only by listening to one another and puzzling over the differences can they come to know the whole elephant. In their bewilderment, they might begin to connect the pieces of the puzzle that each holds. By successfully combining their different perspectives, they will be able to describe more fully an elephant.

Living in a diverse, pluralistic world, we will encounter persons with different connections, experiences, and relationships with God—like the five persons having different contacts with the elephant. God chooses to connect with different communities and persons in different ways according to their cultures and situations. We witness and share how God has connected with us according to our own experiences and contexts while acknowledging God's different ways of working with other persons and communities.

Diversity in community has existed from the early church to now. Paul uses the body of Christ as an image to help us understand the role of diversity in Christ's community. Rather than fight over differences, we learn to listen and appreciate what our differences contribute to the richness of our community.

SUGGESTION FOR MEDITATION: List your gifts and strengths. List your weaknesses. Reflect on how you can share your gifts and strengths to enrich others' lives. Consider how you can invite and appreciate others' strengths and gifts.

Jesus' earthly ministry fulfills the scripture that he reads in the synagogue that day—to bring good news to the poor; to proclaim release to the captives, recovery of sight to the blind; to let the oppressed go free; to proclaim the year of the Lord's favor—Jubilee. Jesus says, "Today this scripture has been fulfilled"—not yesterday or tomorrow, not next month or next year. *Today* begins the fulfillment of Jubilee. From this day on, Jesus acts as if Jubilee were here—forgiving, healing, liberating, empowering. Jesus not only reads scriptures, but he fulfills them with his actions.

The most serious consequence of reading the scripture comes in our taking responsibility to fulfill what we read. We ask how this scripture can be fulfilled *today*—not tomorrow, not next week or month. We cannot go on with life as usual. Every time we read the word of God, God sends a message to guide and show us ways that we can fulfill the commandments. As the body of Christ, we are to fulfill God's commands by acting with our bodies and speaking with our voices.

The Spirit of God is upon *you*; Jubilee is at hand *today*. What will you do today? What will you say to your family and friends? What will you say to your government? What will you say to your community? What will your church community do and say?

Prayer: O God, you sent your son, Jesus, to be among us, to remind us of the essence of what it means to be your children. Help us to follow Christ by reading and listening to your word regularly and in community. Open our hearts to accept your challenge to love mercy, do justice, and walk humbly with you each and every day of our lives. Amen.

The Power of Love

January 22–28, 2007 • *Bob Bettson*[‡]

MONDAY, JANUARY 22 • **Read Luke 4:21-30**

Speaking prophetic words doesn't insure popularity. Jesus was often rejected when he preached the gospel of good news. He cites the text of the prophet Isaiah to tell his friends in Nazareth, people he has known all his life, about his call to bring good news to the poor, release to the captives, freedom to the oppressed, and sight to the blind.

This scripture is fulfilled in your hearing, Jesus says. This news takes the people of Nazareth by surprise. Here is Jesus, the carpenter's son, claiming to be the bearer of a radical gospel message, the kind that will be preached by Israel's long-awaited Messiah. Jesus goes on to state that this prophetic teaching is not only for Jews but for the Jews' hated enemies, the Gentiles. A message of God's inclusive love inspires the rage of the townsfolk as they drive Jesus out of the town; he narrowly escapes death.

Now we face the questions: How will we respond to God's inclusive message of love? How do we respond to prophetic teaching? Do we hear the prophets of our own time?

The good news Jesus proclaimed for the poor and the oppressed is not high on the priority list for many Christians. So engaging in prophetic ministry is as difficult a task now as it was for Jesus in Nazareth. People don't want to hear the good news if it makes them uncomfortable.

Luke's Gospel calls us to see God's intention for justice and peace as an integral part of God's love for humanity and our love for one another.

PRAYER: God, help me hear your prophetic words and be mindful of the biblical call to bring good news to the poor and to let the oppressed go free. Amen.

[‡]Editor of *The Sower*, newspaper of the Anglican Diocese of Calgary, Alberta, Canada.

In 1996 I was news editor for the *United Church Observer*, the monthly publication of the United Church of Canada. I had been a professional journalist for twenty years, eleven of them with the *Observer*. Little did I know that my life was about to come apart at the seams.

That spring my wife left me, taking our nine-year-old daughter to live with her. A few months later my position at the *Observer* was eliminated. I found myself out of a job for the first time in my life, with a year's severance to start over. It was a roller-coaster ride. I plunged into despair and depression. A new relationship soon fell apart. It was a wilderness time.

At that point in my life I really came to understand God as the rock of my life. I continued to attend worship and sing in our parish choir. Out of the desert, by taking refuge in God, I found strength to build a new life. God delivered and rescued me from the dark days of depression.

This wilderness time enabled me to discern the call to ordained ministry. I enrolled part-time in a Master's of Divinity program to test that call. As I write this meditation, I can state that I have been in ordained ministry for four years and happily married for five years.

"For you, O LORD, are my hope. . . . My praise is continuously of you." Psalms like this one often articulate our deepest hopes and dreams, offering particular comfort in times of trial. Sometimes hope is hard to find in the midst of pain and suffering, but we pray for strength to keep hope alive.

PRAYER: God, we give thanks that you are our rock of refuge. We pray for your protection from the wickedness that always seems present in life. You are our hope and our salvation. Praise the Lord! Amen.

"Before I formed you in the womb I knew you." The Lord's call to Jeremiah comes in clear and uncompromising terms—a remarkable commission. Jeremiah feels unworthy and unprepared but receives God's reassurance: "Do not be afraid. . . . I am with you to deliver you." When God calls us, God promises to stay with us.

The structure of this poetic passage outlines Jeremiah's call and commission, which is part of God's plan for the people. It is Jeremiah whom God appoints over nations and kingdoms, not kings. It is Jeremiah who will give the oracles of God's judgment.

We, like Jeremiah, may feel unworthy of a call to ministry for Jesus Christ. Yet God's love for us empowers us to serve. We too need to heed God's call. With all our shortcomings God has plans for us. We are called to love our neighbors as ourselves, to preach the gospel to all nations.

Ministry is not the work of the few. It is the work of the many. If we take seriously our call as Christians, we need to discern what we are called to do. We can't all be prophets. But we can play a role in building the kingdom of God. We can make visible our love for God and our fellow human beings.

We, like Jeremiah, may wonder how we can live up to God's call. But with God, anything is possible. We simply trust in God's love and care for us, knowing that God is with us to deliver.

PRAYER: God, we are called to serve you. But we feel inadequate for this great responsibility we bear as followers of Christ. We pray for strength and wisdom to discern our call to ministry. We ask this in the name of Jesus Christ. Amen.

The problem with this familiar passage, often used at weddings, is that it loses its explicitly Christian message and becomes a poetic ode to love. But Paul doesn't want to talk about romantic love or *eros*. He speaks of *agape* love, the heart of our Christian ethos. He describes the worthiness of selfless love.

We may possess dramatic spiritual gifts. We may understand the mysteries of life and give everything to the poor. All that means nothing if we don't have love, says Paul. This message is difficult for us. We want to believe that we can accomplish so much simply by using our spiritual gifts. Yet the key to salvation is love, a real love of neighbor, whether it's in our own interest or not.

Consider the impact it would have on the world if we took these words to heart and made them part of our lives: "Love is patient; love is kind; love is not envious or boastful or arrogant or rude. It does not insist on its own way; it is not irritable or resentful; it does not rejoice in wrongdoing, but rejoices in the truth. It bears all things, believes all things, hopes all things, endures all things." This scripture clearly connects love of God with love of neighbor.

German theologian Karl Rahner in his essay "Unity of the Love of Neighbour and Love of God" puts it this way: "the primary basic act of [the one] who is always and already 'in the world' is always an act of the love of . . . neighbour and *in this* the original love of God is realised."

PRAYER: God of love, we pray that in our spiritual journeys we may better understand how to love another as you have loved us. May your love inspire us to make love a way of life. We ask this in the name of one who loved us so much, Jesus Christ. Amen.

FRIDAY, JANUARY 26 • Read 1 Corinthians 13:8-13

"Love never ends." This sounds like a phrase from a popular song on the radio; one of the "lite" rock stations that plays a nonstop selection of syrupy love songs.

But Paul, speaking of love in its broader sense as a way of life, tells us that even when the current age ends, love will endure. Love is at the root of our relationship with God, in the current age and in the age to come. The overzealous Corinthians who see themselves as spiritually elite ultimately are judged immature in faith and practice.

Paul speaks of our spiritual journey and compares it to the journey from childhood to the maturity of adulthood. As we grow in our faith, we begin to understand how loving one another is the defining mark of our lives. We move beyond a childlike world where we are cared for by others and focused upon ourselves and take our place in the community of faith as caregivers for others.

As we devote ourselves to worship, prayer, study, and outreach as part of the faith community, it is important to examine how much of our Christian practice is truly informed by a genuine love of neighbor, which Paul teaches.

This isn't an easy task. Loving in this way is countercultural, so different from the love described in many love songs and in our mass media. The love that Paul describes is the self-giving love of those with a servant heart. Let us be inspired by this mature Christian practice of love.

PRAYER: God of love, help us grow in our understanding of the first and greatest commandment: to love you and to love our neighbors as ourselves. We pray for wisdom as we seek to incorporate this into our lives, knowing that while faith and hope are important, love is at the very heart of our Christian journey. Amen.

God stands with us in times of suffering. The psalmist bears witness to that wisdom in this prayer for help. This is a message we need to hear. An eighty-eight-year-old retired doctor in a parish I served told me the advances of modern medicine mean that we are living longer than ever before. This longevity means we will have to learn to deal with more suffering. He knows whereof he speaks, having had two hips and knees replaced in recent years—all in response to chronic pain.

Whether our pain is physical or emotional, this psalm speaks to all who want to be freed from evil and injustice. In response to an experience of suffering, the psalmist alternates prayers of petition with an expression of trust in God as a refuge, a strong fortress, a rescuer, and a rock. This kind of faith serves us well in times of affliction. Like this psalmist, we have to learn how to live with suffering and pain without losing our faith in God's love and care for us.

It is amazing how faith can help us survive suffering. I heard a radio interview with Terry Waite, the Archbishop of Canterbury's envoy, who survived almost five years as a hostage in the Middle East before being freed. He told of saving a bit of bread and some water each day and using the two elements while saying the liturgy of Holy Communion from memory. Sharing in Christ's body and blood gave him strength to survive the isolation and deprivation of being a hostage.

May we respond to suffering with praise and prayer, reminding ourselves that God has been our hope and our strength since our youth and will continue to be so throughout all our years.

PRAYER: God of refuge, we give thanks that you stand with us as our rock and fortress in times of suffering. Strengthen our faith so we may serve you in our weakness. We ask this in the name of Jesus. Amen.

SUNDAY, JANUARY 28 • Read Luke 4:21-30

The people of Nazareth find it hard to hear Jesus' prophetic message. How does he, an ordinary carpenter's son, speak with the authority and wisdom of God? I mean, isn't this the same child who used to play with our kids? Isn't he the one who made that nice table for Grandma?

We too often find it hard to recognize or hear truth from people we know. Familiarity can deafen us to the wisdom offered by those closest to us. After all, we reason, how do they know what's best for us?

As children we often fail to hear the wisdom of our parents. As parents, we may discount wisdom offered by our children. As partners in marriage, we sometimes don't hear the truths spoken to us by spouses.

Pride may prevent us from hearing truth offered in love. Fear of change also may keep us from hearing the truth. If we open ourselves to God's transforming love, we risk having to change something about ourselves or our lives.

So for some in Nazareth the pride of familiarity may cause hardness of heart; for some, Jesus' testimony signals change. Perhaps one of the hardest aspects for the people of Nazareth to stomach is that God's covenant and Jesus' mission are not exclusively for the people of Israel. It is for all who believe.

Jesus preaches a message of inclusivity when the hometown folks want to hear that they are the chosen ones. Jesus tells them that God's love is not only for them but for all. In fact, often God works through and helps persons they might least expect, "outsiders" like the widow at Zarephath in Sidon and the leper Naaman the Syrian.

The people, consumed with rage, threaten Jesus' life. Pride and fear keep them from acknowledging the truth of Jesus' words or from seeing the kingdom among them.

SUGGESTION FOR MEDITATION: What fears and pride blind you to seeing God at work in the world?

Fishing in Deeper Waters

January 29–February 4, 2007 • Judith Jenkins Kohatsu[‡]

MONDAY, JANUARY 29 • Read Psalm 138

How easy it is to give God thanks in the midst of worship—the choir sings, the music resounds, the sanctuary fills with God's praise. Now the work week starts—how easy is it to offer that same praise as one stumbles through morning preparations and sets off to the workplace?

For me Monday is a full day, and I'm not always filled with praise for God. The consideration of prostrating myself before God conjures up an image of falling asleep rather than joyfully acknowledging God's work. You see, I've worked on the sabbath—as a clergyperson. By Monday morning, I am thinking about the next bulletin and sermon, checking up on prayer concerns of the previous day, and preparing for the week's meetings.

James Taylor, in his book *Everyday Psalms,* uses images like extending one's arms in embrace to capture the essence of the NRSV's "bow down." *If I embrace,* I muse, *there must be something there to hold on to.* I haven't entered my workweek alone: it is not just my ministry; it is work shared with God—and others. Slowly I can join in this psalm of thanksgiving. The energy of God and God's creation flows into my bones and soul.

It is Monday—again. We are called into vocation once more. We can take the opportunity to offer God not sacrifices, not completed tasks—just thanks for a new day, for accompaniment, for another chance to be who we are created to be. We are called into living in the space between what was and what will be.

PRAYER: Energizing God, accept our thanks for a day of rest, a time of sleep, a new beginning. Increase the strength of our souls as we face the challenges of a new week. Amen.

[‡]Ordained elder, the New England Conference of The United Methodist Church; pastor, the Federated Church of Sandwich, Sandwich, New Hampshire.

TUESDAY, JANUARY 30 • Read Isaiah 6:1-5

What a great image of God—on a throne, the high and mighty God fills the entire space of the Temple. The choir announces God's glory. What are your thoughts on glimpsing such an image of God? Are you like Isaiah, overwhelmed by your smallness, your inadequacies, and your impurities?

Take a moment and consider your smallness, your inadequacies. Are they truly inadequacies or simply a measure of your humanness? What makes you impure? The Hebrews had a cultic list of impurities. For us today what might comprise that list?

Isaiah describes his situation as living among a people of unclean lips. Some might argue that we find ourselves in a similar situation. In what ways do you consider our society unclean? How do you participate in that uncleanness? For some, cleanliness is a personal issue: having the "right" morals, obeying all the laws. For others, including Jesus, uncleanness is also a societal issue. When persons are in need or oppressed, driven to starvation and ill health, or stripped of their humanity, the society is unclean. How is it for you in your town, your state or province, your nation, this world? In what ways are we a clean society?

Notice the last phrase of the reading: "Yet my eyes have seen the King, the LORD of hosts." Many faithful people in Isaiah's time assumed that it was impossible to see God and live. One might argue that Isaiah's experience is only a vision—so seeing is permissible. Isaiah seems surprised that he is even having this vision. What are your visions of God? This portion of the reading encourages us, no matter our state of cleanliness, to expect such visions. When has God come to you?

PRAYER: Gracious God, come to us in visions despite our inability to be pure, and guide our lives. Amen.

"What do you know? Not much! You?" These are the opening lines of a national radio program—a show about stuff: call-in quizzes, audience quizzes, introductions of guests, and of course a monologue.

Paul raises a similar question with the early Christians at Corinth: "What do you know?" Notice that Paul's interest resides in what you know, not from whom you learned it. In case we are a bit fuzzy, Paul fills in the details of a God of grace and a Christ who died and was resurrected.

So what do you know? Do you know a God of grace and love? How do others know that you know such a God? The Corinthian congregation was often long on talk and short on "do." Paul suggests that when we know God and Christ, we share the good news so others might come to believe. Remember it is in Corinth that Paul cautions people that their actions (inside of "church" as well as outside) speak volumes.

Some of us may believe we are exempt from knowing and sharing because we are plain folks; perhaps we have come to faith a bit late or in less than dramatic ways. Paul reminds the believers in Corinth that even he, who was a bit untimely and who missed the whole Jesus event, can be a carrier of the gospel.

So what do you know? Do you know that even you can share the good news? Do you know that especially you—who have some serious doubts or have made unkind remarks about believers—can share the good news? God's grace includes us all. Unlike the radio audience, our reply to "What do you know?" can be: "Lots. Want to hear?"

PRAYER: Giver of good news, open our hearts to your presence. Open our mouths so that we too might proclaim Jesus Christ risen and among us. Amen.

Thursday, February 1 • Read Isaiah 6:9-10

Have you ever been the bearer of unwelcome, perhaps prophetic, news? This is, in effect, Isaiah's charge from God: Go tell the folks that they are just not going to understand because they neither hear nor see. Eugene Peterson in his Bible translation *The Message* refers to the people as "blockheads."

I've often found myself the recipient of such a message. Even when I profess to want to follow God's way more fully, I can't seem to get my act together. It doesn't help when someone else points out the obvious: my ears are stopped, my eyes shut. I'm not looking at reality as I try to change, "to turn and be healed" as it says in Isaiah. Often I continue moving in a familiar direction without turning toward God's path at all. Whether I like the message or not, I am brought up short and finally begin to confront reality. Walking in God's way means that I let go of *my* way and follow directions to a new course, a new life path.

How is it for you when you find yourself "stuck" on your spiritual journey? Who are the God-sent messengers in your lives who proclaim the obvious? How do you respond to their message? With thanks and gratitude or with an attack upon the messenger? It is difficult to receive such a searing assessment. It is also the first step to new life, a life we say we desire.

Take some time for self-evaluation: how open are your eyes, how unstopped your ears?

PRAYER: Gracious God, thank you for prophets in my life who tell it like it is. Enable me to unblock my eyes, open my ears, and understand the obvious. Guide me in the direction of your truth. Amen.

Only the stump's left—an image of utter destruction. I live in New Hampshire, where people consider stumps in fields as hazards. Stumps can serve as a useful perch, a haven for insects or perhaps small rodents, but what life is left in a stump?

When I lived in Rhode Island a large willow tree graced the backyard. During a late winter ice storm this magnificent tree blew down. The trustee cleanup crew got to work. One person cut fearlessly with his chainsaw. Soon there were many "stumps," or at least two-foot logs. The workers and I discovered that willow doesn't serve much purpose; it's good for cricket bats and interior parts of stringed instruments. A little goes a long way, so a lot of willow stumps or logs sat in my backyard.

Spring came slowly that year. One day as I ducked around the branches on my way to church, I noticed a tiny shoot coming out of the trunk of the downed tree. Quickly small twigs developed, signaling a life force deep within striving to live. It was not just the stump that sprouted. Each log had dozens of sprouts. Deep within this downed, mutilated tree, the instinct to live ran deep.

I learned an important lesson from that downed willow. Even when I feel devastated, utterly cut down, there is a spirit within me that strives to live, to sprout, and to grow anew. I am never devoid of the God-force of life no matter how I am slashed down. God's spirit remains alive inside of me awaiting an opportunity to bud into new life. Isaiah calls it "the holy seed."

PRAYER: Holy Spirit, move within the stumps of my living and break forth into new life. Amen.

SATURDAY, FEBRUARY 3 • Read Luke 5:1-11

"Oh, that will never work." How many times have you heard that as your community poses a new idea, a new ministry? How many times have you said it? "Been there, done that" can be another dismissive reply. "We've tried to feed the hungry, and, look, we have more hungry."

I wonder how many of those responses were on the tip of Peter's tongue as this itinerant preacher tells experienced fishermen where to fish. I wonder what caught Peter's imagination and encouraged him to try again. Perhaps it was the deeper water. Jesus invites Peter and us to "fish" in deeper water where we cannot easily see the fish or the bottom, out into places beyond our depth.

When a community of faith begins a ministry, it generally starts small and grows. Yes, world hunger is a problem, as is hunger in this community. Let's start a food pantry. The pantry succeeds, but the problem persists. What if we dared to fish in the deeper waters? Might the pantry grow into a cooperative farm or a job-training program? The problem isn't lack of food globally but unequal distribution—some have and some don't.

For people of faith who undertake ministries of compassion and justice, this story carries an important message. If we dare to move out into deeper territory (the broader need) the result can be awesome (our nets will be full). The story also suggests that we will need partners to land our catch successfully.

What stands in your way of taking Jesus' advice, of following Jesus' call? What keeps you from casting your nets into the deeper waters? The catch may be beyond your wildest dreams.

PRAYER: Daring God, may we free ourselves of our limited visions and catch a glimpse of your picture of shalom for all. Amen.

46 *Fishing in Deeper Waters*

Today we face the big question: "Whom shall I send, and who will go for us?" The vision is awesome, the message difficult. We are asked to move out with praise, drawing on a depth of knowledge about a most gracious God. We receive the promise of great interior strength and advice to look in unexpected places for our resources. Is this enough for us to answer the call boldly?

Sitting with this week's scriptures enabled me to understand that answering a call is not the end of my life and learning—it is just the beginning. I can volunteer for another segment on God's way because God's spirit will fill me with all that I need. The way will probably be challenging, even dark and scary—but within me lives the "holy seed" that can carry me through to the next stage of my journey. To what is God calling you? What message are you to bring?

As you hear the call, are you ready to run and hide, or will you boldly volunteer? As you consider God's request, what factors do you consider? Often I assume that I must set out with all the answers. After several decades in ministry, I've discovered that the One who calls me into service provides a great deal of on-the-job training.

So behind the smoke, the incense, the flashing lights and giant vision, a voice asks, "Who will go for us?" How will you respond?

PRAYER: Still small voice, you ask a difficult question. Enable me to assess the situation. Fill my frame with your wisdom and strength as I set off to carry the message of love and justice into the world. I volunteer, God, knowing you will be my helper. Amen.

Choices for Abundant Living

February 5–11, 2007 • Hee-Soo Jung[‡]

MONDAY, FEBRUARY 5 • Read Jeremiah 17:5-6

"Cursed are those who trust in mere mortals and make mere flesh their strength, whose hearts turn away from the LORD." Thus spoke Jeremiah of divine judgment against Judah and Jerusalem in the midst of God's outpouring love. The prophet sees God's ultimate desire for human renewal and recovery. The prophetic word captures a future pregnant with hope for an oppressed people.

God's creation is a networking system of abundant life for all, enough for all. But greed and shame coax us to possess more and consume more. We lose sight of the fact that the world belongs to God and is provided as home for all peoples.

Jeremiah's vision offers a strong illustration: trusting in humanity is like a shrub in the desert, in the salt land where no one lives. Human self-pride doesn't sustain much; there is no life-giving water around self-centeredness.

The direction of our life's journey begins to become clear when we claim our own shortcomings. Our desires and ambitions lead us astray, but God comes searching for us on the back roads of our life, bringing liberation that comes only from God. We surrender our own attempts to figure out our lives and turn to the Lord with freedom and joy. We tend to our life in God that we might be in the presence of God with blessing.

PRAYER: We turn to you, God. You have done great things for us and have promised even greater. We confess our failures and shortcomings. We see no hope in ourselves. Guide us to see your love and mercy so that we can continually find freedom in you. Amen.

[‡]Bishop, Northern Illinois Conference of The United Methodist Church; living in Chicago, Illinois.

Jeremiah's word reminds us of the fact that we must make choices about our lives. At the heart and soul of our choices lie questions of whom and what we will trust. Jeremiah perceives that Judah's choice violates the covenant nature of God's reign—the choice shortsighted and twisted by human greed.

Trusting God is like a tree planted by the water that sends its roots by the stream. Its leaves stay green, and it never ceases to bear fruit, a sharp contrast to the shrub in the desert. This fruitful existence reminds us of the nature of genuine relationship with God. As part of God's interconnected world, we engage in mutual relationship. God's love and justice surround us. This fundamental reality "roots" our existence as believers.

Our trust in God relieves our distress and suffering. Gradually we give up self-efforts, become honest about our utter uselessness without God, and live fully by God's grace. John Wesley indicates that this organic relationship brings experience of the divine presence: "God's breathing into the soul, and the soul's breathing back what it first receives from God."

Fruitful living involves faithful relationship with God and solidarity with other human beings. God's life-giving spirit empowers us to be fruitful as we work to restore and heal all creation.

We live in a broken world; we easily fall into isolation and try to become self-reliant. Without sinking our roots into the life-giving stream of God's grace, our lives become barren. Yet God offers restored relationship—a greening of our days and lives.

PRAYER: Gracious God, we pray for those who hope for healing, those who long for justice. May your divine presence and love help us settle like a tree planted by the water so we can bear fruit abundantly. Amen.

We are not at peace until rooted in true relationship with God, an organic and life-giving relationship. Until we reach that place, we may feel restless, tense, and dissatisfied in our soul journey.

Psalm 1 describes right relationship with the Creator as like a tree planted by a stream. The roots move toward water naturally, strongly. Fertile, watered land brings forth healthy plants and trees. The imagery of this passage is a strong invitation to move us forward in our faith journey.

When we look at our lives, sometimes we see ourselves in an uphill battle and find the way difficult. We feel uprooted and vulnerable. Our lives are not refreshed but withering. Israel finds itself in a similar place. God has made covenant with Israel. Israel tries to remain in holy relationship with the Creator God, and its prophets urge no more alienation or separation from God. Even though the people of Israel stray far from their original relationship, they believe that God's redemptive grace will be available as restorative power.

"Happy are those who do not follow the advice of the wicked, or take the path that sinners tread, or sit in the seat of scoffers; but their delight is in the law of the LORD, and on his law they meditate day and night."

Blessed is the one who meditates on the law of the Lord and faithfully pursues right relationship with God. Blessed is the one who desires true relationship with God.

On our life's journey, may we, like trees planted by streams, sink our roots deep into the living water. Then may we gradually be grounded in God's spirit and bear fruit with a peaceful mind.

PRAYER: Creator God, make us a blessing to this earth of yours and all that are part of it so that we may never be detached from you. We desire to bear fruit in your graciousness and abundance. Amen.

When we fought for justice under the military dictatorship of Korea in the 1970s, those of us in the Christian Student Movement witnessed how we could fulfill God's call to justice and transform people's lives. However, our resistance brought consequences. The police registered us on the blacklist and blocked our participation in many free activities, even public worship. The government's disrespect and violence toward us made it difficult to be faithful and keep organizing. We could see no fruits of our efforts; the wicked did indeed seem to be standing—not only standing but prospering. The evil impinging on our lives made it hard to believe that goodness would win out.

This passage invites us to nurture traits of goodness in our hearts and not to lose courage as we stand for justice. This takes discipline. By following God's law daily, we become better and stronger people. Surely God becomes our strength and wisdom in our fight against evil, "for the LORD watches over the way of the righteous."

Our God is gracious and forgiving, yet demanding of justice and right action. The Psalter proclaims God's justice toward the wicked; they will not prosper. Instead, they "are like chaff that the wind drives away." Evil will perish; goodness will flourish.

God dwells in goodness and rejects evil. God created us as authentic selves who yearn to be part of constructive change and moral movement for good. In all circumstances God is with us. The Holy Spirit does not grow discouraged in advancing our commitment to the justice and well-being of society. We can affirm these words from "A Statement of Faith of the Korean Methodist Church": "We believe in the reign of God as the divine will realized in human society. . . . We believe in the final triumph of righteousness and in the life everlasting."

PRAYER: **Our God, who is never far from us, come near and teach us your courage. Justice-making is not simple or easy, but we know you are with us. Remind us that your goodness and mercy are strong and present. Amen.**

God came anew in Jesus Christ. Christ, raised from the dead, is the first fruits of a new creation. God was fully present in this miraculous event.

Some Corinthians, however, were hesitant to accept the general resurrection of the dead. Paul attempts to make clear the risen Christ and his fundamental role in the Corinthians' faith journey. As Paul tells the people of Corinth, "if there is no resurrection of the dead, then Christ has not been raised; and if Christ has not been raised, then our proclamation has been in vain." Christ's resurrection is central to our faith.

The gospel proclaims God is at work in our lives precisely in transforming and giving meaning to our struggles. God suffers with us and for us. In the death of a loved one: a parent, a child, a friend, or in every manner of brokenness, Jesus comes to us with scars that say, God knows. God is not afraid; God does not pull back; and God does not grow distant from the dead. And for Paul, the resurrection is *now* but *not yet*. We experience God's presence in our lives *now,* but we have *not yet* realized God's full intentions for our lives.

Paul preached resurrection as a centerpiece of the faith. When we believe in the risen Christ, we set forth on a new life. When we risk and trust together, we will confidently witness God's renewing power and transformation in our world. But this life is only a foretaste of God's activity at the close of history.

With Paul we say, "I am convinced that neither death, nor life, nor angels, nor rulers, nor things present, nor things to come, nor powers, nor height, nor depth, nor anything else in all creation, will be able to separate us from the love of God in Christ Jesus our Lord" (Rom. 8:38-39).

PRAYER: Creator God, we thank you for your saving grace. Your miraculous act opens doors to a new journey. Help us see in the risen Christ the incredible gift of your coming among us. Amen.

In Luke, Jesus' public ministry begins with preaching and healing. Jesus knows people need his touch to heal their suffering and oppression. He does the work of restoration and healing, the work of bringing meaning to human life. Our yes to God's calling allows us to bring healing to our own communities.

Today the church needs to reclaim the role of bringing hope to people. When persons ask me about my role as a bishop, I always answer that I have been called to hold the hope for the people. I focus on being a vessel of hope.

I'm well-acquainted with wounds. I've been with families who've lost parents, experienced car accidents, and dealt with fire or storms. I've been with victims of violence who often protest: "I don't want this pain. I don't need this wound." And many protest, "I want a God who takes away pain and sorrow and scars." They need so badly to touch Jesus, to claim his power for their living. And God meets us where we are: in the sorrow, through the pain, behind the locked doors of our loneliness.

My father had a socially unacceptable handicapping condition. He struggled to accept his own condition. I felt angry about society's treatment of him; my wounds were deep. One day Jesus met me and said, "I can use your wounds, your pain, your deep emotion, for ministry—to heal, restore, and proclaim hope to others, so your suffering is not wasted."

Healing cannot be an individual matter. Jesus heals people and society by restoring relationship. Truly deep healing comes when we see the crowds pressing in, desperately desiring both the words and the touch of Jesus. The restoration comes when our healing touch meets our neighbor's suffering.

PRAYER: O Christ, free us from our fears and anxieties. Strengthen us with your healing presence. Renew our hope in you and help us to see you through our woundedness. Amen.

I see him most days because he works at the building where I work. He is an elderly man with a ready smile and a strong voice. "How are you this morning?" I ask. "Oh, I'm blessed" is his unfailing reply. *Blessed*, I think as I enter the building. How is it that he, well past retirement age and maintaining a building for a living, thinks of himself as blessed?

Most of the time we consider blessings to be things that bring us pleasure or joy, that make life good or secure. "Count your blessings," we say to someone who has come through a tough time.

Today we read, "Blessed are you who are poor. . . . Blessed are you who are hungry now. . . . Blessed are you who weep now. . . . Blessed. . . ." How could you count these as blessings? No one wants to be poor. No one wants to be hungry or to weep or to be hated or excluded.

Luke's Gospel addresses the issues of wealth and poverty. The rich and poor populate these stories and encounters. Life together in covenant with God requires that all people have the material conditions that make it possible to live with dignity, independence, and self-respect. Hence, the justice of a society will be measured by how it cares for its poor.

Gustavo Gutiérrez, the father of liberation theology, says that God has a preferential love for the poor not because they are necessarily better than others morally or religiously but simply because they are poor and living in an inhuman situation that is contrary to God's will.

Every time I see the man who maintains our building, he says, "I am blessed." And he is; Jesus said so. And so are we when we follow the path of justice for the poor.

PRAYER: Christ, you have promised to bless us. We come to you with hope and expectation. Make us instruments of your blessing to others today. Amen.

Holy Encounters

February 12–18, 2007 • Timothy L. Bias[‡]

MONDAY, FEBRUARY 12 • Read Exodus 34:29-35

An encounter with grace

Is it possible that you and I can encounter God in such a way that the people around us can see the effects of the encounter? Moses' encounter with the holy God brings a shine to his face. The people fear coming near him, so Moses veils his face when he speaks the Lord's commands to the people.

Often my experience of God's presence affects me in ways I find disturbing. Sometimes the encounter takes my breath away, and I cannot speak. At other times the encounter is so deep that tears come to my eyes. In whatever way God's presence affects me, I am no longer the same person.

One such encounter came the day I learned I was adopted. On that day I experienced a sense of chosenness, having been given a name and been loved from the very beginning. This knowledge took me to the mountain where I encountered God's grace through love and acceptance. My life was no longer the same.

In that encounter I began to understand God's grace for all persons. God has chosen us, given us a name, and loved us from the very beginning. We demonstrate our experience of God's transforming grace in our living, our relationships, and our interactions with all persons. Such radical change affects the people around us, frightening some and encouraging others.

SUGGESTION FOR MEDITATION: Reflect upon how your encounters with God's grace have affected you and the people around you. How does your life bear witness to those encounters?

[‡]Directing Pastor, First United Methodist Church, Peoria, Illinois.

An encounter with truth

Who or what is the central focus of your faith? Paul addresses one of the most prevalent issues of our day in his second letter to the Corinthians. Something in our fallen human nature causes us to miss the point of the Christian faith and to become fascinated with the superficial trappings of religion.

Paul, before becoming a Christian, studied the scriptures, worshiped God, defended the faith, and lived a good, moral life. Yet he missed the purposes of God to the point that he orchestrated the imprisonment and death of many early Christians. The truth was veiled; he focused his faith on "right living."

Paul writes, "When one turns to the Lord, the veil is removed," using the veil of Moses to illustrate the difference between the Old Covenant (right living) and the New Covenant (righteousness). He wants his readers to know that truth, which has been veiled, comes from a direct, face-to-face encounter with God in Jesus Christ.

Sometimes we miss the point. We love the Bible more than the God to whom it bears witness. We join the church, through whatever process, without entering into a personal relationship with Jesus Christ. Too often we conform to living a Christian lifestyle without ever changing our hearts. We then run the risk of having the trappings of the faith without experiencing the love, joy, and freedom that come from knowing Jesus.

Paul believed that an encounter with the glory of God in Christ would remove the veil that was hiding the truth. He was convinced that such an encounter would put our faith in proper focus. Has the veil been removed for you?

SUGGESTION FOR MEDITATION: **Reflect upon your encounter with God's truth in Christ. How will you reflect the glory of God in your relationships with those with whom you live, work, and associate today?**

An encounter with holiness

The psalmist helps us understand that in the midst of God's transcendence, God remains involved in the lives of the people. God, the Holy One, is persistently present in our living through forgiveness, righteousness, and justice.

Our holy God differs from other gods. God offers forgiving love to all persons and is not limited to our understandings of relationship. God's shalom includes wholeness, justice, and well-being for all creation and is not limited to our understandings of peace. Just as God's love and shalom were embodied in the life, death, and resurrection of Jesus Christ, so God's love is embodied in the lives of disciples of Jesus and in the ministry and mission of the church of Jesus.

Can you imagine shalom being mosquito netting over the beds of children and adults in remote areas throughout the continent of Africa? When thousands of children die each year from malaria, it is an encounter with God's holy love when mosquito netting provides protection for those who are vulnerable.

Can you imagine shalom being a field of corn in Sudan? When thousands of children, women, and men die each year of hunger, it is an encounter with God's holy love when agricultural projects provide land and farming skills to feed tens of thousands of people.

Can you imagine shalom being a handshake, a hug, or words of kindness? When you and a neighbor or family member or enemy or stranger embrace in forgiveness, reconciliation, and peace, it is an encounter with God's holiness because you are embodying the distinctive love of God.

God is not separate from us in divine holiness. God works with us in forgiveness, righteousness, and justice.

SUGGESTION FOR MEDITATION: Reflect upon how you and your congregation embody the holy love of God. How does your congregation live God's forgiveness and justice? How will you demonstrate God's love today?

THURSDAY, FEBRUARY 15 • **Read 2 Corinthians 3:12–4:2**

An encounter with relationship

What is a church? A collection of rules based on law or a congregation of relationships built on love? Are our action and identity together based on administering the procedures or on ministering to people? I have learned and experienced over my ministry that the stronger the relationship, the fewer the rules. I believe God intends that the church feel and operate not upon an obsession with rules but with deep and abiding relationships.

Paul instructs the Christians in Corinth about the difference between living by legalistic rules and living by relationship. Paul uses the veil of Moses to illustrate his point that the understanding of the Old Covenant, which came through Moses, is fading away. The veil is fading; the teachings of the scripture remain the same. The very heart of the law resides in a relationship between God and God's people. But those who have come to faith through a relationship with Jesus Christ read the scriptures with new eyes and understand with new hearts. Paul felt that when the Spirit of Christ comes into a person's life the veil is lifted, and he or she understands God's message with the heart.

Arguing over right and wrong rules seems insignificant and irrelevant in a world where millions of people starve each year, where nations continue to invest vast financial resources in weapons of destruction, and where people are pushed to the edges of society as unacceptable. In relationship to the love of God we know in Jesus Christ, our rules fade away like the glow on Moses' face. God intends that we operate within deep and abiding relationships.

SUGGESTION FOR MEDITATION: **Reflect on how you and your congregation operate. Is the life and ministry of your congregation based upon a collection of rules or upon deep and abiding relationships?**

An encounter with obedience

Have you ever noticed that Luke's Gospel marks with prayer the major events and critical moments in Jesus' life? After his baptism as Jesus prays, the heaven opens, and he receives the Holy Spirit (Luke 3:21-22). Jesus is praying when he asks the questions that lead to Peter's confession and the first teaching about his coming death (Luke 9:18-20). In today's reading, Jesus takes Peter, James, and John up onto the mountain to pray.

While Jesus prays, the appearance of his face changes and his clothes become as bright as a flash of lightning. Moses and Elijah appear and talk with Jesus about his impending death.

The disciples see Jesus standing with Moses and Elijah, and misinterpret the experience. Peter suggests, "Master, it is good that we are here. Let us build three dwellings, one for you, one for Moses, and one for Elijah. . . ." While well-intentioned, Peter misunderstands what he has witnessed.

Understanding an event is important. Sometimes I misunderstand what it means to be a follower of Jesus. Had I been living then and someone had said to me that Jesus would be executed in a few weeks, I don't know if I would have continued with him. I might have looked elsewhere for someone who fit my idea and image of the Messiah.

The cross, the central symbol of our Christian faith, was not a symbol of success but one of disgrace and weakness. Are you willing to surrender your life and be obedient to the one who died on the cross? Obedience is the only path for those who follow him.

SUGGESTION FOR MEDITATION: **Reflect upon your image of Messiah. Does your image include suffering and death? How are you and your congregation displaying obedience to Jesus? How will you be obedient today?**

An encounter with humility

You have heard the saying that perception is reality; but in today's reading, perception is not reality. Jesus has taken Peter, James, and John up onto the mountain to pray. While he prays, Moses and Elijah appear and talk with him.

Peter's perception of the event leads him to react by suggesting that they build three dwellings and stay there enjoying the light, the glory, and the ecstasy. Instead, Jesus and the disciples return the next day to the valley and the needy crowds. That is where Jesus felt he belonged, and that is where you and I belong. We cannot live on the mountaintop.

Jesus moved from the mountaintop of ecstasy to the valley of need because that is where the gospel becomes relevant. The mountaintop time, while a meaningful and exhilarating experience, is misunderstood by Peter. I can imagine that he began to see himself as an expert in liturgical matters. I am sure he could have drawn up an appropriate order of service complete with hymns and prayers.

But Peter and the other disciples fail when confronted with a father whose small son has alarming and dangerous seizures. Proper prayers in the sanctuary have their place, but if they are not instruments for God's help and healing in the everyday hurts and needs of life, their efficacy is questionable.

Sometimes our experiences of spiritual inspiration and ecstasy are not to make us experts so much as they are to make us humble. Critical moments of prayer connect us to the distinctive love of God, which equips us for making a significant difference in becoming God's instruments of wholeness. As great as the experience might be, it is not for our glory but God's.

SUGGESTION FOR MEDITATION: What meaningful experiences of God have you had in your life? How have those experiences equipped you for ministry? How has humility played a part in your ministry?

An encounter with Transfiguration

The season of Epiphany, which began with the visit of the wise men, concludes with the transfiguration of Jesus. Some people call the Transfiguration a "mountaintop" experience because of its location. But the focus of the experience is actually crucifixion and death.

Jesus has been introducing his disciples to the subject of his coming death: "The Son of Man must undergo great suffering, and be rejected by the elders, chief priests, and scribes, and be killed, and on the third day be raised" (Luke 9:22). He takes Peter, James, and John up the mountain to pray.

While Jesus prays, the appearance of his face changes and his clothes become dazzling. Elijah the prophet and Moses the lawgiver talk with Jesus about his death. In Luke's Gospel all that is written in the law of Moses and the prophets finds fulfillment in Jesus. In other words, the law, the prophets, and Jesus are all part of one story, part of God's plan and purpose.

For Jesus, the Transfiguration confirms that death, rather than being a contradiction of the Messiah, is the fulfillment of being the Messiah. At his baptism, the voice of approval said, "You are my Son, the Beloved; with you I am well pleased" (Mark 1:11). Now the voice of approval says, "This is my Son, my Chosen; listen to him."

Jesus' path is leading him to the cross and to his death. The greatest of all mountaintop experiences are those where we receive confirmation of our obedience. How have you received confirmation of your obedience?

PRAYER: O God, thank you for this week of holy encounters. Fill us with your grace and glory so that all we meet will encounter your holiness in us. Amen.

Lest We Forget

February 19–25, 2007 • *Safiyah Fosua*[‡]

MONDAY, FEBRUARY 19 • Read Deuteronomy 26:1–5

"**D**on't forget the bridge that brought you over." How often I heard these words while growing up. Sometimes they were spoken by an old great-aunt while she sat and rocked on the porch. Other times, they were spoken as an admonition by my grandfather while I watched him work on his car. The old folks hoped that they had seen the last generation of children forced to walk with a stoop because they lived in a room where the ceiling was too low. Through the eyes of faith, they saw a better day coming for black children born in the '50s. The old folks knew, however, that the end of oppression did not always bring out the best in people. They feared that success would spoil us, distancing us from the faith that had sustained us.

Pulpit preachers chased me though my teens with cautions to "remember the days of beans and cornbread." Long before people in the know would talk about the politics of food, street-corner preachers understood that food could fool a person into thinking he or she had arrived and did not need God or the community or even family.

Moses asks the descendants of Jacob to remember their beginnings, just as the old folks and the preacher-folks had warned me to remember the bridge that brought me over. The ritual offering, described in today's passage from Deuteronomy is one of remembrance. The people of Israel were to remind themselves that they had been descendants of a wandering Aramean who went down to Egypt for refuge. Only by the grace of God had Israel become a mighty nation.

PRAYER: God, today I offer thanks for those who endured hardship to give me an opportunity for shalom. Amen.

[‡]Director of Invitational Preaching Ministries for Worship Resourcing, General Board of Discipleship, Nashville, Tennessee.

Remember the bondage you experienced as slaves—and make a place for aliens and strangers to share your faith. After reminding one another of the painful past, Israel celebrates the feast of first fruits with strangers present. Look at the peculiar pairing of painful memories and generous hospitality. It implies that the memory of past suffering enables individuals to empathize with present sufferers and to include them in the feast of the faithful.

I cannot afford the luxury of forgetting the pain of the past. Without those memories I am simplistic, unsympathetic, and all too eager to solve the world's problems with hurried, painless solutions. My grandchildren need me to cry a tear with those who are chosen last for a game on the playground; my children need me to remember the sting of having a professor translate 89.5 into a B on a college transcript. Without these and other memories I risk being distant, disconnected, even dismissive to those around me.

When I visited Dachau, Germany, I was jolted by the late Glid Nandor's grotesque wrought-iron sculpture bearing the inscription "Lest We Forget." It depicts a tangle of skeletons with tortuous facial expressions, placed on the grounds of the concentration camp to remind the human family of its predisposition to inflict pain upon one another. Concentration camps and killing fields are not isolated horrors; they are snapshots of human nature stripped of empathy. We must all remember the pain of personal struggle lest we impose suffering upon others.

Remember the hard bondage you experienced as slaves—and make a place for aliens and strangers to share your faith. Perhaps, before we truly celebrate the feast of life with both familiar people and the aliens that reside among us, we will be required to look candidly at who we are and to remember from whence we have come.

PRAYER: Merciful God, help me remember the pain of suffering and the joy of your salvation, so that I may share good news with both neighbors and strangers. Amen.

ASH WEDNESDAY

I would rather wear the smudge on my forehead than to admit its residence upon my soul. I prefer a crude cross above my eyes to questions about runny mascara. In a society that rewards self-confidence and holds suspect any sign of weakness or emotional predisposition, it is difficult to consider actually following the advice of the prophet to return to the Lord with fasting, with weeping, and with mourning. It is, however, acceptable—maybe even fashionable—to appear in public with a dirty forehead as a sign that I have religion. It is amazing how the symbols of piety, sackcloth and ashes, have been transformed into a mask that hides me from myself and circumvents the intent of Ash Wednesday.

"Blow the trumpet in Zion," the prophet says. Not the trumpet that signals advance to war or the trumpet that celebrates victory, but the one that warns trembling penitents that the day of the Lord is coming. Blow the trumpet that warns penitents like me to wear the smudge of ashes long after their faces have been washed and to admit the smudge on the one place that matters to God, the heart.

"Blow the trumpet in Zion," the prophet says, and "sanctify a fast." Hear the sounds of grumbling need in a world where few are filled—and where we are overfilled. Today I am called to push away from the voracious consumption of everything in my path, for at least a little while, in hopes that I might come to a realization of the inequitable distribution of the world's resources before the fast is over.

"Rend your hearts and not your garments" (RSV), the prophet states. The gift of the day is personal reflection, a season of confession and change. Start the arduous journey from shadow to substance, from ritual to reality, from facade to faith. Today choose the harder course. It is easier to buy new clothing than to mend a soul.

PRAYER: Lord, as I begin this year's Lenten journey, turn my attention to things that matter most to you. Amen.

The construction of the original language text suggests that the temptation of our Lord comes not at the end of his time in the wilderness but rather as a persistent nagging over the course of those forty days. Where does the voice of temptation come from? Jesus is alone in the wilderness. Alone for forty days, with no earthly companions, Mark says, but the wild beasts (1:13). Jesus is alone, with no company save his own thoughts and memories. Alone, by himself, with no one to entice him with a description of his favorite fast food or her favorite beverage. On retreat without cable TV or newspapers or even a good novel. Jesus is just alone. And yet, there alone in the Judean wilderness Jesus hears the voice of temptation.

Where do our temptations come from? Since the time Adam blamed Eve and Eve blamed the serpent, we have become adept at blaming others for giving in to temptation. How convenient to say that people tempt us, that things tempt us, that someone or something else is involved. Then the solution is simply to get away from temptation. Though we may be conditioned to think of temptation as something to escape by a change of venue, this text suggests that if I were alone in the wilderness by myself, I would likely still face temptation.

Does temptation come from without or from within? Perhaps all this time I have wrongly blamed everything and everybody for something resident within me. What if temptation is more an encounter with the unconquered self than the offspring of futile resistance? Perhaps the real issue is myself—not them or it. Forty days of testing and temptation, as alone as one can be on a crowded planet (with a scarcity of convenient wilderness sites) may prove that the voice of temptation comes from within.

PRAYER: Compassionate God, have mercy upon me and teach me the blessings of self-examination. Amen.

The term *compassion fatigue* is creeping into the vernacular of persons who find it easier to pull the covers over their heads than to absorb the tragedies of each morning's news. Of late, there seems to be no shortage of calamity: unprecedented floods, history-making hurricanes, freakish tornadoes—the kind once reserved for filmmakers and wild-eyed talk-show guests have now swept and lapped their way into our living rooms. In spite of so-called superior technology and refined minds, we cannot escape the terrors of this world by changing the channel; they have come to roost on our porch.

Some say that the earth is too warm, hence the unpredictable outbreak of storms and floods. Unlike new cars that lose their smell and begin to amass repairs or houses that show wear and tear within the first five years, the earth was built to last. She is not newly old; she has been old for quite some time and has, until of late, aged in a majestic sort of way. I refuse to accept that the earth is having hot flashes and has become cranky and irregular with age. I have reluctantly joined the whisper that the earth is too warm because we have done something to her.

If it were not for the Lord, this story would be sadder still. God created the earth and has been present with the earth and its peoples through every era. When the Black Death swept through Europe, God was there, preserving humankind. God continues to be made known in human history. While AIDS sweeps through Africa and seeps into the water table of other continents, God is still at work, preserving humankind. Here lately, instead of avoiding live narrations of the human drama, I am beginning to turn up the volume to hear what people are saying about God. Their testimonies are more frequent. God is our refuge. God is our fortress. In God we trust.

PRAYER: O God, we need you more than we have ever acknowledged. Teach us how to find refuge and hope in your presence. Amen.

Confess and believe; believe and confess. Paul repeats this as though it were possible to do one without the other—to confess without believing or to believe without confessing. He could easily have been writing to twenty-first century Christians.

I taught one confirmation class that I will never forget. The class was unusually large and fun loving, so I invited the members' parents to participate in the confirmation retreat. Many of the parents came, and we had a wonderful weekend of games, food, Bible study, and worship. That night at worship something happened! I do not know if it was the song or the sermon; I only know that the light bulb came on for those youth, and the faith that they had been studying suddenly made sense. You could see it in a collage of nodding heads, awestruck faces, and misty eyes. Whatever happened to them also happened to several of their parents who later confided that they found faith that night. Serendipitously, the closing hymn for that evening was "Lord of the Dance." As we sang, some of the girls came to the front, near the communion rail and began to dance! Before long nearly everyone was dancing in the aisles, clumsy gym-shoed boys, parents, and pastor.

I invited the confirmands to help me write the worship bulletin and was not surprised when they chose "Lord of the Dance" for the closing hymn. A few weeks later the class members stood before the congregation to be confirmed; they confessed their faith with a firm belief in what they were saying. As the closing hymn began, it surprised the congregation when the confirmands started dancing, just as they had danced at the retreat. The number of people who danced with them was an even bigger surprise! The newly confirmed confessed what they believed and believed what they confessed. They also chose to dance unashamedly in front of a reserved congregation.

PRAYER: Loving God, help us believe and confess our faith. Amen.

FIRST SUNDAY IN LENT

Throughout the season of Lent, we become more acutely aware that temptation waits for all of us. It waits like an animal in the shadows ready to pounce upon its prey. This experience has always been so for the human family. Temptation waited for Cain before he slew Abel. It crouched until the right angry, jealous moment. Before Cain knew it, he had been overcome. Temptation also waits for you and for me when we are angry beyond words—providing an excuse to do some harm to those who anger us. Perhaps for this reason Jesus suggested that an angry person was just as culpable as a murderer.

Jesus is in a wilderness for this particular time of temptation; temptation also waits for us in the wild places of life. Wild places take the form of circumstances so out of the ordinary that we could be persuaded to suspend the rules, to respond to the seduction of the moment, or to sin for the good of the order. Temptation waited for Moses in a wild place. In a wild moment of realization that life was not fair, Moses willingly looked, first this way, then that, before slaying an Egyptian. The wild places are many; the temptation to exaggerate, to bend the truth, to outright lie waits around every bend in the road.

Temptation waits for us, but we are not powerless. Jesus is not powerless. As a hungry mortal, he refuses the justifiable self-indulgence of turning stones into bread. As a person with hidden strength, he refuses an ostentatious show of power. As a person of royal destiny, he does not require the attendance of angels to prove his worth to onlookers. The One who pitched a tent among us proved by example that yielding to temptation is not inevitable. Jesus teaches by example; neither moments of weakness nor wild places need give way to temptation. Even in the wild place, temptation waits for Jesus in vain!

PRAYER: Lead us not into temptation, but deliver us from evil. Amen.

Stand Firm—But Keep Moving

February 26–March 4, 2007 • John Indermark[‡]

MONDAY, FEBRUARY 26 • Read Genesis 15:1

Life can present a complicated array of confusing choices and overwhelming situations. How can we find our way through—or trust God's way through? *Put first things first.* Remember where and in Whom our lives are grounded. For Abram, the bedrock upon which he stands firm and from which he finds it possible to move forward in faith is God's first word to him: "Do not be afraid."

Fear, far more than doubt, is faith's opposite in the biblical witness. In Abram's case, fear had caused him to pass off Sarai as his sister. Fear drove Abram to discount God's promises of an heir and of a place. Abram had undertaken the journey from Ur, but now it hangs uncertain in Abram's fear of delays in the details of the promises portended. So God announces a word equivalent to putting first things first for Abram: "Do not be afraid."

Do not live in fear. Journeys of faith still stumble on account of fear, which tells us that we are alone, that whatever is not under our control or in our grasp will be lost.

The gospel of God to Abram is a message of community, soon to be enacted in the covenant that follows. It tells us that life resides not in what we may or may not grasp but in whose grace and promise we are held. It is a message that affirms our trust in the One who offers such gracious covenant.

We need not fear, not because there are *not* things to be afraid of in life. We need not fear because God's presence and promises accompany us, empower us, free us.

SUGGESTION FOR MEDITATION: Make a list of your fears. Beside each one, note a promise or experience of God that encourages you not to be afraid. Use this list in your daily prayers.

[‡]Minister, United Church of Christ; writer of Christian education curriculum and devotional books; living in Naselle, Washington.

Do you know your place? "Knowing your place" can be a phrase used to limit or control another's life—or our own. We don't like others rocking our boat. Persons don't appreciate our meddling in their affairs. "That is not your place."

Paul, on the other hand, speaks of knowing our place in a positive sense. Paul counsels the Philippians, and through them us, to "stand firm in the Lord in this way." I take "in this way" as a synonym for knowing our lives are anchored in the place made for us in the love and grace of God. If we know *where* we belong and to *whom* we belong, we can live with values and purposes that differ from those that deny hope or belittle life.

Tradition holds that Paul wrote Philippians while imprisoned. Yet the whole of Philippians is one of Paul's most joy-filled epistles. Gratitude for God and for the community to whom he writes fills its chapters. How can that be? Paul knows his place in life and does not allow imprisonment to define it. His place is defined by life in Christ and citizenship in God's realm.

Do you know your place? Do you know where and to whom you belong: even when life seems confining, even when hope seems distant, even when circumstances spiral out of your control? To live in Christ is to know our place as anchored in love, grace, and hope. Such an awareness of place in our lives frees us to live out our days in actions and words that embody those same qualities.

Do you know your place in Christ?

SUGGESTION FOR PRAYER: Pray this day for those who experience life without place: the homeless, the refugees, those whose grief leaves them in this moment unable to gain their bearing or find their footing. Pray that both they and you will find the gift of place.

One of my seminary professors presided at his daughter's wedding. After the prospective son-in-law offered his vow of fidelity, my professor turned to his daughter and asked, "Do you believe him?" After his daughter took her vows, he asked his son-in-law the same question.

That question cuts to the heart of Abram's wonderings. Time has passed since the promise of child and land. Sarai remains childless. The couple remains sojourners in tents with no place to call home. How can Abram be sure that God will fulfill God's promises?

Then again, how can *we* be sure? How many times have we prayed "thy kingdom come, thy will be done, on earth as it is in heaven"? Faith confesses God's realm and rule to be among us now. But we also know and experience its not-yet quality. The experiences that remind us that we are not yet there move us to question whether we ever will be. Like Abram, we long for some tangible assurance, a guarantee that all will be well.

God offers that assurance to Abram . . . sort of. A covenant is struck. An oath is made. But notice: God does not magically produce an heir out of thin air. God does not hand over a notarized deed for land. God says, "I give, . . ." but the gift is not yet in hand. The gift is in word. Which means, among other things, the gift relies on trust. The journey forward by Abram, and us, is not based on irrefutable proofs that remove all questions. The journey forward is made by trust in the promises and in the One who promises.

Do you believe that?

PRAYER: God of grace and promise, cultivate in me the gift of trust; trust, not as a way of avoiding the responsibilities you entrust to me—but trust as the ground upon which I stand and walk, knowing I can depend upon your word and your presence. Amen.

THURSDAY, MARCH 1 • Read Psalm 27:1-6

Do you have a place of refuge in your life: a place of safety, a place of sanctuary?

I once served as an associate chaplain at a juvenile detention facility in our community. At one chapel service, several youth flashed gang signs. Chapel was one of the few times when youth from all of the lodges were in the same location. That mix, combined with the close quarters, made the signing a potentially dangerous act. Over the next week, I talked with several counselors about what had happened and what we might do.

At the next chapel service, my message expressed a simple theme: sanctuary. Sanctuary not only as a place of worship but as a place of safety. The chapel had to be a place where the things that normally threatened were removed. Otherwise, chapel would provide no sanctuary. Many of these youth intuitively knew about sanctuary or the absolute lack of it in their experience of life on the street. I closed with these words: "When we come into this room, we seek God's presence in worship; we hope for the experience of sanctuary. God will be faithful to the promise to draw near—and God leaves the rest to us. Chapel will be as much or as little as we make of it. So let us keep this a place of worship, a place of safety: our sanctuary".

We never had gang signs again, not because the sermon worked but because the youth needed sanctuary. They needed refuge.

Do you have a place or person of refuge in your life? The psalmist affirms that Yahweh serves as such a refuge in his life. What say you?

SUGGESTION FOR PRAYER: **Seek out a place of refuge. Be aware of the presence of the Holy One in that place and sanctuary. Pray for those who seek refuge. Decide on action or advocacy that offers refuge to persons in need of it.**

"Imitation is the sincerest form of flattery," so the old saying goes. Thomas à Kempis wrote *The Imitation of Christ* to encourage Christians to live in the example of Christ. Who would argue that we should do otherwise?

But take a closer look at this day's verse. Paul counsels the Philippian community to "join in imitating *me*." Whoa, just a minute here! Imitate *me*? Wasn't Paul the one who wrote in 1 Corinthians 3 to stop falling prey to the cult of personality that divides the church into factions? And now he says, imitate *me*!

Keep in mind the traditional context of this passage. Paul is imprisoned. He does not ground his appeal in the egomania of "me first" in all things. He asks the Philippians to live the faith even when circumstances seem to deny it. Beyond that, his appeal acknowledges a fundamental truth about Christian witness. If others are to see (and imitate) Christ in this world, they sometimes will have only our lives as example. We can easily portray the negative side of this aspect. Too often people make a case for remaining uninvolved in Christian community by pointing out how church members treat one another and the world around them. On the positive side is the ancient begrudging admiration of the early church in the words of a would-be critic: "See how these Christians love one another!"

Imitate me. There may be moments when imitating Paul might not be the best example to follow as when he states in First Timothy: "I permit no woman to teach or to have authority over a man" (2:12). We are all human. But Paul rightfully reminds us here of our call as individuals as well as communities: to be the body of Christ on this earth for the sake of others.

SUGGESTION FOR MEDITATION: How might your life imitate Christ this day, and who might benefit from that? Give thanks for those whose lives have been an example of Christ for you.

Waiting is not a virtue of this age. I recall the minutes it would take my first computer to load in preparation for use. Now I can become impatient waiting for it to reach the desktop screen, although the wait is measured in mere seconds. Some of us gleefully latch on to leaders and candidates whose wisdom can be reduced to sound bites. Others of us do not have time or patience to wait for solutions that will take time, much less sacrifice. We want things now. Attention deficits are not limited to adolescents dealing with learning disabilities.

The psalmist too speaks with an undertone of urgency. A hearing is needed. A fear of God's absence ("do not hide your face") marks this plea. Trouble in the form of false witness and violence is just at the edge, around the corner.

Yet the psalm concludes by affirming not once but twice: *wait for the LORD*. Waiting can be difficult, especially when misunderstood as detachment or as flight from responsibility. The waiting spoken of by the psalmist is neither of those. The psalmist's waiting is trust that acknowledges not all things are ours to control. Or manipulate. Or determine. Waiting for God can be a radical act of obedience in a culture primed on "It's always up to you"—because sometimes it's not. For those whose faith always seems to turn on activism, waiting may be the needed reminder of sabbath and renewal. Waiting is not about inaction. Waiting is not about resignation. Waiting is about trust in the sovereignty of God. Waiting is a life lived with integrity to fulfill those expectations. Such waiting can bring strength and courage when the time comes—and come it will—to move from waiting into action.

SUGGESTION FOR PRAYER: **What do you need to wait for? Use the following breath prayer as it seems appropriate throughout this day: Wait for God (breathe in); be strong (breathe out); take courage (breathe in); wait for God (breathe out).**

SECOND SUNDAY IN LENT

It is said that water will follow the path of least resistance. Discipleship does not—at least, not the discipleship modeled by Jesus. "I must be on my way."

In the face of Herod's threats (and remember, Herod's capacity to kill had recently been demonstrated in the execution of John the Baptizer), Jesus stands firm. Yet standing firm does not mean paralysis. The way he must go is not one dictated by fear of Herod but by faithfulness to God. The absence of fear motivating this way becomes clear in Jesus' perception of what awaits in Jerusalem. Had he feared Herod, Jerusalem would have been the last place he would have gone. Herod was a sideshow in comparison to Pilate and the power of Rome. But Jesus stands firm in his resolve to keep moving in the direction of faithfulness and ministry.

This week we have explored texts and stories that affirm faith's twofold call: stand firm—but keep moving. That affirmation emerges out of trust: trust in God's presence to stand with us, trust in God's invitation as we move on our path of discipleship to not be afraid. Or perhaps, we might better say: to not *live* afraid. As noted in Monday's meditation, we will always have reasons to *be* afraid. Herod and Pilate provided ample reason to be afraid in Jesus' time. We might summon similar causes to fear from the crises of world and nation—and our own communities. However, we choose whether to *live* afraid. Jesus chooses to live on the basis of trust, not fear. So may we choose: to stand firm and to keep moving, in the grace of God's presence and toward the light of God's promises.

Vaya con Dios—go with God!

PRAYER: Holy God, plant my feet and faith when I need to stand. Stir my heart and spirit when I need to move. In Jesus Christ. Amen.

Repentance—A Way of Life

March 5–11, 2007 • *J. Thomas Laney Jr.*‡

MONDAY, MARCH 5 • **Read Luke 13:1-5**

While Jesus is teaching one day, someone in the crowd brings up a much talked-about event—the killing of some Galileans who were in Jerusalem to offer their sacrifices. Pilate had likely ordered the killing and the mixing of their blood with that of their sacrificed animals in a brutal display of power. We are not told why the person raises the issue, but Jesus' response indicates that the real reason lies in revisiting the age-old question "why?" Why did this happen—and to these people?

Whenever we wrestle with these profound questions we are attempting to understand the moral order of things. Our hope is that if we can fathom the why, then we can learn a clear lesson from the tragedy and perhaps avoid a similar fate by taking the lesson to heart.

If Jesus is ever going to answer this fundamental question of life, this is the perfect occasion. But he does not. In fact, Jesus never attempted to answer fully the questions we struggle with about evil and suffering. His silence indicates his contentment and willingness to let stand the great insights and perspectives found in the prophets and the book of Job.

A major milestone along the journey of faith is the acceptance that there is no neat answer to the "why" questions related to evil and suffering in this world. We come to realize that if we make our relationship with God contingent upon a satisfactory answer we will surely be disappointed. Jesus chooses not to give a simple interpretation, and we must take it on faith that there is none.

PRAYER: Dear Lord, as I continue on this journey of faith, grant to me such faith that accepts that there is no simple answer to the age-old question "why?" Amen.

---

‡Pastor, West End United Methodist Church, Nashville, Tennessee.

In responding to an inquiry about tragic death, Jesus mentions another disaster, the collapse of a tower in Jerusalem that killed eighteen people. Unlike the deaths of the Galileans, these people were victims not of human malice but of a freak accident. In both cases, Jesus declares that those killed were no worse sinners than any others in Galilee or Jerusalem. Their fate was not God's vengeance for an egregious sin.

But Jesus then says something that sounds strange to our ears: "Unless you repent, you will all perish just as they did." It seems as if Jesus is saying that our repentance will protect us from such tragedies. But that, of course, is not true. There is no immunization from sorrow and pain.

We must look closer to see that Jesus is speaking not of the manner of their deaths but the fact that they died unexpectedly, suddenly, without having time to reflect on the full scope of their lives. The only faithful response to these kinds of events is to examine one's own life in awareness of the inevitable, ultimate reckoning. Turn back to God, turn around, return to the source of your life—personally and communally. Repentance does not inoculate us against tragedy, but in that turning—returning—to God, we are able to live with life's uncertainties and unanswered questions.

To appreciate Jesus' response on that occasion, we also have to recognize that he was talking at that time a great deal about judgment—about the reckoning God will bring about in the final days. He is reminding all of us that we cannot keep on going our own way and be right with God. But more than that, he is saying that even religion, in the sense of doing and saying religious things, is not enough. Only by following Jesus, going with him, learning from him, trusting him do we know truly what repentance and salvation are.

PRAYER: Show me, Lord, how faithful repentance can be an ongoing discipline in my spiritual life. Amen.

Repentance, a major theme of Lent, is often misunderstood because the call to repentance often seems like a command to feel bad. Biblically speaking, though, repentance is much more profound than simply feeling remorse or groveling before God. Repentance entails an attitude of honesty, truthfulness that willingly acknowledges the painful realities about our lives—not simply specific misdeeds but our misalignment with God's purposes. It admits our need for God's corrective love to bring us back into harmony with the reign of grace and justice. Repentance, therefore, is never simply a private, personal activity—though it incorporates the personal. It is also a communal activity intended to heighten our awareness of the pervasiveness of sin and the ease with which we forget God's purposes and, instead, try to chart our own course.

Christian worship has traditionally included a corporate confession—not because we are all guilty of each sin but because the church understands repentance as a discipline that strengthens our resistance to the seduction of our private agendas.

Another corporate action that enhances the discipline of repentance involves the recollection of stories of disobedience and faithlessness. Paul reminds the Corinthian Christians of examples from the scriptures of people who had received God's blessings but strayed from God and suffered because of it. He hopes that the believers in Corinth will take these lessons to heart and not assume exemption from succumbing to temptation.

Using stories of others' failings as lessons can be tricky. Sometimes we grasp the appropriate message and truly learn from others' missteps. Other times we mistakenly assume that our knowledge of their fate means we could never make the same errors. Pride can impair our ability to identify properly with those whose failings are well known. True repentance hears the lessons of the past with openness, humility, and gratitude.

PRAYER: Guide me, loving God, in appreciating the lessons of faith passed down in scripture and Christian tradition. Amen.

Paul's instructions to the Christians at Corinth also include a clear warning against smugness: "So if you think you are standing, watch out that you do not fall." The discipline of faithful repentance includes a proper sense of vigilance against overconfidence and self-righteousness. As soon as we think we have it made, we are most vulnerable to being toppled by our own hubris.

Nor are we to think our trials and temptations are worse than anyone else's. Paul reminds the Corinthians that the world assaults the faithful everywhere with all kinds of enticements to turn away from God. A proper spirit of repentance keeps us from trying to compare our ordeals with those others face.

God is faithful, says Paul, and will not let us be tested beyond our strength—another confirmation of the scriptural assurance that God will not give us more than we can handle. Speaking out of his own experience and conviction, Paul has felt God's presence and help in all of the crises he has endured. Yet each of us knows persons and situations that seem to contradict that claim. Some people succumb to temptation and despair. How do we make sense of this fact in light of Paul's assertion? We accept that in freedom we can ignore or resist the encouragement God offers. Paul believed wholeheartedly that God provides the way out of the temptations that come to us. Simply put, Paul remains convinced that God will never set us up to fail.

This then returns us to the dynamic of the discipline of faithful repentance. In humility and gratitude we turn back to God, knowing that God wants us to draw strength and hope from the Holy Spirit. God is never a skeptical bystander watching to see if we will fail a spiritual test. Instead, God always actively seeks to assist us in any way to which we're receptive.

PRAYER: Let your Spirit intercede for us, gracious God, in ways that enable us to navigate the trials and temptations that come our way. Amen.

FRIDAY, MARCH 9 • Read Luke 13:6-9

This short parable uses the familiar metaphor of a fig tree to convey the sense of urgency regarding the day of judgment Jesus has been speaking about. A fig tree's reason for being, of course, is to bear figs, a staple of a Middle Eastern diet. When the owner of the fig tree sees that this one is barren for the third year in a row, he is through with it. "Time to cut it down," he tells his vineyard keeper. "No more need to waste good earth with this fruitless tree."

But Jesus says the keeper is not quite ready to give up on the tree. "Let me dig around it and put fertilizer on it and see what happens next year," he requests. "If it is still barren, then you can cut it down."

The telling of this succinct parable after the call to repentance in the preceding verses underscores the fact that the fruit God desires is precisely that of repentance, realignment, and acceptance of God's grace. Yet evidently the people hearing Jesus do not respond to God's invitation to genuine repentance. Even so, Jesus wants to make clear his commitment to interceding on behalf of everyone, to giving another chance to hear the judging—and saving—word of God.

The call to repentance does not come in a spirit of angry condemnation. Through Jesus God asserts the divine longing for our return to righteousness and the divine willingness to do everything possible to help us make that decision.

PRAYER: We thank you, holy Lord, for the patience you show us and the world when we do not bear the desired fruits of repentance and righteousness. Amen.

Jesus' expression of commitment to help us with our repentance, renewal, and new fruitfulness echoes a venerable scriptural affirmation of God's graciousness. Centuries earlier God had invited all of Israel to come to the wondrous bounty of God's goodness. Fresh water, delicious food, wine, and milk would abound. There was no need to waste money and labor for rewards that would not satisfy. God only asked that Israel listen carefully and follow God's guidance in order to have the full life God wanted to share with them.

Isaiah then restates the invitation: "Seek the LORD while he may be found, call upon him while he is near; let the wicked forsake their way and the unrighteous their thoughts; let them return to the LORD that he may have mercy on them." Isaiah simply asks that the people acknowledge that their path is the wrong one. God will be merciful, Isaiah assures the people, and will abundantly pardon.

The reason for this graciousness lies far beyond our understanding. Forgiveness and mercy of this magnitude do not make sense in human terms. Our natural inclination is to focus on merit and worth. How can God possibly be so welcoming? God's reply is simple: "My thoughts are not your thoughts, nor are your ways my ways. For as the heavens are higher than the earth, so are my ways higher than your ways and my thoughts than your thoughts."

We can never hope to fathom God's mercy. That part of God's essence differs completely from our human nature. While we might worry, for instance, that people will take advantage of that grace, God is utterly confident that divine mercy will yield the faithfulness that God longs to see in our lives. All we have to do is celebrate this remarkable truth of God as we respond to this irresistible invitation.

PRAYER: Loving God, we rejoice that your gracious ways and thoughts are beyond our imagining. Amen.

THIRD SUNDAY IN LENT

The discipline of faithful repentance is one way we awaken in our souls the deepest longing for reconnection with our loving Creator. Few passages in scripture express this longing in such vivid ways as Psalm 63, and yet we do not readily acknowledge this profound desire in our lives. When we confidently focus on our own abilities and powers, the thought of hungering for God seems absurd. We know what we hunger for—success, prestige, wealth, happiness.

The spirit of repentance punctures this self-delusion. Instead of letting us convince ourselves these worldly "blessings" will satisfy us, faithful repentance makes us pay attention to the nagging voices that know the truth: none of the offerings of this life is a fulfilling objective for our souls. We are, indeed, made in such a way, as Saint Augustine said, that our hearts are restless until they find their rest in God.

Psalm 63 describes the ideal spirit of worship—beholding God's power and glory, praising God with our voices and lifting up our hands as we call upon God's name. Even as we admire this expression of faith, we admit it does not reflect our experience most of the time. Burdened with responsibilities, weighed down by cares and problems, we often come to worship distracted and preoccupied—simply hoping for strength to get through another day and week. The sheer delight the psalmist describes in being present to God sounds like a foreign language.

The psalmist's very approach invites our repentance—not because we have necessarily done wrong things but because we see the gap between how we want to approach God and how we actually do. The reassurance of all the passages this week is that God eagerly welcomes us back, provides encouragement and strength for the turning, and celebrates with us when we return to where we truly belong.

PRAYER: Let my worship this day, dear God, focus solely on your glory and love. Amen.

Lost and Found

March 12–18, 2007 • Kim Cape[‡]

MONDAY, MARCH 12 • Read Joshua 5:9-12

The rhythm of the Christian year quickens in Lent. As Advent prepares us for Jesus' birth, Lent prepares us for Jesus' death and resurrection. Being human, we are not equipped for either theophany. In our Joshua text, the people renew their commitment to their covenant God. By celebrating the Passover they reenact their parents' story of deliverance; the current generation recalls God's deliverance from slavery in Egypt.

The eyewitness generation has died; this is the first celebration of Passover by the new generation. The parents' rebellion at the border of the Promised Land had condemned them to wander in the wilderness until they died. Even in their wilderness wanderings, God sustained the people with manna, literally giving them their daily bread. Every day reminded them that their very existence depended on God. No matter how faithless we humans are, God is faithful. God knows our needs. Whether manna in the wilderness or produce from the land, God provides with grace that goes ahead of us.

I often feel that going through life is like driving a car and looking in the rearview mirror. We see the significance of events after the fact, not before. "We have always done it this way," is not a faithful response to each new day given us by the Creator. God has been faithful in our past. Can we not trust that God will continue to care for us in the future?

PRAYER: God you are always faithful. You make a way when there is no way. As you have led us in the past, lead us into the future. Give us the courage to trust you even when we cannot see the new thing you are doing. Amen.

[‡]Austin district superintendent, Southwest Texas Conference, The United Methodist Church; living in Port Mansfield, Texas.

John Wesley wrote, "Our affections are alienated from God and scattered abroad over all the earth. All thy passions, both thy desires and aversions, thy joys and sorrows, thy hopes and fears, are out of frame, and are either undue in their degree, or misplaced on undue objects." Sounds like Wesley is saying that we are a mess. We listen to every voice but God's, and we get ourselves "out of frame."

And we can't fix our "out of framedness" without God. We try to fix our condition. We try with food, drink, sex, smoking, children, church work, Little League, law school, houses, success, status, boats, drugs. We exhaust ourselves and one another by looking for someone or something to fix us, to save us from the misery of being out of frame. Yet we look outside ourselves for help, to misplaced objects, in vain.

Our "strength was dried up as by the heat of summer." It's as if the psalmist acknowledges before God, "OK, I give up. You win. I was killing myself my way. I need you, God, to be my life's compass." The psalmist confesses wrongheadedness, being like a horse or a mule without understanding. This is one size that fits all. When we confess to being "out of frame," we are not telling God anything that God does not already know. Confession requires having the courage to recognize and admit in God's presence that we have lost our way. We acknowledge our own condition of being in rebellion and ask God to save us from ourselves.

PRAYER: O God, you know us better than we know ourselves. Help us to open the hands of our hearts to release what is destructive that we hold so tightly. With your help, let us receive what you would give us for our healing. Thank you for this assurance that we are safe and can trust you. In Jesus' name we pray. Amen.

Thomas Merton said that the two enemies of the spiritual life are laziness and cowardice. Ouch! Self-deception is one place that laziness and cowardice combine to blind us to what God calls us to be and do. Most people do not get up in the morning, look in the mirror, and say, "I am going to make choices today that will mess up my life, betray my best self, and generally insure that I and those I love are miserable." But we lie; we cheat, steal, and commit adultery anyway. Laziness is the enemy of the spiritual life through self-deception. We avoid looking at what we don't want to see.

Maturity is having the courage to attend to our inner lives, confess our sins of omission and commission, and invite Jesus to heal our hard hearts. When I was ten years old my parents gave me, against their better judgment, a BB gun for Christmas. I was the only kid in a six-block radius who got a BB gun that year. In my joy I went out in the front yard and started shooting. I picked various targets, and then decided I would try to shoot a leaf off a tree. *Bad* idea. The leaf I chose to shoot was directly in front of our next-door neighbors' picture window. I ran home, guilty and terrified. I knew I would be killed. It didn't shatter the window; it just made that little crater. When my mother confronted me and asked if I had committed this crime, I lied. I could not confess because I knew I would be killed, and I knew that replacing a picture window was a debt I could not pay. I could only confess if I knew I would be forgiven. I did not know at the time that there were lesser penalties than death. I never did tell my mother. Like God, she knew what I had done, but I could not tell her. And because I could not confess, I could not receive forgiveness. Because Jesus paid our debt and forgives us, we can receive the forgiveness already given. What a relief! What is preventing you from laying your burden down?

PRAYER: **Merciful God, like children we fear the consequences of our actions. Quiet our fears. Meet us in our terror. Forgive our guilt. O Lord, you are our Rock and our Redeemer. Amen.**

Usually the need for reconciliation implies a serious conflict between parties. Rancor, abuse, abandonment, and addiction wreak havoc among us and cause great pain. We speak of couples on the verge of divorce being reconciled. We hear of estranged children who seek reconciliation with their parents.

South Africa established the Truth in Reconciliation Commission to deal with the crimes committed during apartheid. Archbishop Desmond Tutu chaired this commission. Both Archbishop Tutu and Nelson Mandela knew that reconciliation would not come without confession and forgiveness. The future of South Africa depended on this hard, painful work.

Likewise, in many ways the quality of our own future depends on the work of reconciliation. Our text states that God has reconciled the world to God's self through Christ Jesus. God has done this for the world. God, in Christ, forgives everyone, everywhere. This is good news! God has done God's part. Our part of the ministry of reconciliation is to accept the forgiveness that God offers us and then offer forgiveness to those who have wronged us. This is easier said than done.

What relationships in your life need reconciliation and healing? What burdens of anger, hatred, and deep hurt does God desire you to release? In saying the Lord's Prayer we pointedly ask God to forgive us *as* we forgive those who have sinned against us. We will receive the measure of forgiveness that we mete out to others. Sobering thought, isn't it? Most of us collect the wrongs others do to us and conveniently forget or discount the harm we do to others. According to Paul, we cannot claim peace with God until we are at peace with our neighbors. And we cannot claim peace with our neighbors until we are at peace with God.

PRAYER: **Merciful God, help us to pray sincerely the prayer Christ taught us. Give us the grace to be reconciled to you. Give us the peace that we can find only in your love. Amen.**

The words of a hymn keep playing in my head: "My life flows on in endless song, above earth's lamentation. I hear the clear, though far-off hymn that hails a new creation." The hymn points to a haunting hope, the hope of being a new creation in Christ. Don't we all long to be changed, cleansed, redeemed, saved, transformed by the love of God in Jesus Christ?

It takes maturity and life experience to realize that we cannot create our own meaning. It takes the experience of failure to know that we cannot by ourselves save ourselves. We have to reach the point where we can't touch bottom before acknowledging our need for a Savior. A paraphrase of the beatitudes captures this sentiment beautifully: Blessed are those who know their need. The word *transformation* in Greek derives from *metamorphed*. This transformation, this metamorphosis is something God does in us, if we allow it. Wesley talked about "sanctifying grace" as the grace that transforms us and moves us from the image to the likeness of God.

In 2001 I went with a team of people to South Africa. During our stay we visited the John Wesley Seminary in Pretoria, where we met Sidwell, a United Methodist pastor and dean of the school. Sidwell took us to a church in Soweto, the scene of an anti-apartheid rally that dissolved into a massacre when the police panicked and started shooting the students. There were still bullet holes in the walls and ceiling. While we ate lunch, Sidwell told us his story. Because of his anti-apartheid participation as a student activist, he was jailed and tortured. He told his story with such an amazingly gentle spirit that I asked him, "Sidwell, after all that you suffered, why aren't you bitter?" His reply? "You are right. I am not bitter. It was too heavy. I could not carry it." Sidwell is a new creation. Because he is at peace with God, he has made peace with his enemies.

PRAYER: God, look upon us with mercy. Heal our broken hearts. Transform our experiences into encounters with the living Christ. Amen.

We find this story only in the Gospel of Luke. Chapter 15 tells the story of the lost sheep, the lost coin, and the lost son. Each successive story escalates the stakes. Is a lost sheep important? Is a lost coin important? How valuable is a lost son? Jesus addresses these stories to the Pharisees as he tries to teach God's perspective: *all* people are in need of God's grace and redemption. The Pharisees, in their inability to recognize their own sinfulness, are equally lost; they are "out of frame."

To understand Jesus' meaning, put yourself in the place of each of the characters in the story: the father, the prodigal, the elder brother. I began praying this text as one who believed it had nothing new to teach me. But I thought, *What the heck, I will be the lost child.* In my scenario I went to my father, asked for my inheritance, and had a good time wasting it. Then I found myself in the pigpen—muddy and stinking. I was so hungry that the pig slop looked good. It came time for the lost child to come to himself, and at that moment (like a weather advisory warning scrolling across the bottom of a TV screen) I saw: "Get up out of the pigpen! You've been there for the past five years!" And, I said, "Oh, I have been in the pigpen for the past five years." So I got up out of the pigpen and began walking home, stinking and filthy, rehearsing my little speech: "Father, I have sinned against heaven and against you and am no longer worthy to be called your child. Just let me be a servant." But the Lord God Almighty saw me from a long way off, ran out to meet me, *hugged* me, and and put an arm around my shoulder. As we walked back to the house, God said, "Kim, we are going to skip the robe and the ring part. What you need is a *bath!*"

PRAYER: O God, help us put ourselves in your story. Call us from the pigpens we have made of our lives. Receive us home with joy. Bathe us in your love and mercy. Help us know that we are your precious children, and you are doing everything you can to save us. Amen.

FOURTH SUNDAY IN LENT

As I reflected on my pigpen experience, I was struck by the fact that what had kept me in the pigpen so long was my pride. Ironic, isn't it, that pride would keep me in the pigpen? The name of my pigpen was self-pity. Remember that Paul acknowledged himself as the chief of sinners? Oh no, I was! I felt determined to punish myself for my sin and failure. I'm proud of my suffering. Get up out of the pigpen? *No way!* I am having too much fun punishing myself.

Here is the catch. If I'm punishing myself, am I not playing God? Isn't judgment God's job? Repentance means letting God be God. And the good news comes in God's mercy. Gordon Cosby once said that when we hold onto suffering past its season, we have an idolatry in our life. And so we ask, "What is the idolatry in my life?" Can you name your pigpen? Once we can name our pigpen, then we have enough self-awareness to get out of it. Remember, Jesus says that the lost son "came to himself." When we come to ourselves, we can hear God's summons to "get up out of the pigpen!" God is both Savior and Judge; the judgment is mercy. Can you handle mercy? If not, aren't you playing God?

The parables of the lost and found have more to teach us. Our lostness is not a one-time experience. We are always stumbling into pigpens. We find new ways to get lost. Thanks be to God that God is always searching for us, watching for us. Are you hiding from God in a pigpen? Isn't it time to get up and come home? Life is hard enough. Jesus has already paid the price for you. Not to accept his offer of forgiveness is the sin of pride. Some things we cannot do by ourselves, and we don't have to.

PRAYER: God, you have made your love and redemption known through Jesus. Take away our false pride, and give us the humility to follow him. Amen.

A People of Hope

March 19–25, 2007 • Bronson C. Davis[‡]

MONDAY, MARCH 19 • Read John 12:1-8

Some days the pressures of daily life can overwhelm us. We often try to do the proverbial "twice as much in half the time" and run ourselves ragged trying to inculcate speed, productivity, and dependability into our working lives. We live by deadlines and find ourselves at the mercy of expectations from coworkers, family, and friends. No wonder we find ourselves easily distracted, unable to focus on what is happening right before us.

We would like to think that life was a lot slower and easier in Jesus' day. Yet, somehow I think Jesus feels equally burdened when he goes to a supper in his honor in Bethany where Martha serves; Lazarus, Mary, and some of his disciples are present. It is six days before Passover, and Jesus senses that his ministry will soon culminate—possibly not in the triumph his disciples imagine. He knows his opponents lie in wait. Jesus has to be thinking about his next move. How can he best deliver God's message to a world so headed in the wrong direction?

In this story, Jesus exhibits a quality that all of us need to embody as we move through our busy lives. Despite his many concerns, he is absolutely present for Mary as she anoints his feet with the precious ointment. He fends off Judas Iscariot's criticism and recognizes her simple act of kindness. Jesus isn't distracted by the meal, by the challenges of his ministry, or the criticism of the cost of the ointment. Rather, he focuses on Mary and her special gesture of gratitude.

PRAYER: Dear God, in the hurly-burly of our lives, help us be attentive to those around us and to give thanks readily for the many blessings that come our way. Amen.

[‡]After thirty-two years in university fund-raising and publications, now retired and working with the stewardship programs of First United Methodist Church, Fort Worth, Texas.

The notion that we would always have the poor among us was difficult to accept for those of us who came of age in the idealism of John F. Kennedy and carried forward the hope embodied in Lyndon Johnson's War on Poverty. Much in Jesus' ministry pushed against this fatalistic notion. Did he not say his purpose was to bring life and to bring it abundantly? Is it not up to us to somehow make that happen in the here and now?

The years since the '60s, however, have not seen the eradication of poverty. We have come to know the problem of homelessness firsthand, which in light of the great prosperity of the 1990s is simply difficult to comprehend. And we have seen widespread droughts, hunger, and death in Africa—not merely in one country but in five different countries at various times in the last fifteen years. Natural disasters have also impoverished communities, such as the tsunami in Thailand; hurricanes Katrina and Rita on our Gulf Coast; and earthquakes in Iran, Turkey, and Mexico.

We also celebrated the end of the Cold War and truly believed that peace was at hand only to witness subsequent wars in the Balkans, in Rwanda, in the Sudan, and twice in Iraq. A prime by-product of war is poverty. Just when we think we are making progress, events conspire to make us wonder.

Yet pessimism and fatalism are unnatural states for Christians, who are a people of hope. We are Easter people who continue to feel the imperative to somehow make this world better. Faced with the intractability of poverty in our world, we can only adopt the stance encouraged by John Wesley in his admonition to "Do all the good you can, By all the means you can, In all the ways you can, In all the places you can, At all the times you can, To all the people you can, As long as ever you can."

PRAYER: Gracious God, may I embody Wesley's admonition in my life. Amen.

The importance of forgiveness is certainly one of the Bible's themes. In this passage from Isaiah, God says to the Israelites, in essence, let's forget past indiscretions; I will give you a new opportunity. "Do not remember the former things or consider things of old. I am about to do a new thing; now it springs forth, do you not perceive it?" Starting over with a clean slate is an enormously attractive state of being.

Numerous other examples in the Bible relate God's forgiveness, as well as human forgiveness: Joseph forgives his brothers for selling him into slavery twenty years before. Jesus extends the notion of forgiveness even further than his Jewish forebears when he declares his power to forgive sin. Additionally, Jesus' admonition to turn the other cheek and forgive enemies is particularly radical for the time. By including the concept of forgiveness in a prayer, Jesus underscores its importance: "And forgive us our debts, as we also have forgiven our debtors" (Matt. 6:12).

Why does the concept of forgiveness figure so prominently in the Bible? Possibly our early development as humans hardwired us for revenge and made us partisan and tribal by nature. We know from the study of psychology that we will go to extremes to defend our ego, and such defensiveness weighs against our being quick to forgive. At the same time, we know that carrying a grudge exacts a toll on us; remaining bitter over past wrongs can poison the soul. The everyday admonitions to "get over it" and "let it go" are common recognitions of this problem. However, forgiveness in its best form needs to be active. This involves a "reaching out" to the source of affliction, identifying the pain, and then simply, sincerely saying, "I forgive you," or (paraphrasing God's words to the Israelites in Isaiah) "Let's let bygones be bygones. Let's do a new thing together."

Prayer: Dear God, as we move through our days, help us to be quick to forgive, guided by the example of your son, who, in his last difficult hours, said from the cross, "Father, forgive them; for they do not know what they are doing." Amen.

Since childhood Paul had wanted to be a rabbi and a Pharisee—a leader in the Temple—though he had come to study in Jerusalem from a small town in Asia Minor. He was well on his way to that goal, exhibiting ferocious dedication and soon rising to the attention of Caiaphas, the high priest in the Temple. It was he who sent Paul on his mission to Damascus, delivering letters that denounced the teachings of Jesus. En route, Paul was struck by a blinding light, the revelation that completely altered his life. The Christian persecutor became the Christian proselytizer and for years neither side trusted him. Paul turned his back on his achievements and headed into an uncertain future buoyed only by his "knowing Christ Jesus my Lord."

In our life's struggle to make meaning and to find order, value, and structure, we encounter the Bible and, with luck, discover Paul and his profound faith: "For [Jesus'] sake I have suffered the loss of all things, and I regard them as rubbish, in order that I may gain Christ and be found in him, not having a righteousness of my own that comes from the law, but one that comes through faith in Christ, the righteousness from God based on faith."

The irony is that we can recite the creeds, attend church, live a godly life, and still not experience the grace of God or the power of faith. Only a commitment to our faith—a leap empowered by a sudden understanding of who Jesus is and what his message is for us and how it offers meaning and truth for our life—makes the difference. We may not understand exactly why we are making the commitment. It just feels right. And later, while we are "living" the commitment, we come to understand. We are what we commit to, and this commitment to Christ's message brings the faith and joy Paul describes so vividly.

PRAYER: God of us all, may we not only allow Paul's words to guide us as we move through this time of Lent but may his conviction and faith motivate us toward a life of meaning and grace. Amen.

FRIDAY, MARCH 23 • Read Psalm 126

This psalm comes to us following one of the darkest periods in Jewish history, the Babylonian Captivity. During that time the Jews believed that, with the destruction of both the Temple and Jerusalem, God had abandoned them. They not only lost their homes and their freedom but also their God. However, they gradually discovered that life would right itself and that much good would come from what seemed to be their darkest days. God had been with them all along, both in the darkness and in the light.

The early followers of Jesus experienced similar feelings. Most probably believed that Jesus' ministry had died with him on the cross. Like the Jews in Babylonia, Christ's early followers were convinced that God had abandoned them. Only with the passage of time did this community begin to understand the Easter experience and to realize God's presence with them through the darkness of Good Friday and the brilliance of the Sunday that followed.

Today we manifest many of the same attitudes. We believe God is with us in our triumphs but somehow disappears during our failures. In this view, God resembles a capricious parent who rewards good behavior and brings misfortune or no fortune for disobedience. Therefore, we must work to get on God's good side so things will go our way. We hear prayers seeking victories in football games, changes in the climate, and success in the job search. These prayers use God as a talisman. But God is so much more than a parent or puppet master. God is the ground of our being, the agent who empowers us, the source of the love who makes life meaningful, and the wellspring of hope who pushes us to make a difference for others in this world.

PRAYER: Dear God of us all, we take comfort from your continuing presence. Guide us by your Spirit to look within our hearts and to do the right thing in advancing your reign here on earth. Amen.

The Jerusalem church headed by Peter and James, Jesus' brother, never envisioned that Jesus' ministry would be more than a reform movement within Judaism. They gave no thought to a new religion. On the other hand, Paul, a practicing Jew his whole life, comes to understand Jesus' ministry to be to *all* humankind. For Paul, faith in Christ as Lord becomes the critical element that circumscribes all other requirements.

Paul's understanding of the universality of Christ's message and ministry did not come at the time of his revelation on the road to Damascus. These ideas developed over many years as Paul pursued his own ministry. By the time he writes his letter to the Philippians, however, these notions have become central tenets of his belief system.

Paul's willingness to struggle with his brothers in Jerusalem over the meaning and thrust of Christian ministry reminds us of our own responsibility to confront our faith and construct its meaning for our own time. Through the ages, the message of Christianity has had many interpreters, all of whom wrestled with the scriptures, their own revelations, the history of the Christian era available to them, and the thought forms of their world. Only then might they discover the true meaning of Christ's message and ministry. Yet many of their interpretations are no longer relevant for our time. An ever-changing dialogue exists between our experience of God as a presence and the practical and intellectual understanding of the world in which we live. The faith of Christianity has never been stable or static. The struggle of each generation keeps our faith alive and relevant. We may find the faith of our forebears absolutely right for our own time, but only in our struggle to realize this do we make that faith our own.

PRAYER: Dear God, help us to better understand our faith and to examine it in the light of our time, the scriptures, and our experience of you. We press on to make it our own, because Christ Jesus has made us his own. Amen.

FIFTH SUNDAY IN LENT

Speaking through the prophet Isaiah, God reminds the Israelites of their salvation from the bondage of Egypt through a series of miracles, the last of which was making a way through the sea for them and causing the extinction of the Egyptian army. But God doesn't want to dwell on the past. When the Israelites find themselves captive in Babylonia, God again speaks through Isaiah, saying, "I am about to do a new thing." God hasn't given up on the people, even making "a way in the wilderness and rivers in the desert" to create a new day, a new opportunity, for the Israelites to redeem themselves.

No matter how much we disappoint God, other people, or ourselves, we always have the opportunity to make things right—to make that 180-degree turn. As Jesus would later state, "for God all things are possible" (Mark 10:27). God needs every one of us to make this a better world and so breathes hope into the darkest corners of our existence to help make this happen.

God is always looking to "do a new thing"—to help redeem humankind and move this world in a more positive direction. While we understand Jesus Christ to be God's most radical "new thing," God's efforts to lure us in a positive direction did not end in the first century. God continues to work through us to achieve hope for this world—a world of possibility and a world in process waiting on us to move it forward.

Our modern world can easily discourage us; events conspire to overwhelm us, and despair seems the only rational emotion. But we cannot surrender or admit defeat. We must continue to push the boulder up the hill but not in a Sisyphean struggle in which we then watch it roll back down. Our destiny is to keep pushing until the boulder rolls over the hill.

PRAYER: Dear Holy One, give us the strength to push through the welter of everyday life and to focus on those things that make us better people and this world a better place. Amen.

Holy Friendship

March 26–April 1, 2007 • Pamela Hawkins[‡]

MONDAY, MARCH 26 • Read Isaiah 50:4-9a

As we approach the end of the Lenten journey, I am stopped at the beginning of verse 7 of this chapter from Isaiah: "I have set my face like flint. . . . " Through the prophet's imagery, I imagine the face of Jesus, jaw jutting forward and eyes strong, as the time draws near to complete the journey begun earlier, when he first "set his face to go to Jerusalem" (Luke 9:51). I wonder if Isaiah's words cross the Lord's mind. Do they inspire courage? Can they settle his heart?

Our reading spreads before us words of untainted confidence in God. At other times the prophet laments the suffering and humiliation that fall upon God's servant, but not now. Here, Isaiah draws upon all that stirs in the depths of his spirit, all that solidifies his rock-hard confidence in God's presence, even while in the hands of hard-hearted enemies.

And so, I imagine Jesus setting his face "like flint" toward Jerusalem. He knows what stretches before him, that he will be scorned and spat upon. He knows that some of his friends will be threatened, and some will become a threat. It is enough to harden anyone else's heart but not the heart of Jesus. Instead, he will only harden his face, compelled to move forward by an unflinching confidence in God.

In any circumstance or struggle, whether personal or global, we have the promise of God's presence with us. Yet most of us have faced circumstances where God has seemed absent. But if we, like Jesus, will make a home for God's word in our hearts, our confidence in God can be strengthened for whatever waits ahead.

PRAYER: God of north, south, east, and west, point our lives this day in the direction that you desire for us. Amen.

[‡]Associate pastor, Belle Meade United Methodist Church, Nashville, Tennessee.

TUESDAY, MARCH 27 • Read Luke 23:1-49

It is a stark absence. Not once in the forty-nine verses describing Jesus' trial before Pilate will Jesus' disciples stand out in the crowd. They will all but vanish, disappear into the nameless sea of faces until the worst is over. The ones closest to him will distance themselves. His best friends will huddle in the shadows or feign disinterest in anything other than just being one of the crowd. To do anything more, especially in the days and hours leading up to the Cross, will be too risky.

Friendship marks us. We know this. We notice to whom our children are drawn. We worry about whom our youth will want to date. We decide, even strategize, about whom we will invite into our communities or to our homes or to our tables. And if the ones we have called friends begin to struggle with some issue—if they are accused or suspected, if they are addicted or rejected, if they begin to be seen as different from most or to seem dangerous to some—we have to choose all over again whether or not we still will be their friend.

It is telling that in these same verses of scripture where Jesus' best friends will become invisible, the only friendship we see is between his accusers. "That same day Herod and Pilate became friends with each other; before this they had been enemies."

Friendship marks us. We know this. And we know that claiming to be a Christian friend will lead us to be present with many whom others will not choose, will not stay with, and will not stand up for. May we, this Lent, become true friends in the way that Jesus calls us.

PRAYER: O God, guide and friend, deepen our love for you and for each other today and every day. Amen.

"I guess it's in God's hands now, isn't it, pastor?" It was a mother's question—half plea, half statement. She was seated on a worn-out sofa in the back of the house as far away from the front-room television as she could get. That way she could not hear the latest news report about her son's pending execution. Imprisoned for murder, her son was out of appeals; his final clock was set.

"I guess it's in God's hands now," the woman said again, not really to anybody in particular; but I heard her, as did my son who had gone with me to share food and presence with this woman and the few friends who had stuck by her through the day-by-day loss of her son. A pretty thin crowd gathered behind pulled blinds. Humiliation by association had worn them down over the years; you could see it in their eyes. They had heard the whispers and seen the jeering looks from other neighbors. And yet, there they were, holding on to thin threads of friendship and a thick trust in God as if their future depended on it.

"My future is in your hand," writes the psalmist, voicing the same thick trust in God as had the heartbroken mother, while strength and hope thin away in misery.

In Luke's account of Jesus' passion and death, words from this psalm are on the Lord's lips as he breathes his last. In the life of the church, words from this psalm most often find their way into liturgies for remembering the dead. But let us not forget that this psalm is also for remembering the living, especially those who live in deep anguish or sorrow. This psalm is for any of our friends who need to find refuge in God. May we bear God's trustworthy word to someone who needs to be remembered today.

PRAYER: O God, may we find refuge in your steadfast love and call upon your name. Amen.

She would slip into the back pew right after the service began. She must have stood just outside the doors listening for that first note of music, entering when she would not have to speak to anyone. She simply came to be present for the Lord's Supper.

And then, right before the service ended, she would slip out again. Her timing was perfect; it never failed. Week after week she would slip in, sit in the back, come forward to share the bread and cup, and then slip out into the night.

When she did approach the table, hands ready for the broken bread, she did not look down but instead always looked right at me. For all of her desire to be anonymous in coming and going, she revealed a vulnerability to be known at the table. Up close, I saw evidence of a hard-lived life—her eyes and face revealed a scarred, haunted presence. But in the dim lighting of the back pew, no one could see it.

Then one night at service's end, she was still there. I saw her smiling in my direction, so I excused myself from a conversation and went to her. All she said was, "I love it here. Something happens." She then told me her first name and said, "See you next week" as she slipped out the doors.

"When the hour came, he took his place at the table," begins Luke's account of the Last Supper. "Then he took a loaf of bread, and when he had given thanks, he broke it and gave it to them," and something happened. From that night on, when any gather at the Lord's table, something happens. Often we fail to remember this. May we be reminded that something happens in the gifts of bread and cup.

PRAYER: Lord Jesus Christ, may we accept the invitation to your table and greet all who come to receive. Amen.

"Let the same mind be in you that was in Christ Jesus," Paul writes to the church at Philippi—a deceptively simple invitation into the Christian spiritual life. How hard can it be to begin to think like Jesus? After all, simply through his thinking Christ brought good things to life.

The mind of Christ was compassionate—he cared for the vulnerable and the lost, drawing people to him like lambs to a loving shepherd. The mind of Christ was quick—quick with simple parables, pregnant pauses, and perfect comebacks, causing even the hardest hearts to look at situations in new ways. The mind of Christ was wise at an early age, seasoned before his time, and clear in the middle of chaos. And the mind of Christ recognized the unjust, untrue, and unacceptable, shifting the eyes of many to see what had been overlooked. How can we not desire to have this same mind?

But if we stay close to the rest of Paul's text and stay close to Jesus on the road to Jerusalem, we will discover that God takes an interest in far more than our minds. Soon, verse by verse, this beautiful hymn from the early church reminds us that to become imitators of Christ requires that we use all aspects of ourselves.

God desires our minds and our attitudes to be Christlike, yes; but also our actions. God attends to our feet and our knees, our hearts and our hands. God takes interest in the words on our tongues and the prayers of our lives. But God also longs for us to step out in faith, dismantle injustice, and put sweat equity into peacemaking. This God, known to us in Christ Jesus, is our all-and-everything God—our God who desires that all and everything about us reveal to the world that we are the body of Christ.

PRAYER: O God, may we learn to love you and all of creation with our whole selves. Amen.

It has taken my whole life to notice the beauty of broken seashells. For years my beachcombing routine has been predictable. As the surf rolls back, I search around my feet for a shiny edge of something lovely, something partially revealed between sand and sea that I can quickly pinch before it disappears again. And with just a moment in my hands, I decide whether the shell is worth keeping. Imperfect, broken ones I usually reject—returning them to the sand with a disappointed toss.

But lately I have begun to notice a different beauty in broken shells. My eyes are being caught by the color of a fragment or the shape of a fractured edge. For some reason I am drawn toward wonder about the life created for the shell's intricate space—what did it look like? Where, in the depths of the sea, had been its home? I cannot say why, after all these years, I can no longer walk past what I have been rejecting, except to say that something has changed the way I see.

As I read from Psalm 118, my eye is drawn to verse 22 and my imagination to those tossed-back shells of earlier years. What had appeared unappealing and imperfect to me, have been, in the eyes of God, treasures not to be rejected. So too, this text reminds us, is the treasure and gift of Jesus, the cornerstone of our faith. He was set down in the tides of power, poverty, and politics; but many could not see him for what he was. And so, he was tossed back—rejected—at least, so it seemed, until a few days later he appeared again to some whose eyes were opened to see in new ways. May the light of God illuminate our journey with Christ in new ways this season.

PRAYER: O God of light, pour out your mercy on us that we might see with new vision any whom we have cast aside. Amen.

PALM/PASSION SUNDAY

It is a most intimate moment in the text, one almost hidden in the ups and downs and comings and goings before Jesus' final entry into Jerusalem. As a young colt nervously stamps the dust and jerks against the lead, cloaks are quickly thrown onto his back. And then, while dust and hooves settle, the strong arms of the disciples set Jesus on the colt. Jesus does not climb up alone, according to Luke; he places his life in the hands of his friends as he faces the road into Jerusalem.

For the disciples to set Jesus on the colt requires getting close to the Teacher, to grasp an arm or brace a shoulder. It means being close enough to feel Jesus' breath on their skin, close enough to smell the sweat on his cloak. At least one friend will be to Jesus' back; others will be eye-level, looking him square in the face. Jesus could have found a nearby wall to stand on without leaning toward his friends, but Luke describes a different kind of friendship.

For Jesus, once he enters the city, there will be many intimate moments of discipleship. There will be bread-breaking and wine-sharing. There will be foot-washing and truth-telling. And at what would appear to many as the end of the road, there will be time once again for a few to put their hands under his arms and their faces to his face as they set him down from the Cross. Intimate moments, all.

The Christian's journey to Jerusalem and beyond calls for extraordinary acts of intimacy. Discipleship requires vulnerability, closeness, and a willingness to lean in the direction of others. In this Lent, may we give thanks to God for those who stand ready to love us.

PRAYER: O Christ, may we lean toward you this day, as you lean toward us; may we rest upon each other, head to head and heart to heart, strengthened for the journey. Amen.

A Play within the Play

April 2–8, 2007 • W. Paul Jones[‡]

MONDAY, APRIL 2 • Read Isaiah 42:1-9

The church divides its year into two "rehearsal" periods for a drama that discloses the meaning of everything. The plot unfolds in three acts: promise/gift/response. The first rehearsal is titled Advent/Christmas/Epiphany and the second Lent/Easter/Pentecost. During the intervening thirty-plus weeks, we live out that drama in our "ordinary" daily life.

Thus Lent crescendos this week as a play within the play. Excitement is rampant as we dress for our parts, ready to pass in triumph with Jesus through the Jerusalem gate—anticipating a victory over repressive authorities. Isaiah's dream is about to happen, for God "will bring forth justice to the nations." Now is the moment, for "the former things have come to pass, and new things I now declare." But our cheers drown out Isaiah's hints that this week may not end as we hope—for he will not "lift up his voice or make it heard in the street." In fact, "a bruised reed he will not break." What kind of a liberator is this?

The plot intensifies. The night before his entry, Jesus dines with friends. Unexpectedly, Mary anoints him with costly ointment as Jesus whispers something about its being for his burial, while a "friend" prepares to betray him. And Hebrews warns that although Jesus will enter triumphantly, the temple sacrifice will be *his* blood, no longer that of goats.

The week ahead will plunge us into the question that undid the disciples: "Who do you say I am?" Equally important is a second one: "Who does Jesus say that we are?"

PRAYER: God, are the mixed messages I receive your doing or mine? Amen.

[‡]Emeritus Professor, St. Paul School of Theology; Trappist Family brother; author of twelve books, including *The Art of Spiritual Direction* (Upper Room Books, 2002) and *An Eclectic Almanac for the Faithful* (Upper Room Books, 2006); living as a hermit/priest near Pittsburg, Missouri.

Unfortunately we cannot track Jesus' precise activities during these first days of our Holy Week drama. The Gospels agree on his triumphant entry, but then uncertainty sets in. In one Gospel Jesus cleanses the Temple that evening, while for others it happens the following day. For one he spends his nights on the Mount of Olives, while others have him with friends in Bethany. What they do agree upon is that he spends his days teaching in the Temple, deliberately provokes the authorities, privately prepares his confused disciples, and seeks safety outside the city nightly.

Viewed from our comfortable distance, the whole scene becomes surreal. A peasant carpenter who spent over thirty years in total obscurity suddenly makes his appearance, and in one year (no more than three) exhibits such amazing charisma that he is either passionately loved or lethally hated. By claiming to incarnate who God is, he mirrors painfully back who we are.

Today's scripture moves toward a shocking climax, so total that this Jesus with a "mouth like a sharp sword" must have been chosen from his "mother's womb," called before he was born for a lead part destined to overturn not only Temple tables but everything about life as we know it. Yet is it possible that our liberator will do so as a slave—as foolishness to our world, a stumbling block that shames our wisest and strongest? Subversion is about to take place, because the very pulse of our society is to "be someone" by competing for power, prestige, and possessions—winning by making certain that others lose. But here, astoundingly, Jesus is about to be destroyed for the opposite: losing one's life to gain it, dying in order to live, giving away in order to receive. No wonder Peter cries out for all of us: "Don't do it!" But when Jesus refuses, it seems easier to crucify him than to follow.

PRAYER: Christ, couldn't you have figured out an easier way? Amen.

At my ordination, I was startled to hear the words of Isaiah 50:1 read: "The Lord GOD has given me the tongue of a teacher, that I may know how to sustain the weary with a word." I knew how to teach by talking, but Isaiah goes on to describe teaching the word by action—giving "my back to those who struck me," "my cheeks to those who pulled out the beard," and not keeping "my face from insult and spitting." I was being called to "set my face like flint." This week's drama is about all of us called for cross-carrying duty.

Understandably, monks for centuries have begun their worship with the words of Psalm 70: "O God, . . . deliver me. O LORD, make haste to help me!" Our calling discloses us to be "poor and needy." The incredible difference between Christ's cross and ours, however, is that he had to carry it alone—because "all his acquaintances . . . stood at a distance." Not so for us. While Jesus is "the pioneer," we can "run with perseverance the race that is set before us" because "we are surrounded by so great a cloud of witnesses." The Christian is never alone because the church is far more than a few individuals meeting in a building down by the gas station. The church of Jesus Christ is an amazing panorama of persons living and dead, among whom we are called to take our place with their support as a multitude of companions.

Even so, John's Gospel reminds us that only God is trustworthy, for in each heart resides the makings of betrayal: "Is it I?" It almost seems that Jesus chooses Judas to do the deed, for when Judas goes out, Jesus insists that now he "has been glorified." Without Judas there is no good news! Paul spoke of the fortunate fall, for without sin we would never know God's forgiving grace. Perhaps we have here the "fortunate betrayal," witnessing to a God who can turn our worst deeds into redemptive ends.

PRAYER: God, I am so sorry but thanks for somehow making it right. Amen.

THURSDAY, APRIL 5 • Read 1 Corinthians 11:23-26; John 13:1-9

MAUNDY THURSDAY

We enter the climactic days of our play, called the Triduum ("three days"), so crucial that they consume half of our earliest Gospel (Mark). Persons ignorant of Christianity would need only participate in the church's worship from tonight through Sunday in order to understand it all. In fact, all our worship is a richly textured drama through which we participate in this meaning of God's actions on our behalf.

Various threads of history begin to converge in today's scene. The Exodus reading (12:1-4, 11-14) for Maundy Thursday portrays the founding Jewish event of Passover that liberates God's people from slavery through the blood of a lamb. Correspondingly, Paul's Corinthian letter portrays the founding Christian event of Eucharist, giving this day its name: Maundy Thursday (mandate—"do this in remembrance of me"). Protestants commemorate this night in sadness as the "last" supper with Jesus. Catholics provide the joyful thread by celebrating it as the "Lord's" supper, which originates our communing with Christ as Real Presence. The Triduum is not just in the past, for as Psalm 116 insists, it is ongoing whereby "precious in the sight of the Lord is the death of his faithful ones."

Then Jesus makes his move, introducing an act so unique that the church has at times regarded it as a sacrament. The one about to be slain takes a towel as his vestment, and, before our eyes, God becomes our servant. Incredible. I remember a time when our board of ordained ministry was so internally split as to be inoperative. Not knowing what else to do, the chairperson brought in a basin. As he washed our feet, he asked that we wash the feet of the person from whom we felt most alienated. "I have set you an example . . . that you love one another." Ashamed and humbled, we sang a hymn and went out—reconciled.

PRAYER: Jesus, "you will never wash my feet!" But would you, please? Amen.

GOOD FRIDAY

Centuries before Good Friday ever happened, Psalm 22 provided the blueprint. The psalm describes a person taken by God from his mother's womb, only to have his hands and feet pierced, lots cast for his clothing, and mocked with taunts about letting God "rescue the one in whom he delights." He is to be "poured out like water," his tongue cleaving to his mouth, crying out, "My God, my God, why have you forsaken me?" Totally broken, he is laid "in the dust of death."

We can understand this amazing correlation in three ways. The first is prophecy: God discloses what will happen. The second is that Jesus, searching scripture for what God would have him be and do, found in this psalm God's intention for his Jerusalem finale. The third is that the disciples, devastated by Good Friday, devour scripture in order to understand why God allowed such a tragedy. They find clues not only in this psalm but also in today's Isaiah reading. The promised one will be "despised and rejected." He will bear our griefs, be bruised for our iniquities, and be led like a lamb to slaughter. Then it will make sense to the apostles, in a manner distilled from a story of two of them on the Emmaus road—when a "stranger" interprets the scriptures. In having the scriptural dots connected, they finally hear what Jesus has told them before and they have not understood— that he *had* to die, that he *would* rise, and that their eyes would be opened to see all things as *new*.

Only then will the disciples dare to call this Friday good. But at this point in our drama, there is only bad news. Jesus' cry of "Why?" is the cosmic scream of billions of suffering humans throughout history. If only something more than human could be going on here. Could this actor be God in disguise, whose primal line is this: "I will remember their sins . . . no more." But today we can only wait, hoping against hope that the play is not yet over.

PRAYER: Jesus, when I'm not sure about God, I trust you. Amen.

SATURDAY, APRIL 7 • Read Job 14:1-14; 1 Peter 4:1-8

HOLY SATURDAY

Today's psalm provides Jesus' last words and the reality every human faces. "Into your hand I commit my spirit" (31:5). None of us knows with certainty if it is God or nothingness that awaits in the darkness. Holy Saturday makes very clear that faith is simply a thread on which we Christians dangle over life's tragedies. Thus it is appropriate to begin with Job, witnessing to life as full of trouble, our days fleeing like shadows, our withering like a flower. Look away, Job screams at the darkness, that I might enjoy at least one day before I lie down never to "rise again." Yet he dares to ask: "If mortals die, will they live again?"

On Holy Saturday, the odds overwhelmingly favor death's finality. Nietzsche is right: "God is dead." The disciples know it is all over—betrayed by the God whom they had betrayed. We, the audience, ready ourselves for the houselights that end our pitiful drama—as Pilate posts guards against foolish talk about resurrection and the broken disciples walk sadly to their fishing boats.

Yet precisely at this point the imagination of the church becomes staggering. Scripture gives a clue with these strange words: "The gospel was preached even to the dead." And the church dares to declare in the Apostles' Creed that on Holy Saturday Jesus "descended to the dead." Often we ask the question, "What of those who died before Christ?" An ancient sermon describing this day portrays Christ with spit on his face, his hands and side still bleeding, looking for Adam and Eve in order to free them. He "harrows hell," leads them out and all the damned who will come—to be enthroned in heaven. The banquet is ready; the eternal dwelling places prepared; and the crucified God discloses his favorite game as "lost and found." We are stunned. What makes the gospel so hard to believe is that it is too good to be true. But it all depends on tomorrow.

PRAYER: God, I thank you that your imagination is greater than your anger. Amen.

Sunday, April 8 • Read 1 Corinthians 15:19-26; John 20:1-18

Easter Sunday

Scripture is definite: death ends every life. That is why "the last enemy to be destroyed is death," declares Paul. Enemy indeed— so much so that "if Christ has not been raised," those "who have died in Christ have perished" and we are "of all people most to be pitied" (1 Cor. 15:17-19). Our one hope is that if God actually raised Jesus from the dead, he will do so for us who believe in his dream.

The Gospel lesson begins with a foot race. John, the younger disciple, wins. But frightened at what he might find, he pretends to bow to age and lets Peter enter the tomb first. Scripture speaks of seeing and believing; but they just go home, for they did not understand. If they had, they could never have gone home again. Rumor of a dead man walking around might be an interesting phenomenon but hardly significant beyond the evening news.

But Mary refuses to go home, and that makes all the difference. Yet even talking to the walking dead man is insufficient, for one tiny word is missing—"Mary!" Only when each of us is addressed by name will our shattered world be transformed. Psalm 118 anticipates: "The stone that the builders rejected has become the chief cornerstone." And standing at that garden corner, what does our world look like through resurrection eyes? Isaiah dreamed of it: "A new earth" where no longer is heard "the sound of weeping" and "the cry of distress," for none shall "hurt or destroy on all my holy mountain." What an incredible resurrection vision.

Yet there is more. "The cloth that had been on Jesus' head" was "rolled up in a place by itself." This is the resurrection cloth (called a corporal, meaning "body") on which we in the Roman Catholic tradition serve Holy Communion. On it the resurrected one is ongoingly present in "the breaking of the bread."

Suggestion for meditation: Meditate on the Resurrection as the ongoing incarnation birthed in each of us.

God's Human Speech

April 9–15, 2007 • *Barbara Bate*[‡]

MONDAY, APRIL 9 • Read John 20:19-23

We tend to think of language as the essential element of communication, but it's not. Eye movement, tone of voice, physical gestures, volume, space, and time play a larger part in the meaning we take from other people's messages to us and the ways our conversations are heard and interpreted by others.

Imagine the disciples huddled behind a door that has been "locked for fear of the Jews." They apparently don't believe what Mary Magdalene has told them about Jesus being raised from the dead—perhaps because of the speaker herself. Jesus comes to them with a powerful series of nonverbal and verbal messages that revive them. First, he moves through solid matter and open space to stand among them.

Second, he speaks to them with four simple words, "Peace be with you." His third message is again nonverbal as Jesus offers his hands and side to them to see. In the fourth message Jesus repeats the earlier verbal blessing, but this time he adds the rhetorical crux: "As the Father has sent me, so I send you."

The crucial nonverbal message occurs when Jesus breathes on the disciples, giving them the experience of the *ruach* or breath of God. This nonverbal essence of life receives added emphasis when Jesus speaks these words to the disciples: "Receive the Holy Spirit." It starts at that moment to empower them to become a new community, offering the forgiveness of sins that Jesus alone could offer prior to his death.

SUGGESTION FOR MEDITATION: **Think about a time when someone who has been a God-connection for you offered a longed-for blessing. Breathe in God's holy and life-giving presence.**

[‡]United Methodist local pastor, pianist, retreat leader, and mental health advocate; teacher and writer about communication, gender, preaching, and spirituality; living in Ocean Park, Washington.

The Revelation to John begins much like one of the letters from Paul to the individual churches. In this case, though, the sender of the letter is not in the midst of community but banished to an isolated island, writing on command to seven distant churches.

The opening verses make the writer's purpose clear: "Blessed is the one who reads aloud the word of the prophecy, and blessed are those who hear and who keep what is written in it" (1:3).

This qualifies as rhetoric: the words are meant to be spoken, to be heard, and to be effective. For those of us living in the twenty-first century who know the Bible as a written document, it's easy to forget that this rhetoric or human speech served as the primary means of communication many centuries ago. People might never read from a scroll, but they were likely to hear the voices of prophets, preachers, and storytellers.

This introductory section of Revelation weaves together the talk of humans and the talk of God. Seven churches bound to earth are trying to survive and thrive. The voice and vision of "One like the Son of Man" lifts up each church by name (1:12). The writer has already stated the reasons for communicating. God's emissary Jesus Christ has loved and freed us through his blood. And those who knew him, whether as seekers or persecutors, will be affected in the time when Christ comes in the clouds. It is prophecy, not just a reminder of the earthly life and death of the Human One.

SUGGESTION FOR MEDITATION: **Read aloud verses 4 through 7. Listen as you speak, getting a sense of the potential power of this spoken introduction for people not yet met in person. Notice the rhetorical essentials: who is the source of the message, who are the receivers; why does this source have ultimate credibility and what are the communicator's expectations for the future? As you finish reading aloud, close your eyes and slowly say the words in verse 7: "So it is to be. Amen." Do you feel certain or tentative as you speak those words?**

In one sentence at the start of the Revelation to John, we read many different identifiers for God, most of them rooted in the Old Testament: "'I am the Alpha and the Omega,' says the Lord God, who is and who was and who is to come, the Almighty." Notice how these words give variety and fullness to the language identifying the Holy One.

1. Moses is told to identify God to the Hebrews suffering in Egypt by the words "I AM has sent me to you."
2. *Alpha* is an adaptation of the Hebrew word *aleph*, which can mean either ox or leader.
3. *Omega* is the last letter in the Greek alphabet.
4. *Lord* is often used in the Old Testament to denote the personal deity, ruler of the Hebrews with sometimes capricious qualities.
5. *God,* as translated from the Hebrew, denotes the more transcendent deity, creator of the universe and of all beings. [See *God: A Biography* by Jack Miles, Knopf, 1995, for details about the distinction between Lord and God.]
6. *Who is and who was and who is to come* is a rhythmic phrase that sums up the God of all history—past, present, and future.
7. *The Almighty* is a Hebrew word used widely in Genesis and Job but never in the New Testament Gospels.

In merely twenty-three English words in this introduction to Revelation, the writer gathers up seven aspects of God in terms that spread throughout the rest of the Bible. As a rhetorician John of Patmos opens the door for receivers unknown to him to connect to his Source by using many terms. Could he have been that clever? In 2007, could we follow his lead?

SUGGESTION FOR MEDITATION: Which of the words or phrases in Revelation 1:8 do you find challenging or problematic? Which offer hope and give life?

PRAYER: O God, may I become more open to unfamiliar as well as familiar words and images for you. Amen.

God's human communication depends on individuals being willing to speak up for God, even in risky circumstances. Astounding actions by Peter and the other apostles indicate that Peter is now free of the fear that had led him to deny Jesus.

The story's rhetorical situation pits Peter and the apostles against a high priest of the Sadducees. The disciples have been imprisoned for speaking out. The high priest supposedly would have the upper hand by being able to arrest the troublemakers. But the prison door has been opened, and the angel has sent them out to speak in the Temple to "tell the people the whole message about this life" (Acts 5: 20). There's nothing like a miracle story of a prison break to show that the high priest's orders are powerless in the face of these gospel witnesses.

One essential rhetorical task is to sum up a situation in a few words. In this case the summary gathers up the facts of the Jesus story in forty words. Peter speaks of God's work in raising up Christ despite the human authorities "hanging him on a tree," with the ultimate impact of Christ's being on earth to "give repentance to Israel and forgiveness of sins."

In a rhetorical situation, the persuaders note the constraints of their setting. It may seem that the apostles would feel constrained by the high priest and the Sadducees; but in fact, the reverse is true. The apostles are now the credible ones who speak the truth as they see it, knowing that the people around them have seen the evidence of new life in the healings and other miracles. The strength and urgency of their rhetorical message cause the high priest to enforce "strict orders not to teach in this name," but silencing these excited, hopeful people is impossible. Conflict inevitably rises between legalism and the spirit.

SUGGESTION FOR MEDITATION: **Where have you seen a person in conflict try to restrain another person by citing a rule against communicating? If a so-called gag order is unsuccessful, what alternatives might you suggest to address the conflict?**

Thomas has missed the miraculous moment in the locked room. No words can convey Jesus' nonverbal actions when he passed through the door, showed his hands and side, and breathed the Holy Spirit into the other disciples. The language Jesus *spoke* that night was only a small part of the whole experience. Thomas must have felt tremendously isolated from his ten compatriots when they related their versions of the night's events. Was Thomas unreasonably skeptical? I don't think so. He knows that a visit from the risen Savior is an unparalleled event. A second-hand report is just that, secondhand.

A number of people who deal with addiction or substance abuse try with all their might to find sobriety and a productive life. Often key to positive response to an addiction counselor is the advisor's having experienced addiction and struggled to walk away from the highs and lows toward balance and survival. As human beings we long for direct experience, whether it is the experience of awe and amazement in the disciples' case or the recognition of what fear and desolation feel like in the recovering addict's case.

Jesus responds to Thomas with empathy, not judgment, offering himself just as he had done with the disciples a week earlier. Given that gracious understanding, Thomas exclaims, "My Lord and my God," like others who have seen and recognized God in front of them. The verse that follows in John's Gospel seems to have been written for members of a later community. Its rhetorical intent is to remind people that faith does not depend on being an eyewitness. But I treasure and count on the story of Thomas's being left behind and then drawn back into the circle of Jesus' love.

PRAYER: I thank you, God, that your story includes not only miracle and mystery but also loss and recovery. May I experience Jesus' love wherever I am. Amen.

Christian leaders in many African nations experience the polar opposites: energetic new congregations *and* major repression by governmental authorities. While living in Harare, Zimbabwe, in 1997, I noticed that the single government-owned television station broadcast only two programs from the United States. Communication from Zimbabwe to the rest of the world has also been limited since the 1900s. Most American citizens have no idea what people's daily lives are like in Harare or the rural areas.

Late in 2005 the bishops of The United Methodist Church's Central Conferences received equipment and training to help them reach other Christians around the world. When I received my first e-mail message from the Zimbabwean Conference Office, I felt the Holy Spirit, God's breath or *ruach*, bringing words and new life from across thousands of miles and years of enforced silence.

At the end of the first century CE, the writer John, exiled to the island of Patmos for his Christian preaching, writes to seven mainland churches in Asia Minor. The members of these churches face persecution and possible arrest by officials under the Roman emperor Domitian. John may never see the letter's recipients, but he wants to encourage them to hold on to their commitment as Christians. Twenty centuries later, the risk of speaking truth to power remains a reality for Christians in Zimbabwe. Bishop Nhiwatiwa's letter to other Christians was transmitted via the Internet, an approach Americans may take for granted but African Christian leaders cannot.

Despite the huge difference in the means of transmission from Patmos and Harare, the heart of both messages is the same. They are God's human communication, sent out to expand the power of God's love and justice in the world.

PRAYER: Thank you, God, for showing us the power of your communication, then and now. May we not hang back from speaking words of life to the world. Amen.

"May everything that breathes praise the Lord!" Saying those words immediately brings to my mind the twirling bodies and grinning faces of sisters Grace and Lindsay. Ages four and one, they fill our small church sanctuary each Sunday with an infectious delight.

Rhythm instruments such as a tambourine, rain sticks, and gourd shakers are kept at the front of the church for children to pick up and use as we sing the first hymn. Each of the sisters has a favorite. Gracie likes the rain stick, a long section of wood filled with seeds that sound like raindrops when the stick is turned over. Lindsay often chooses the tambourine, shaking its metal disks and drumming on its surface at the same time.

Psalm 150, last of the book of Psalms, sums up the exuberance that Lindsay and Grace exhibit, free of self-consciousness. While we choose quiet music for our community prayer time, we often begin or end our worship with gospel tunes that lend themselves to rhythm instruments and clapping.

Loud noise does not automatically lead to godly reflection, to be sure. High-decibel amplified sound can drown out the sound of human singing and speech, whether in a worship service or on a radio broadcast. Keeping the praise connection personal and direct seems to foster a balance between exuberance and quietness.

Children can truly lead the adults when it comes to gathering with joyful noise. The spontaneous singing and dancing of Grace and Lindsay bring energy into our Sunday worship, whether they are sitting on the chancel steps or dancing to "Jesus Loves Me" as they go off to Sunday school. Their contagious joy makes each person feel a part of "everything that breathes" in God's creation.

PRAYER: God of all music and all children, give me ears to hear and eyes to see your love in the exuberant sounds of children. Help me remember that I am a beloved child in your eyes so I can praise you with every breath of my being. Amen.

Transformations

April 16–22, 2007 • Thoburn F. Thompson[‡]

MONDAY, APRIL 16 • Read John 21:1-14

This passage is so rich in images—disappointed fishermen, slow recognition of a beloved master returned from the dead, nets not torn by a huge catch, 153 large fish, a lakeside charcoal fire, and an invitation to share a meal of roasted fish and bread.

I live in Minnesota. Folks in my part of the country know what it is to fish and not catch. We know about torn nets and the "big" fish. We tell others the number caught, the species, and how many we lost or released. When there is a catch, one companion expertly fillets the fish, another friend cooks; we invite one another to taste the best portion, and together we finish the last morsel.

A few years ago seven fishing buddies stood together on a Boundary Waters Canoe Area lakeshore: fathers, fathers-in-law, sons and sons-in-law. It was cold and pouring rain. We had caught only one fish that blustery day. With no dry spot to sit down, we stood and shared the one fish, bread, and one another's company—a time of special sharing. It was enough! All of us remember the meal, the fish, and the bread we shared. For my part, a wet and cold long paddle out of the BWCA was small price to pay for the enduring companionship of that "shore lunch."

This powerful story of Jesus and the disciples on the lakeshore is not about the details of fishing but of the relationships that were reinforced and transformed at that post-Resurrection meal. It was and is sacramental, our shared meal.

PRAYER: Dear Creator God, we gratefully acknowledge shared experiences. Teach us to share our bountiful food with those who hunger, and give us who have bread a hunger for justice and peace. Amen.

[‡]Retired missionary and surgeon; layman, United Methodist Church, Albert Lea, Minnesota.

Some of our best moments come after a good meal. Jesus addresses impetuous Peter, asking three times, "Do you love me?" Each time Peter declares his love, Jesus tells Peter to "feed my lambs," "tend my sheep," and "feed my sheep." The repeated question frustrates Peter and hurts his feelings. Peter affirms love of Jesus and faithfulness to the task. But Jesus recognizes Peter's youthful impetuosity and indicates that the journey to maturity will bring difficulties not even imagined by Peter. This is the paradox of discipleship: seeking the kingdom of God on earth, as Jesus taught, will lead to dangerous situations. Yet even this warning did not dissuade Jesus' followers. The disciples and early apostles did suffer persecution, jail, and death.

Charles Butler and his wife went as young missionaries to Panama. They faithfully taught, preached, and shared the gospel in a culture not their own. They witnessed political strife in Central America in the latter half of the twentieth century, strife marked by brutal military dictatorships, disappeared clergy, paramilitary and rebel massacres of civilians. Peace and justice were in short supply. Upon retirement, Charles protested the role of the U.S. School of the Americas in training Latin American military personnel in counterinsurgency techniques. The School of the Americas trained hundreds of men who became agents of violence, intimidation, and assassination in their own countries. Some became dictators.

Charles Butler ended up in federal prison as a consequence of his repeated public protest. I believe that Charles, like Peter, had "a belt fastened around" him, to lead him "where he did not want to go." I believe that going to prison can be the price of answering the call of Jesus to "tend my sheep."

PRAYER: **Loving God, show us that where we do not want to go is often where we must go if we are faithful to the commission of our Lord Jesus Christ. Give us courage. Amen.**

We find images of sheep and shepherds throughout the Bible. In the earliest scriptures, lambs are a most precious sacrifice, an offering to God. In Isaiah, the new creation is envisioned as a time and place where the wolf and the lamb shall feed together. In the Gospels, we come to know Jesus as the Good Shepherd. And Revelation views Jesus as the slaughtered Lamb worthy of our praise.

In today's passage, a myriad of angels sings loudly, "Worthy is the Lamb that was slaughtered to receive power and wealth and wisdom and might." Jesus is the lamb in the vision, the sacrificial offering. However, his power was not and is not the contemporary image of power. His life and teachings indicate that faithfulness to God does not depend on wealth, guns, or an imperial political agenda. His death and resurrection confirm this through his suffering love and power used to reconcile the world with God. Jesus' power is one that empowers us to love as God loves, even though we know it leads to the cross.

In my faith journey, I have developed an awareness that Christ's power is made manifest in loving relationships, downward mobility, forgiveness, and faithfulness to God. Lech Walesa, Nelson Mandela, Dorothy Day, Mahatma Gandhi, Martin Luther King, and Oscar Romero all exemplify this type of power. Each of them had no conventional armies, no personal wealth; but each one did Jesus' work and ministered to the persecuted, the homeless, the oppressed, and the dispossessed. Three of them were assassinated. I believe that as much as Jesus died *for* our sins; Jesus was killed *because of* our sins.

Today let us confess our sins, opening up more room to let God into our lives, transforming us to be bearers of Christ's empowering love to our world in need.

PRAYER: Dear God, our faithfulness may cause us discomfort, ridicule, or even death. Give us more courage and more faithfulness to walk in the ways of Jesus our Christ. Amen.

My wife said, "A man and a boy are at the door. I think they are selling something, but they want to speak to you." When I went to the door, I recognized the father and his young son. The father had a cloth-wrapped package, which he opened. It was a lamb, killed, dressed, and ready to cook and eat. It was not for sale; it was a gift, an offering, an expression of gratitude.

Some time previously the boy had suffered greatly from tuberculosis; it had destroyed his hip joint. The hospital staff of which I was a part had been able to give medication, clean the joint, and then fuse it. The boy, now full of smiles, could run with the help of a simple crutch and not suffer pain. This boy and his family lived in a distant Andean village in primitive conditions. Even though they had a small plot of land and a courtyard shared with a few animals, the gift of their lamb was indeed a sacrifice. I could not refuse their gift. This was not a payment for services rendered. We find ourselves humbled by such generosity from those who live so precariously.

Our Christian doctrine and tradition explain that God gave God's son as a sacrificial lamb. The power of that sacrifice, the power of Jesus' life, makes us thankful and humble. We too fall down and worship. As disciples of Christ we are reminded that power comes from love and faithfulness to God. Praise God for this marvelous gift to us. We are not worthy of the sacrificial Lamb, but our gratitude is endless.

PRAYER: Dear God, fill us with gratitude for your gift to us. Make us a people of sacrificial generosity, compassion, and an humble spirit. Amen.

This psalm praises God's faithfulness. Buried in the rejoicing and thanksgiving one verse indicates disheartenment: "By your favor, O LORD, you had established me as a strong mountain; you hid your face; I was dismayed."

Mortimer Arias was the first bishop of the Iglesia Metodista Evangelica de Bolivia when it became autonomous. He was instrumental in the empowerment of Aymara and Quechua leaders for the church and served as a public spokesman for justice. A powerful pastoral role model, Arias spent time in jail for writing a Christian manifesto for the common people. He was a spiritual leader beyond the borders of his adopted country.

In 1976, Bishop Arias resigned to allow the church's indigenous majority to elect its candidate at the Asemblea General (Conference). Those in attendance, including my wife and me, watched Bishop Arias accept the vote and heard him eloquently state his readiness to accept any appointment by the new bishop and cabinet. He received no appointment! Imagine his dismay and feelings of rejection, the failure of collegiality. Yet those of us present witnessed no anger, no harsh words from him, and no threats of dissociation from the people or mission of the church. Mortimer Arias may have been dismayed, but he has continued to witness to the faithfulness of God by teaching, writing, and preaching in North America, Central America, South America, Europe, and Africa.

Praise of God's incredible faithfulness in the ups and downs of life can be the theme of our lives. "You have turned my mourning into dancing; you have taken off my sackcloth and clothed me with joy, so that my soul may praise you and not be silent. O LORD my God, I will give thanks to you forever"!

PRAYER: Dear God, we praise you for your faithfulness in all of life, through thick and thin, through delight and disappointment. When one path of discipleship closes, help us walk confidently into another. Take our moments of mourning and turn them into a dance of joy. Amen.

Saul, struck blind on the road to Damascus, asks, "Who are you, Lord?" Ananias, a resident of Damascus, hears the Lord speak and responds, "Here I am, Lord." Ananias knows Saul of Tarsus as a persecutor of the saints in Jerusalem. This dominant, powerful person suddenly becomes pliable in response to an experience that leaves him unable to see, disoriented, and confused. Saul, led to Damascus, is found by Ananias who reluctantly heals this enemy.

Saul receives shelter, food, and the companionship of followers of the Way in Damascus. He regains his sight and is filled with the Holy Spirit. When his strength returns, Saul enters the synagogue to proclaim Jesus as Son of God!

Ananias and his friends served as agents for God's transformation of Saul the persecutor to Paul the evangelist to kings, Gentiles, and Jews from Jerusalem to Rome. Might Ananias's role have given Paul insight to write to the Romans: "If your enemies are hungry, feed them," and "Do not repay anyone evil for evil" (12:20, 17)?

Not many of us listen to Jesus' voice telling us to seek out those who have wronged us, and seldom do we choose to act on their behalf. Champions of causes we deplore seem like enemies if they oppose our deeply held positions of faith, politics, and moral values. Ananias responds in faithfulness and trust to God's request, hoping against hope that his action will indeed serve a divine purpose. Ananias answers God's call despite his fear and perhaps hate of Saul. And Saul receives healing in body and spirit.

PRAYER: Dear Lord, give us courage to approach persons we perceive as enemies. Your Spirit can change us and others into instruments of healing and praise. Reform us, transform us. Amen.

Fellow travelers witness Saul's fall to the ground. Then comes a three-day period of suffering—no sight, no food, and no drink. When Ananias arrives at Saul's side, he represents a network of Jesus people. Rarely is good accomplished in a solo performance!

But networks of faithful and skilled persons can accomplish incredible feats. Many years ago a flood destroyed an entire poor barrio in eastern Bolivia. Catholics and Protestants, government and private organizations, and many health workers responded, although they previously were not noted for collaboration. The workers established a temporary camp for over six hundred people who no longer had homes or land. They received help in organizing their new community: schooling, food, public health education, medical attention, and vaccinations. By the time the government had found a safe but remote location for a new settlement, the six hundred had become a unified, healthier, more literate, and hopeful community.

Today, decades later, that colony of flood victims remains productive and more cohesive because of the initial delay in relocation. Equally important is the fact that most of the cooperating agencies of the resettling effort still work together in this poor and stressed region.

Saul suffers for three days before Ananias arrives. Here too the delay in needed help perhaps serves a good purpose. Both Saul and Ananias experience God's presence during that time. Then Saul, cared for and nurtured in the community of faith in Damascus, receives his sight, his baptism, and his voice among these committed followers of the Way. Only then can he proclaim: "[Jesus Christ] is the Son of God."

PRAYER: Faithful God, give us courage to answer your call, especially when it requires us to confront difficult situations and people we do not know. Give us confidence that we do not work alone. We rejoice and praise you for giving us friends and neighbors to be enlisted for acts of compassion and service. Thank you for Ananias. Amen.

I Shall Not Want

April 23–29, 2007 • Kim Poole[‡]

MONDAY, APRIL 23 • Read John 10:22-30

Growing up in the Texas panhandle, my family drove many miles across wide open spaces for vacations or to visit family. My brother would read and I would sleep. My grandmother sat between us to keep peace in the backseat. After a while the monotony of the miles would take its toll, and one of us would start the eternal questions: "Are we there yet?" "How much longer?" We were impatient passengers along for the ride.

"How long will you keep us in suspense?" In today's reading the Jews express impatience as well. "If you are the Messiah, just tell us plainly." Some commentaries mention that this is less a question than a statement of irritation: "How long are you going to annoy us like this? End all of this cryptic nonsense and just tell us what we want to know."

Along my spiritual journey I have cried out to God in impatience: "How much longer, God?"; in fear: "Where are you, God?"; in anger: "Why this? Why now?" Many times I obliviously missed the answers to my questions. Caught up in the turmoil I failed to take the moments of silence to listen for the answers. Like the Jews who question Jesus, perhaps I have heard the answer but failed to believe or did not receive the answer I desired.

Along life's journeys, questions will rise within us. If we are honest with ourselves we will find the courage to ask the question. In trusting the process, we will hear the response. The decision then becomes ours to act on that response in faith.

PRAYER: God, open our hearts and our minds to ask questions; give us the patience and wisdom to wait for and understand the answers. Amen.

[‡]Hospital pharmacist, spiritual group leader, retired United Methodist minister and missionary; living in Juneau, Alaska.

Individuals in each community stand out as examples of giving beyond what is required in order to help others. Tabitha is one such example in Joppa. She served the community of widows by making garments for them. When she dies, the widows help wash and lay her body out for visitation. The widows' tunics and other garments visibly display Tabitha's ministry to them.

Over the years I have seen a change in the way we honor people at the time of their death. In the early years of my ministry the services were traditional funeral services with the personal touches coming in the music selections and perhaps the words from the minister in reflecting on the person's life. In the past decade or two the services have become more a celebration of life: picture boards and mementos of the life of the deceased decorate the sanctuary and fellowship hall. Persons share stories, and the gathered community eats a meal together rather than the church providing a meal for the family.

I like the change. Life and service deserve celebration. Yet I mourn that so often we wait until the person's death to offer such testimony to their ministry. What a gift it would be if we found more ways to celebrate people's lives while they could still hear our words of gratitude and admiration.

I encourage each of us to find a way to show or tell one person in our community how much his or her service, presence, and giving has meant to the community.

SUGGESTION FOR MEDITATION: **Consider those whose lives and services have influenced you. Picture them in your mind. Hold them in your heart. Offer a prayer of thanksgiving. Write a note, make a phone call, or pay a visit to thank them.**

During children's sermon one Sunday I asked, "What is a miracle?" One young person thought for a brief second and replied, "A miracle is when God touches you, and you feel different." Great thinking—simple, truthful, and easy to comprehend.

Peter sends everyone out of the room and kneels down by Tabitha's body. There he prays, and when he says, "Tabitha, get up," she opens her eyes and sits up. Lending his hand, Peter helps her to stand and calls her friends in to greet her.

Oh, how often we wish for this type of miracle in our lives! I have volunteered in various hospice settings and witnessed some miraculous occurrences. I have prayed *with* families and *for* families as they face the last moments of life of someone close to them. Always we pray for healing. Yet we do not anticipate that our hospice clients will get up from their beds and live again. The miracles we pray for are miracles, nonetheless. People live their last hours in good ways, supported and surrounded by families and friends in the comfort of their homes.

When we pray for miracles, it seems we expect the supernatural to occur. Yet, often a miracle occurs within the smallest moment of time: the moment we hear the pathology report that says "benign"; the moment the doctor says, "It's a girl"; the moment someone says, "It's over." These are the miracles that surround us.

In each of these times we feel touched by the hand of a loving God, a touch that tells us we will be fine, no matter what. God loves us and cares for us. That is the greatest miracle of all.

PRAYER: Loving God, touch us today with the miraculous works of your creation, your redemption, and your sustaining holy power. We trust that in you all will be well in this day. Amen.

I live in an isolated community. Our connection with the outside world comes via plane or boat. The week after September 11, 2001, no traffic passed into or out of the community. During those days our prayer vigils crossed the faith-community barriers that had existed before September 11. Christians, Jews, and Muslims prayed together for strength and understanding, for healing and hope.

Out of these times of prayer developed dialogue and a celebration with a combined choir called "The Children of Abraham." We shared the unity of our faiths rather than the differences, by using prayers from the Jewish, Islamic, and Christian traditions. The night ended with an amazing rendition of "Down by the Riverside." It was a time of healing and celebration.

When I read the words of Revelation that describe the varieties of people who will gather at the throne of God, I believe that this picture moves us beyond an exclusive heaven toward an inclusive community of God. I claim Christianity as the ground for my understanding of God. I have friends who stand on the faith tradition of their Jewish and Islamic heritages. Together we form a strong community of faith that cares for one another. Together we learn to love God, our neighbors, and ourselves.

I am grateful that our community leaders chose to extend the hand of fellowship to one another at a time when they could have easily turned against one another. I look forward to the time when we will all stand before God and sing praise in our multitudes of language from all the corners of the earth.

PRAYER: God of all people, we give thanks today for all people of faith, for their communities and their leaders. May we live together in peace today and work together for peace in the days to come. Amen.

Two letters rest on my desk, each from a dear friend. I admit that with the advent of e-mail I have become a poor letter writer. I won't remove these letters, however, until I reply with pen and paper. The importance of their messages cannot be pushed aside. One letter comes from a person with whom I shared a house. She writes asking me to pray for her family as she keeps watch with her sister in the sister's last days of cancer.

The other letter is the Christmas letter from a former class-mate. She usually sends a wonderful message of hope. But this time the message contains the sad news that her young nephew was killed in Iraq this year. The letter is heavy with grief. I have delayed my writing because I lack the words to say to either of these dear friends who experience so much pain and grief.

The writer of Revelation reminds us that pain and grief are not the end of the story. There is hope for those who have endured great ordeals in life. For thousands of years persons have experienced periods of persecution, war, hunger, illness, pain, and grief. In the presence of the eternal glory of God, those who have suffered will find a world far beyond what we can compre-hend: "They will hunger no more, and thirst no more; the sun will not strike them, nor any scorching heat; . . . and God will wipe away every tear from their eyes."

Renewed with this hope I will shut down the computer and take up the more personal pen and paper and write my friends today. There is good news for those who have endured trials and tribulations in this life. There is consolation for those who grieve and remain behind. Thanks be to God who heals the heart.

SUGGESTION FOR PRAYER: **Pray for those who mourn and grieve today.**

She was angry about life, about everything that was "wrong" in the church, about everything that was wrong in the world, it seemed. She brought folders of parish newsletters, worship bulletins, and minutes from meetings— all highlighted and marked up. "If you don't change, I will call the superintendent on Monday and demand your removal!"

I responded the best I could. "I am sorry if I seem to be a problem to you. I will think about what was said today. But I cannot promise to act on your last words. To me they were an ultimatum that leaves no room for dialogue or for us to repair what is broken in our relationship."

She gathered her papers and left. I returned to the parsonage to ruminate and eventually to seethe. Over the weekend she called church members and stated her case to as many as would listen. By Sunday morning I wanted to call in sick rather than go to church.

Sunday was Communion in our church. As I led the liturgy I looked at the congregation and there she sat, glaring at me. "Lord, don't let her come to my aisle to be served," I prayed. But she did.

As I served her I looked into her eyes and saw an angry woman, coming into the presence of God, being offered the gifts of God by someone she viewed as an enemy to her faith. I realized that I was beginning to think of her as the enemy as well. We were at an impasse. But here we were dining together, invited to a table prepared for us by God in the presence of our "enemies."

I can't say our relationship was healed that day or in the days that followed. She did not call the superintendent, and I stayed four more years. Over that time, we dined at God's table frequently, in the presence of God's love.

PRAYER: God, in the presence of my enemies I seek your love and protection in the bounteous feast you prepare for all of us. May I find your peace there. Amen.

Rabbi Harold Kushner wrote a book on Psalm 23 titled *The Lord Is My Shepherd*. He writes that the Hebrew words for the second line of this psalm might be more accurately translated as "I shall lack for nothing." Yet we who lack for nothing want or desire more than we have: more hours in our days, more excitement or joy in life. We may desire more material possessions or yearn for better relationships.

In the wake of tsunamis and hurricanes we have witnessed those who had little to lose, lose everything, including the lives of family members and friends. Watching the news stories tugs at our hearts as we acknowledge our affluence. Many of us truly lack for nothing.

Yet Kushner turns this phrase in a different direction as he writes about the desires of our hearts and the empty spaces in our lives. At the close of the chapter he says that he might choose to rewrite the phrase as, "The Lord is my shepherd; I shall *often* want. I shall yearn, I shall long, I shall aspire." We do yearn for a closer relationship with God, with others, and even with ourselves. We openly desire many things: the spirit of joy, the sound of laughter, the gift of tears. We yearn to sit at the table prepared for us. We desire the cup that overflows and long for the goodness and the mercy that accompanies us all the days of our lives.

The Lord is our shepherd. We lack nothing; we yearn for much.

PRAYER: **Loving Shepherd, you have cared for us in so many ways. You have led us through dangerous paths and times of trial. You have provided for our needs and sheltered us along the way. We yearn today for the goodness and mercy that we find in your presence and desire to settle ourselves into the arms of your loving-kindness. Amen.**

Praising God

April 30–May 6, 2007 • *Bo Prosser*[‡]

MONDAY, APRIL 30 • Read Psalm 148:1-6

Creation is groaning and has gotten our attention recently. The fury of hurricanes, tsunamis, and tornadoes; the rumblings of volcanoes, earthquakes, and mud slides; warming of polar caps, destruction of acid rain: all this and more demand that we pay attention. If we listen closely, we will hear the groans of our world—not just its inhabitants but also the trees, the stones, the water, the air! Are we listening? Are we responding?

God commanded, and the heavens were created. God commanded, and all was established. We didn't have anything to do with the creation of the sun, moon, and stars. We had nothing to do with the blue of the sky or the black of the thundercloud. The heavens declare with praise the greatness of God. The angels sing praise. We must pay attention! We must hear the groanings and respond appropriately.

Today the psalmist calls us to pay attention to the groanings of creation and to honor its praises. Yet we pollute the air; we poison the environment. We consume and discard without thought. The psalmist asks that we care as much for our natural resources as we care for our own families. It's not about hugging trees; it's about fulfilling our role as caretakers!

Take a moment and listen to the sounds of creation. Hear the groanings; hear the praise. Join the created order in praising God and praying for the redemption of God's world.

PRAYER: God of heaven and earth, help me pay attention to the groanings of your world. Help me to be more caretaker than consumer. May I honor your created order even as that created order honors *you*! Amen.

[‡]Coordinator for congregational life, Cooperative Baptist Fellowship, Atlanta, Georgia.

When did you last pay attention to the world around you? Recently I traveled to a major city and marveled at the beauty and majesty around me. Towering buildings, miles of connecting highway arteries, and sprawling greenways of parks and trails filled the "city proper." On the way to the airport, about five miles out of the city, we encountered some of the most beautiful farmland I've ever seen. The horses and cows were of prize-winning quality. The barns looked like mansions. The fields looked manicured and emerald green. Somewhere I think God was smiling! Creation was singing!

We can go nowhere on earth that we won't see the beauty of nature. The brightness of the snow-capped Rockies reflect God's praise. The mists of the Smoky Mountains whisper praise. The roar of the ocean upon the shore shouts with praise. Just as the heavens declare with praise the greatness of God, so also does all the earth. And we are called to pay attention.

This springtime the azaleas, the dogwoods, and the lilies declare God's handiwork, shouting with praise to the Lord. We are called to "hear" the praises of all of the earth, to be caretakers not consumers. Our duty is to till the earth, to harvest the offerings, and to praise God through it all. We are here to maintain the praises of all of nature, not to destroy the land in our selfish consumerism. God's glory is greater than all of the beauty of this world.

Take a moment and glance out your window at the world around you. See the beauty of the flowers in your yard. Praise God for the green grass growing as testimony to God's greatness. Hear nature singing in the earthly choir of birds and breeze. Let everything praise God.

PRAYER: God of heaven and of earth, help me to praise you in the beauty of this wonderful spring season. Let me praise you in the freshness of this day! Amen.

WEDNESDAY, MAY 2 • Read John 13:31-32

When have you witnessed the glory of God? The apostles witness the glory of Jesus firsthand. The splendor of God shines through Jesus the Christ that moment in the midst of confusion, anger, betrayal, and worship. If God can be glorified in confusion and betrayal, then just imagine how much more the glory in our praise and love! Yet, most of us in the good times forget about the grandeur of God. The apostles have come for a time of fellowship and a meal. They receive a servant's welcome from God and witness the majesty of God's son.

The Gospel writer reminds us of God's glory and how it manifests itself in our midst. Judas's betrayal must have filled everyone who witnessed it with anger and pain. His sudden exit sets into motion a series of events that will fulfill the life calling of the Son of God. The apostles see the glory of God not as a shadow on a rock, not as a rainbow in the heavens, not as an angelic messenger but as the one and only Son of God! Jesus' exalted state glorifies God.

We are challenged to see the glory of God in our lives. As good things happen to us, glorify God. When anger threatens relationships, glorify God. In the midst of pain and betrayal, glorify God. In all things—good, bad, angry, sad, even in the midst of confusion—glorify God. Recognize the glory and give praise!

PRAYER: God of all life, help me to recognize your glory in all things and to give you praise. Even as I feel pain and joy, let me claim your glory in my praise! Amen.

The young man was dirty and smelly and asking for a handout. My pastor asked the young man about his plight and his story. He told us of drug abuse, physical abuse, and lonely nights on the street. He told us of his hunger and promised to use our money to buy food. I was skeptical. My pastor gave him a ten-dollar bill! "Why did you do that?" I asked. He replied, "Our job is to love others, not judge them. God knows their hearts. We know their needs. We respond in love."

The preacher, full of ego and arrogance, told a group of gathered pastors what we had been doing wrong in ministry. He told us his secrets for church growth. The man related God's blessing him with prosperity and a strong retirement fund. He then passed the offering plate for us to help his ministry continue. My young associate was cynical. I put a ten-dollar bill in the plate as it passed. "Why did you do that?" he asked. I replied, "Our job is to love others, not judge them. God knows their hearts. We know their needs. We respond in love."

The Gospel writer calls us to a new accountability: to love one another regardless! Jesus and Judas have exchanged words; Judas has left in anger. The glory of God has manifested itself in the midst of it all. And Jesus calls us to be intentional in love. Surely the apostles are passing judgment on Judas and the interaction they have just witnessed. Yet Jesus gives them a new commandment. Jesus knows what Judas is up to and calls for love.

We bear witness to the glory of God as we love others, even those whom we might judge with cynicism, skepticism, or even anger. So let us love one another that all may see that we are disciples of our Christ and children of our God. Our job is to love others, not judge them. God knows their hearts. We know their needs. We respond in love.

PRAYER: God, heavenly parent of us all, help us to love others as Jesus loved us! Help me in my love to bear witness to your glory and to bear witness of my praise. Amen!

I love the modern-day Pharisees. They know everything about everything. They "know" the mind and heart of God and quickly judge the rest of us. They tell us of the love of God and the judgment of God. They tell us how God works, when God works, and with whom God works. Being a Pharisee must be fulfilling!

But what happens when God works in ways we don't understand? God loves with a love that is bigger than the Pharisees, bigger than me and you too. God loves those in the world whom the rest of us don't love. God even loves the Pharisees. God is love.

The writer of Acts reminds us that we don't know the mind of God. The apostles and other believers, while young in their faith, seem to know exactly how God works, whom God loves, and to whom God's love is meant to go. They are angry with Peter for his missionary journey to the Gentiles, those who are unclean and unwanted. The young believers didn't understand.

Peter anticipates the "Pharisees" and readily tells his story. God has expanded Peter's understanding of divine love. God has broadened Peter's understanding of freedom in Christ. God's revelation reminds Peter of both the Creator and the created. Peter trusts in the fullness of God's glory and shares witness in praise. He testifies that God's love is greater than our understanding of that love.

Peter ministered to the Gentiles, the Pharisees, and his critics. And through his love, he praises the greater workings of God. The only way we can undo the Pharisees is to love them in our praise of God. Easier said than done.

PRAYER: God of love, help me to see with the heart of Christ and to love those who criticize me. Help me love the Pharisees in my life that you might transform them into your disciples. Amen.

The praise of God begins in the halls of heaven and echoes throughout all of creation. John's vision of the praise of heaven resounds in our hearts today to fill us with the hope of glory. What a day this must have been for John! What a day this will be for us! However, today we focus on our praises on this earth in this time.

Today as I listen to the news, war rages across the world; AIDS is at an epidemic level in Africa; famine and drought are causing hunger throughout the world. The world today seems besieged by conflicts, pollutants, limited resources, and selfish world leadership. This is hardly the hope of glory. Yet, even as we hear creation crying out, "Come, Lord Jesus" (Rev. 22:20), we also hear the psalmist, "Let everything that breathes, praise the LORD"(Ps. 150:6).

How can we praise in days like these? you wonder. We praise because the "home of God" is with us. Jesus the Christ is with us today, even as the Christ will join us in the days of glory. And John tells us that not only will Jesus dwell with us, God will be with us!

Let our praise not be in vain! Let our struggles be praises to God. Let our limitations be praises to God. Let our searches for solutions be praises to God. As we live within the praises, God inhabits our praise and joins us in the living of these days. And God's presence with us gives reason for praise—both today and in the days to come.

PRAYER: God of today and tomorrow, help us to praise you in the good and the not-so-good. Help us to praise you in the ease and the struggle. Help us to praise you from today into the glory of what will be. Amen.

SUNDAY, MAY 6 • Read Revelation 21:4-6

"There's no crying in baseball!" Those immortal words chortled by Tom Hanks in the movie *A League of Their Own* echo in my head as I read this passage. Just as there is no crying in baseball, the author of Revelation anticipates no crying in the new world to come. Heaven is in a league all its own; we can hardly imagine the glory.

The promise that comes to us from John's prophecy implies that nothing will make us sad or move us to tears when the new created order arrives. Can you imagine no tears of sadness or death or pain! Every day in the world to come will be like the wonders of springtime we experience today. God promises to completely redeem and renew the world.

The hearers of John's prophecy, in the midst of ridicule and persecution, need a good and strong word from the Lord. Their spirits sag and their witness is being tempted. They are being beaten, tortured, and killed because of their faith. Their tears and cries for compassion are great.

You and I do not face the same persecution and torture as did those first-century Christians. However, we still face hurt, temptation, and ridicule. Christian influence on the world seems to lessen everyday. Some reduce our testimony to Christ to a set of superstitions. The world looks at us as if we are crazy; or worse, as if we do not matter at all. And that is a cause for tears. But God says, "A day is coming when the only tears you shed will be tears of joy." And that is a word worth praising!

PRAYER: God of heaven and of earth, of past, present, and future, help me give you praise through my life, through my work, through my tears. Hear my praise today in my anticipation of the hope of glory. Amen.

Persuaded by God

May 7–13, 2007 • *René A. Perez[‡]*

What amazing ways God employs to persuade us to follow! The book of Acts tells of Paul's vision of a man in Macedonia who begs him to come and help. Although Paul and Silas conclude that God is calling them to Macedonia, I can think of numerous undertakings I considered to be of my making before I realized that it was God's idea all along.

For Paul and Silas, it begins with God's vision. As with all healthy visions, God's vision for our lives possesses a purpose greater than what we intend or imagine. We can read about Paul and Silas or about Joseph in the book of Genesis and discover that none of them knows exactly where God will lead them. Paul sees a man in need; Joseph, on the other hand, is a man in need. But for both, God had a much greater purpose. In each case, they had to decide to trust God.

The German theologian and martyr Dietrich Bonhoeffer said, "As a follower of Christ, I don't always know where I am going but I know I am following Jesus." God casts a vision for our lives and persuades us to follow. Although it might be difficult to grasp God's blessings in the midst of our realities, we must understand that God's ways, though obscure to our apprehension, will lead us like Paul and Silas to God's greatest gift of purpose for us and for those God has chosen to bless through our revelation.

PRAYER: God of all, I know your ways are higher than mine. Help me see my way through your eyes. Remind me that my life is in your hands. As I grow certain of your love, let me be a blessing to others. In the name of Jesus I pray. Amen.

[‡]Worker with Latino ministries, ethnic ministries, and new church starts, Eastern Pennsylvania Annual Conference of The United Methodist Church; living in Lancaster, Pennsylvania.

TUESDAY, MAY 8 • Read John 5:1-6

Have you ever lost hope?

The man has been an invalid for thirty-eight years. Every day, he lies next to Bethesda's pool (NIV) hoping that someone will help him into the water to be healed. Of course, he is not alone. Many blind, lame, and paralyzed persons join him in the hope that someone will help them. But no one comes.

Imagine living with a debilitating condition and a sense that no one will help you. When have you believed that no matter how hard you pray or try, nothing changes? Have you ever decided to stop trying and praying and accept your fate?

Many people today find themselves next to the pool of Bethesda—people who want to experience wholeness but carry physical, emotional, or spiritual scars. Some scars come from abuse, some from hunger, others due to illnesses or uncontrollable addictions.

At moments in my life, I have experienced situations so dark that I lost hope, even times that convinced me that no matter what I did or how fervent my prayer, I could do nothing more.

But Jesus passes by Bethesda and sees this invalid man who feels as desperate as I have felt many times. The man does not flag Jesus down or call to him; Jesus sees him and asks, "Do you want to get well?" (NIV)

If you have ever lost hope, remember that even when we don't call on God, the Holy One is with us. The One who became flesh among us can restore our hope and offer healing for the wounds we've received.

PRAYER: Dear God, you know who and how I am and what I've been through. Forgive me for not believing when you are so near. Like the man at Bethesda, I want to get well. Help me find forgiveness, healing, and peace in your presence. Amen.

Are you willing to stay and help?

From time to time I think about the job I had before I entered church ministry. The pay never kept me there; the people did. Most of them were Latino immigrants who knew little or no English. I saw myself as an advocate for them, speaking on their behalf against issues and treatment I considered unfair.

In 1992 God called my wife, Wanda, and me to ministry in Philadelphia. I often wonder what would have happened if I had been willing to stay and keep working among the immigrant population. I could have continued helping some of the people, perhaps leaving a legacy of justice in the workplace. I don't know.

Today's passage of the paralytic takes me back to those days. Some of the sick persons I worked with in my previous job really had no one else to help them. Until today I did not consider accepting God's call into the ministry a selfish act; I saw it as God's will. But the fact is that leaving that job gave me a sense of freedom. I did not have to deal with the injustices I saw or run the risk of losing my job for the cause of others—none of that. God was leading us to a better place.

Have you been there before? An opportunity presents itself, and you figure it's time to pack and go. Yet you know you are leaving others behind, others who have no one to put them in the pool. In retrospect, I realize we need people to stay and make a difference. God doesn't always take us to new places; sometimes we stay right where we are, either in a present job and ministry or in the city where we live.

PRAYER: **Creator of all that exists, I thank you for the place you have given me to be right now. I continually desire to be in your presence and to follow you no matter where you send me or where you have me stay. Help me see what you see and go where you would prefer that I be. Amen.**

The authority of love

A conversation about the fragility of marriage led a young man to pose the following question to his future wife, "What if you wake up one morning and don't love me anymore?" She immediately responded, "There's always obedience."

Although obedience is part of the love we owe one another, it certainly does not precede the love we have for others. Rather, obedience is a result of love. We obey our parents because we love them. We comply with our spouses' requests because we love them and want to enjoy our marriage. We obey God out of our love for God rather than out of self-interest or requirement. As Jesus states, "Those who love me will keep my word."

Many of us are lost in the realm of self-gratification. We obey God expecting to receive some blessing or profit out of that exchange. Yet we too can be loving and obedient if we allow the Holy Spirit to lead us, teach us, and remind us of all that God has done and is doing.

By ourselves, we often fall short of living life well, loving others, and loving God. We fret and fear. Obedience scares us. It means doing things we would not normally do. It means trusting God in all things at all times in every situation of our lives. Obedience really means believing that God loves us beyond our wildest thoughts or imaginings.

PRAYER: Loving God, I often fall short of loving you and trusting you. Bless me every day with the power and counsel of your Holy Spirit so that I may accept your love for me. Amen.

Blessed by God

Many years ago I heard about a high school teacher whose husband unexpectedly died of a heart attack. About a week after his death, she shared some of her insight with her students: "Each of us is put here on earth to learn, share, love, appreciate, and give of ourselves. None of us knows when this fantastic experience will end. It can be taken away at any moment. Perhaps this is God's way of telling us that we must make the most out of every single day. So I would like you all to make me a promise. From now on, on your way to school or on your way home, find something beautiful to notice. It doesn't have to be something you see, it could be a scent—perhaps of freshly baked bread wafting from a house or the sound of the breeze slightly rustling the leaves in the trees or the way the morning light catches one autumn leaf as it falls gently to the ground. Please look for these things and cherish them. For these things are the 'stuff' of life, the little things we are put here on earth to enjoy, the things we often take for granted. It becomes important to notice them, for at any time it can all be taken away."

This teacher learned a valuable lesson about gratitude, and so can we. The psalm for today also reminds us of our many blessings. Although the psalmist asks something of God, he confidently believes he is on the receiving end of God's blessings. "God, our God, has blessed us," he writes.

God, through little and big things, continually blesses us. Even when our days seem somber and gray, there is an unseen blessing ready to transform us and brighten our day.

PRAYER: God, you are an awesome God! Today, help me be appreciative of everything you've already done for me so that, with a positive attitude, I may unveil the great things you have in store for me. As you have blessed me, allow me to bless others. Amen.

A city for all

It is perfect! Even with room left for imagination, every detail is included to perfection: angels, gates, beautiful and precious stones, inscriptions of the twelve apostles and tribes. This passage of scripture reveals to us the awesome wonders of God's creation.

I remember growing up listening to my grandmother tell Bible stories, particularly about that day when Jesus would come back and take us to a better place where the streets were of gold and a river was like crystal. It was amazing! Who could imagine God had so much gold and water would be so clean and transparent? It was definitely something to look toward.

This awesome place described for us in Revelation symbolizes the restoration and transformation of God's creation. God continues to envision a people who live restored and transformed lives worthy of the One who calls them.

The holy city of God is a visualization of the future but also a potential of the present. The streets of gold are not only for the wealthy but also for the poor. There will be no VIP list—only the names of the faithful. There will be a judgment, but we will not be judged by what we wear or what we look like or what language we speak, because we will be able to see how God sees us. A perfect day, a city for all! It will be a place for you and me.

PRAYER: Dear Lord, thank you for your promises. Thank you for allowing me to believe that the evil I see today will not last forever. I know you will return one day and, together with you, I will live in your holy city where people from every nation and tongue will worship you. For now, let me live a life worthy of your name, loving others as much as you love me. Amen.

Something more

Most Sundays after church we pick up fast food. Usually we go through the drive-through to bring the food home. It never fails that whenever we go, the same homeless man approaches us to ask for money; and every time, if we can, we give him a few coins.

One day I realized God was asking me to do more. I did not hear a voice out of nowhere; I simply felt a tug in my heart. That day I ordered an extra meal with coffee and gave it to this man. I watched him enjoy a long-desired meal. My heart cries to this day when I think about it. It hurt me that day when I saw people ignoring him, and it hurts me now when I realize God continues to ask me for more. When has God asked more of you?

This passage in Revelation describes such a beautiful scene of sunny days, clear running water, and the tree of life full of leaves for the healing of the nations. I know that on that day, God will heal every broken heart, feed every hungry stomach, and give drink to anyone who thirsts. But for now, God is asking me for more. God needs me to help feed the hungry, clothe the naked, welcome the stranger, give drink to those who thirst, and mend the brokenhearted.

While my soul desires to see God on that day in God's glory, right now God wants us to help others envision that day of hope. My best guess is that, as one of my seminary professors said, "Many people are so heavenly minded that they are of no earthly good." My prayer is that we may give more and more of ourselves to God and others until that day when we find ourselves realizing that it isn't all about us.

PRAYER: Dear God, forgive my apathy for the pain of others. Help me share your enduring hope with those who have little or none. Amen.

Ascension Power

May 14–20, 2007 • John E. Anderson[‡]

MONDAY, MAY 14 • Read Acts 1:1-11

Luke divided his storytelling of Jesus' life into two installments. Book One (The Gospel of Luke) describes the life of Jesus. In this volume, we read of Jesus' entering our world as a nursing child, teaching with Spirit-resonating power, and healing people. We watch from a distance as bystanders mock Jesus on the cross. And as the words "He is risen!" sink deeper and deeper within us, we choose to believe that Jesus can forgive our sins as well.

Book Two (Acts) relates the reign of Christ. We read how the Spirit was poured out upon waiting disciples and Gentile believers alike. The disciples speak with Jesus' authority and heal many who are sick or demon-possessed. Jesus' followers multiply, mature, and then scatter throughout the Roman Empire.

One event divides Luke's two-volume account: the ascension of Jesus. This defining moment removes the limits of Jesus' earthly ministry. In volume one, Jesus teaches and heals only those he can see and touch. Location limits his kingdom. But when Jesus is carried into heaven before the witnessing gaze of his disciples, a new era begins. Jesus speaks with authority, heals with compassion, and liberates the oppressed through those who follow him!

Luke's second volume is a work in progress. Book Two is being written upon the pages of our lives as we allow the reign of Christ to continue to unfold through us. Thursday, May 17, we remember Jesus' ascension, the day when Jesus began to extend his kingdom through each of us. Meditate for a moment upon this turning point in Jesus' story, in your story. Choose to let Jesus' story continue through you today.

PRAYER: Lord Jesus, show me how you might speak, heal, or liberate through me this day. Amen.

[‡]Pastor, Trinity Presbyterian Church, in suburban Denver, Colorado.

Luke narrates this second volume on the life of Jesus in the third person. He tells his story from the anonymity and objectivity of the historian. But at this point in Luke's biography of the ascended Jesus, Luke abandons the third person "they" in favor of the first person "we." He wants us to know that this book is based on more than interviews and research. It also records first-hand experience. When Paul and Silas get to Troas, Luke is there. And now he joins in the story!

As you read today's scripture, let Luke's shift in pronouns invite you to enter this story as well. To do so, you might want to read this passage again more slowly. As your eyes register the words, let the Spirit guide your imagination. Picture yourself walking through the streets of Philippi with Paul and Silas. A young girl hovers at your heels. She shouts and attracts attention. What happens next? As you take in this experience from an eye-witness perspective, be aware of what Jesus does and does *not* do for Paul and Silas.

As we celebrate the ascension of Jesus, we discover that we are written into his ongoing story. Since the Spirit of Christ continues to deliver, proclaim, and heal through us, we too will find ourselves in awe-inspiring and terror-filled situations. Today might be a good day to talk with Jesus about your readiness or reluctance to live into his story. As you do so, listen quietly for any response Jesus might offer you.

PRAYER: Lord Jesus, fix within me a confidence in your name. Whether spoken over the needs of others, uttered in times of fear, or affirmed as a statement of faith, convince me of the power of your name. Amen.

Every Christian spends some dark nights in damp cells. We all experience seasons when evil people seize control. They lead us with shackled feet to places we don't want to go. Being cut off from the support of family and friends can rob us of hope. That is the intent in Philippi—to lock Paul and Silas so deep within the prison that their cries for help cannot be heard. To be out of earshot in times of distress can break the human spirit.

How do Paul and Silas cope? They pray. They pray to the ascended Jesus who understands their need, because he is still the God-man. When Jesus ascended to the Father, he did not as a spirit leave his disciples. Rather, he returned to heaven in his resurrected body. Jesus is still God incarnate today! In a mystery too profound for the limits of time and space, Jesus is present with the Father. He ascended bodily and for all time and eternity will forever be fully God and fully man.

When the dark nights in damp cells take us captive, we can remember that we are never out of Jesus' earshot. He understands when we feel threatened, humiliated, or discouraged. Jesus empathizes with us because he is forever united with us, bone of our bone and flesh of our flesh.

It may help to visualize the ascended Jesus when you pray. Picture him in his human flesh, powerful but personal. He knows, he feels. He understands, he responds.

PRAYER: Thank you, Jesus, for hearing us. No cell is too deep or too dark to hide us from your care. Shake the foundations of all that holds us. We pray this in the power of your name. Amen.

A good story when read will paint a picture in our mind's eye. This picture imprints itself upon our imagination. Visualizing the events as they unfold helps us order the story so that we don't miss its truth. This may not be the first time that you have read the account of Jesus' ascension. What is important today is to examine more closely the mental portrait you have created of Jesus' return to heaven. Is your illustration vivid enough to capture the truth of this story?

How have you pictured Jesus' ascension? Does his body seem to evaporate into spirit right before your eyes? Is he beamed up into Star Trek static? Luke set the stage for the ascension (Luke 24:36-43) with Jesus proving to his disciples that he was flesh and blood, not a ghost. In his Easter appearance, Jesus seems most concerned about convincing the disciples that he is truly alive. He begs them to examine his wounds, touch his body, and give him something to eat to prove that he is no mere spirit. This real and physical Jesus ascends before their very eyes.

Many of those who have pictured Jesus' ascension in this way feel a joy similar to that of the first disciples. Why? Because when Jesus returns to heaven in his resurrected body, he leaves the door cracked open for us. He makes a way so we can be physically present with our Father as well. Because Jesus has taken his humanity into heaven, we can picture our humanity there too. Ponder this promise for yourself or someone you love.

PRAYER: Lord, help me to live into the sure and certain hope of my resurrection as well. Amen.

As twenty-first-century believers, we sometimes feel jealous of the twelve disciples. We yearn for Jesus' physical presence. We are convinced that if we had heard Jesus teach or had seen him walking on the windswept sea, we would have believed. But maybe not! We know from personal experience how much easier it is to describe something as a coincidence rather than a miracle. Perhaps seeing isn't believing after all.

The ascended Jesus is present to us in a manner that wasn't accessible to the twelve when he was *physically* present with them. We have longed for Jesus to be "before us," but he offers us something better: Jesus "in us." When Jesus returns to the Father before the awestruck gaze of his disciples, he gathers all future disciples in tow. Instead of leaving us behind, Jesus draws us with him into the Trinity.

In Jesus' prayer for all believers of every age (John 17), he prays into reality God's deepest longing—an intimate communion between God and each of us. We are pulled into the mystery of the Trinity as the Father, Son, and Spirit are poured into us. We are able to know the ascended Jesus from the vantage point of our inner experience. Jesus is in us in a way that the twelve didn't experience until Pentecost. Just as the three persons of God dwell within one another without losing their unique identity, they also dwell within us without overwhelming our identity. Just as the Father, Son, and Spirit honor one another with a self-giving love, they also readily give themselves to each of us. "As you, Father, are in me and I am in you, may they also be in us." The ascended Jesus offers us far more than the twelve or the women who followed Jesus could ever have known while he was with them—Jesus in us!

PRAYER: Lord Jesus, awaken me to all that is you in me. Amen.

Every now and then we need to be reminded of what is real. Psalm 97 describes reality as "The LORD is king," awesome, mighty, and in charge! Jesus shared this glory with the Father and the Spirit prior to his incarnation and again after his ascension. But these words create such a different picture of Jesus than we have of him during his earthly ministry.

In the Gospels we see a humble Jesus. As he walked among us, Jesus traded his glory for the humiliation of a jilted lover. Jesus used his strength to persevere in the face of our rejection. He loved those who could take it or leave it. To the uninformed, Jesus looked weak. At first glance, he appeared to be no match for the neighborhood bully. But this would be a "before-the-ascension" conclusion.

Psalm 97 exposes our misconceptions about Jesus. The mountains melt before the one who would not speak in self-defense. And the one who ascended into the clouds surrounds himself with tumultuous storms. His humility has exalted him above all gods!

All who follow Jesus are called to exercise strength through humility. They too may be misjudged as weak. But the power and the glory of our ascended Lord now serve those who walk in Jesus' shoes. Psalm 97 reminds us that God loves the upright and rescues the faithful. How might you be called to flex your muscles by joining Jesus in his long-suffering love today?

PRAYER: **Jesus, help me desire the strength to love as you do. Amen.**

The Revelation given to John is a peek at Jesus in his ascended glory. Only two times in the book of Revelation are we directly addressed: in Revelation 1:8 and here in Revelation 22. In both instances, Christ's message is the same: "I am the Alpha and the Omega, the first and the last." Christ not only surrounds the beginning and ending of time but every moment in between. The whole of our lives is filled with Christ's presence and purpose. Though hidden from sight, he is there. If Jesus were to speak just one reassurance to us in the midst of a crisis, what better thing to say than, "It is I, Jesus"?

Many of us do not fear our ultimate end in life. We feel confident about our eternal destiny. It is all of the in-between time that causes anxiety. We believe that we will live with God forever in the end, but we question whether or not Jesus will live with us in the here and now. Will he share the pain of our diagnosis, our fears about retirement, or our sleepless nights as parents? By granting John this vision, Jesus makes a surprise appearance in an in-between time in the first-century church. Jesus shows up and says, "It is I, Jesus. I have been here all along."

This revelation, granted to John, is intended for you. What aspect of your life needs this midcourse reassurance the most? How can you welcome the knowledge that Jesus reigns in your in-between time?

PRAYER: Come, Lord Jesus, now, when we most need you; and in the end, for needs we can't yet even anticipate. Come. Amen.

What Does This Mean?

May 21–27, 2007 • Marty G. Bell[‡]

MONDAY, MAY 21 • Read Psalm 104:24-34, 35b

In the summer of my eleventh year, my family vacationed in Florida. I encountered the ocean for the first time. Driving to the beach near Jacksonville, I will never forget my first glimpse of the mighty Atlantic. To say that I was overwhelmed doesn't do justice to my experience. Almost forty years later, I'm still awestruck when the ocean first comes into my view on a trip to the beach. This past spring as I came within sight of the ocean on the coast of South Carolina, once again I exclaimed, "There it is!"

From the primeval period to contemporary times, humans have experienced the ocean emblematically as a mysterious sign of the divine. In Psalm 104 the writer exclaims: "Yonder is the sea, great and wide." I love the word *yonder*, probably because I heard the word used in the rural South where I was raised. One of the meanings of the term is being at a distance but within sight of something. Among the various ways that we experience God is the perception that God is yonder: at a distance but within our sight. Such a perspective of God is like viewing the ocean from the shore.

From that vantage point, God is great and God is wide. As a reflection of the greatness of God, the ocean tells me that God cannot be fathomed, cannot be controlled. However, God can inspire awe within us, and God remains the one constant in the ebb and flow of our lives. As a reflection of the wideness of God, the ocean says to me that God cannot be reduced to our constricted thinking or limited by our narrow prejudices. However, God can evoke bold ideas, and God can explode our provincial view of the world.

PRAYER: "May the glory of the LORD endure forever; may the LORD rejoice in his works." Amen.

[‡]Professor of Religion, Belmont University, Nashville, Tennessee.

I've always been fascinated by the fact that the words for spirit, wind, and breath are the same in the biblical languages. The Bible points to an invisible life force from God, in God, through God—use whatever preposition you wish—that animates us. That God gives us spirit, wind, breath is a given. As Carl Jung, the eminent psychoanalyst, said, "Bidden, or not bidden, God is present." However, we can cooperate with the presence of God in our lives, or we can struggle against it.

Thinking of the Hebrew word *ruach* and the Greek word *pneuma* as wind offers some interesting possibilities. Assuming that God is like a constant wind that blows and that our lives are like wings, I would like to make a few observations. I'm indebted to Huston Smith, the famous scholar of world religions, for the basic idea that follows. The tilt of our wings makes all the difference in the world. If our wings are tilted at the right angle, we can soar. When we cooperate with the wind of God's presence, we discover our true identity as children of God. If our wings are not tilted at the correct angle, we set ourselves up for a crash. Then we struggle against God and allow fear to rule our lives.

The disposition of our lives is like the tilt of wings into the wind. Cooperating with the invisible presence of God, we not only find God to be trustworthy, but we come to experience God in intimate relationship—what Paul calls the "spirit of adoption." Struggling against the invisible presence of God, we conclude that we can only trust ourselves. We consider ourselves the pawns of fate, and we despair at the meaninglessness of life— what Paul calls the "spirit of slavery."

PRAYER: Give me courage to tilt my wings to rise on the wind of your love, Abba, Father. Amen.

Philip said to him, "Lord, show us the Father, and we will be satisfied." If we're honest with ourselves, there's a bit of Philip in all of us. Why can't our faith be more straightforward and tangible? Of course the standard answer that we often receive or give is this: if everything was perfectly clear and obvious, we wouldn't need faith. One problem with the standard answer is that it seems to prioritize faith over God who is the object of that faith.

Jesus responds to Philip's request with questions designed to help Philip reflect on his own experience of Jesus as a manifestation of God. At the heart of the exchange is the experience of incarnation—not just the notion of incarnation but the experience. In fact, Jesus tells Philip that if he can't accept Jesus' words about it, he should accept Jesus' works.

Maybe Philip's problem and ours is that we haven't absorbed the reality of incarnation. Incarnation, a radical notion, becomes an even more radical experience—God getting with us in the nitty-gritty of daily life. Some part of us would rather have a God who conforms to our ideas of the divine, who satisfies our desire to have clear mental categories that the reality of everyday living can't contaminate. The reality of incarnation not only points to God in the life and ministry of Jesus, it also points to our responsibility to enact the works of God as the followers of Christ. The only way to do the works of Christ and "do greater works than these" is by being incarnational people, daring to believe that God lives through us as we minister to the world.

PRAYER: Ever-present God, put us in touch with all our senses that we may experience you in the ordinariness and the extra-ordinariness of our daily lives. Amen.

Thursday, May 24 • Read John 14:15-17

Jesus never allows us to confuse sentimentalism with the demands of authentic love. Loving God and loving neighbor as we love ourselves are not easy matters. We need all the help that we can get. We need a paraclete. Unique to the Johannine literature, the term *paraclete* has several possible meanings. In its oldest usage the term probably referred to someone called into a situation to provide help, an assistant of sorts. Eventually, the term came to be associated with legal assistance.

The Gospel of John makes it clear that Jesus is our first Paraclete. While he lived on earth, Jesus was frequently called into the lives of people to help. Through his preaching, teaching, and healing, Jesus assisted people. He advocated that those who acknowledged their need for help in facing life would find it.

Jesus taught that he would send another Paraclete to aid his followers, the Spirit of truth. Jesus speaks of the world's inability to receive this Spirit of truth. In the same way that Jesus threatened the value system of his generation through his courageous living out of the truth, so it happens today when his followers live out the truth. But, then and now, those who bear witness to truth find that God's Spirit is a powerful helper.

We make two basic mistakes in trying to obey the commandments of Jesus to love God and our neighbor. One mistake is believing that we have no resources beyond our own willpower to make it happen. The other mistake is to assume that we can substitute language about Spirit-filled lives, thus alleviating our responsibility to act.

PRAYER: God, we need all the help we can get to bear faithful witness to truth in a world that is betrayed by deception and denial. Forgive our arrogance when we think we can be bearers of truth without your Spirit's advocacy. Forgive us when we shirk responsibility while claiming your Spirit's guidance. Amen.

Traditionally we view Pentecost as the coming of the Holy Spirit and the birth of the church. It's worth noting that this remarkable experience occurred while "they were together in one place." Although profound spiritual experiences occur in private moments, the truly historical events of our faith usually occur in community where we share a common life. At its best, church is an experience of interdependence, where the Holy Spirit empowers us to live out our calling as the disciples of Christ. We can't live this life without one another and without the power of the Spirit.

Pentecost has an older history than the birth of the church. Literally meaning "fifty days," Pentecost concluded the Passover season and began the season of harvest as the Feast of Weeks, one of the three great holidays in Jewish life. Pentecost celebrated the first fruits or the spring grain harvest. Later it came to be associated with the giving of the Torah to Moses at Mount Sinai. These older understandings of Pentecost richly underscore the importance of community.

Reaping the spring grain harvest took the efforts of the whole community. Men and women vigorously participated in the various tasks that had to be accomplished in order to bring in the harvest. Without communal participation, the harvest could not be reaped. Nor could they reap the harvest without the help of the wind (*ruach*, the same word for "spirit") which blew away the chaff from the grain at the threshing floor.

Living the life demanded by the Torah also took the efforts of the whole community. By its very nature the Torah is social in orientation. Six of the Ten Commandments deal with how humans treat one another. Authentic community always requires a commitment to interdependence and a responsibility to the "least of these." Consistently, the Bible reminds us that we cannot love God unless we love our neighbor.

PRAYER: **God of all people, make us true community. Amen.**

"All were amazed and perplexed, saying to one another, 'What does this mean?'" The mighty acts of God that Acts 2 describes are nothing short of amazing and perplexing. Ultimately, like those who originally experienced Pentecost, we are led to ask: What does this mean?

I enjoy what I do as a professor of religion and as a pastor. I constantly ask my students and parishioners in a variety of ways some version of this question. I want them to move from an inherited theology to an acquired theology. It's not enough to accept uncritically what others have told us about Christianity; we must find our way through our own experience. John Wesley took the three-legged stool of Anglicanism—scripture, reason, and tradition—and added a fourth "leg" as a basis for religious authority: experience. The Wesleyan or Methodist quadrilateral serves as a tool for theological exploration. Our heritage is "to think and let think."

The exploration of faith takes time for reflection. One of the disturbing aspects of our contemporary culture is the expectation that we can have what we want instantly. A 24/7 world demands instant access and immediate gratification. Mature and seasoned theology is not like a prepackaged meal we pop in the microwave; rather, it's more like gourmet cooking in which the meal starts from scratch and contains all sorts of wonderful herbs and spices. By taking time to explore the meaning of our experience of God, we will be amazed and perplexed. More importantly, we will find a deeper satisfaction in our quest to fill our spiritual hunger. Yielding to the temptation to find easy and convenient answers, we miss the point. Then and now there are those who sneer at questions of meaning, desiring the quick conclusion.

PRAYER: God, may we not be afraid to ask, "What does this mean?" May we see that our amazement and perplexity grow our faith more deeply. Amen.

Pentecost

Peter's sermon at Pentecost is a response to a question asked in the midst of the experience, "What does this mean?" His answer involves two assertions. First, Peter rejects the easy and false answer. Those filled with the Holy Spirit are not drunk. Second, he dares to believe in the possibility of the prophetic vision of Joel. The time has come for the Spirit of God to gift all people as agents of liberation and empowerment.

Like the cynics who scoffed at what was happening on the day of Pentecost, we too are prone to seek an easy explanation for that which makes us uncomfortable. Academics, like me, often make use of "Occam's razor": the simplest of two or more competing theories is preferable. All things being equal, it makes sense to go with the more straightforward explanation. The problem, however, is that the Spirit of God can't be reduced to a simple theory or a provable experiment.

Besides cynicism, we also face the problem of conformity. Holy Spirit power in the lives of people shakes things up. The activity of the Spirit is anything but business as usual. Young and old, men and women, slave and free are included in Joel's vision that Peter quotes. The Spirit includes all—a radical inclusion that by its very nature topples structures of conformity.

Pentecost demonstrates that we cannot reduce God to a manageable force. God explodes our prejudices and thwarts our expectations. God doesn't fit into our programs, our finances, or our long-range plans. Furthermore, the success or failure of programs, finances, and long-range plans does not necessarily indicate the Spirit's blessing. Pentecost is about us getting into God's work in the world, not about getting God into our work.

Prayer: God, surprise us and forgive us for our cynicism and conformity. Keep us open to the great inclusion of your Spirit. Amen.

Godly Guides

May 28–June 3, 2007 • Ulrike R. M. Guthrie[‡]

MONDAY, MAY 28 • Read Proverbs 8:1-4, 22-31

This week, plenty of guides have called me to follow their particular paths. A writing Web site lists its tutors but nary a word on what they've actually written and how they do it. An ad in a window down the street galvanizes me with its promise of a life coach. But the ad speaks all about my dreams and lostness without suggesting what the coach can train me in.

By contrast, Lady Wisdom in this chapter of Proverbs is neither elusive nor uncredentialed. From the most prominent and the most ordinary places of our daily lives she beckons us. Her pedigree is unmatched: She is the one who was there "when [God] had not yet made. . . . the world's first bits of soil." She is the one who hung around God "like a master worker," or, depending on your translation, "like a little child."

Both images ring true for me: I've known my children sticking close to me, observing, learning. I've also had mentors who've allowed me to be apprenticed to them as I learn a particular craft.

This week's biblical texts speak of various godly guides on whom we can rely on our life journeys. Like the Trinity, which we particularly celebrate on Sunday, these guides are several and yet one. They speak not on their own but what they hear from God. Down through the ages we remind ourselves of their collective yet unified wise guidance when we gather weekly as a community of faith.

SUGGESTION FOR MEDITATION: From what source do you gather the wisdom for your daily living?

[‡]Freelance book editor for The Pilgrim Press, Cowley Publications, and the Hispanic Theological Initiative at Princeton University; contributor to several books and to *Alive Now*; member of St. James' Episcopal Church in Old Town, Maine; living in Bangor, Maine.

After seventeen years of living in the United States, our family is spending my husband's sabbatical year in England, my homeland. Our children drink milk delivered to our doorstep along with the paper and walk along the hedgerows to attend local public schools where they have assemblies with prayers. We buy crumpets and clotted cream, Cox orange pippins and pearlike russets (apples), and parsnip and beetroot flavored crisps (chips). In this small market town of Saffron Walden, we have the country's oldest medieval turf maze or labyrinth, a youth hostel that's over six hundred years old, and a stately home on whose rolling parkland we take our evening walks. It's all pretty incredible.

It's a poor comparison, really, but at least a small daily reminder of what awe feels like—amazement, surprise. As my children might exclaim, "Holy!"

The very words of this psalm, the rhythms and images, all conspire to express the awe and glory and majesty of which the psalmist speaks. "How majestic is your name in all the earth!" Even psalms that go on to speak of our deepest despair often begin and end with this hymnlike refrain, as if helping us to deliberately reframe our present experience.

When our emotions aren't quite in tune with the words, the mere saying of words of praise (to God, or for that matter to our neighbor) can change our being. Indeed, hormones do change our brain chemistry and consequently the way we feel. Like the psalmist here, it often happens that as we begin, perhaps reluctantly, to praise God, we actually come to praise God truly. In other words, sometimes we praise others and God because we feel like it; but other times by praising others or God, we actually begin to feel different—and then begin to act differently also.

PRAYER: With my heart filled with praise, I will bless you, O God. Amen.

WEDNESDAY, MAY 30 • Read Romans 5:1-5

An e-mail from another guide, this time my bishop in Maine, advises our diocese of a former bishop's death. She writes: "Bishop Moodey lived deeply and richly with cancer in his life. The disease robbed him of little, repaying him with the knowledge that life is not endless and that opportunities for time with family and friends, trips to unknown places, and glorious Maine days were to be seized and celebrated."

Such words of assurance have integrity, coming from a woman who has known a great deal of grief and suffering herself, a woman I trust to relay rather than dress up the bishop's own experience. Hers are words of faith and survival well worn by experience.

Paul too in our reading today has been through the wringer. Knowing this about him, his assurance that suffering produces endurance becomes credible to us. My mother might call it developing a tough skin or a strong heart to cope with what life brings. Paul specifically means steadfastness in the hope that Jesus has brought us, the hope of sharing the glory of God, the hope of salvation. And that is what we want when we are brought low— to know God's transformative healing and love in those depths.

Living now not far from Norwich in England, I think often of the fourteenth-century mystic Julian of Norwich, whose words "All shall be well, and all shall be well, and all manner of thing [sic] shall be well" in her *Revelations of Divine Love* might be familiar to you. What integrity they gain when we realize she survived the horrors of successive waves of the Black Death or plague that decimated almost half the population of her town, the second largest in England at the time. To still have the confidence that all shall be well shows enduring faith and hope indeed.

SUGGESTION FOR MEDITATION: **Our hope does not disappoint us.**

We continue the theme of godly guides. Today Jesus tells his disciples that after he goes, the Spirit of truth will guide them into all truth. Like Wisdom, this is no independent guru-come-lately, no go-it-alone life coach or personal trainer. This guide isn't making it up as he goes along.

In this passage we meet a guide who is a teacher. Like most good teachers, the Spirit is also a pupil—of Jesus. Jesus the Teacher twice repeats that the Spirit will "take what is mine and declare it to you." We're going to get the same story from both Jesus and the Spirit, not alternatives. The same wisdom passed along. The same good word about justification by faith not works, about hope not fear, the same instruction to love God and our neighbor.

Yet a teacher worth his or her salt discloses differently according to what the student can bear. What I tell my thirteen-year-old about death or sex or the challenges of the year living abroad differs from what I tell my nine-year-old. For she "cannot bear" some things yet, and it's my responsibility as a parent to be wise to her limits.

What did Jesus feel his disciples were not ready to hear? We find out more as Jesus' farewell teachings continue.

How is the Spirit-Teacher guiding us into all truth today? To whom and to what is the Spirit urging us to attend? Regularly encountering the teachings of scripture reminds us of God's revelation in the Bible, through Jesus, in our church traditions, and now through the Spirit and one another. What old, familiar word are we being called to hear anew today? What people, what truths in our midst are we squinting to avoid seeing fully?

SUGGESTION FOR MEDITATION: To what is the Spirit-Teacher reminding you to attend?

> *When I look at your heavens, the work of your fingers,*
> *the moon and the stars that you have established;*
> *what are human beings that you are mindful of them,*
> *mortals that you care for them?*

We have reflected on how this psalm creates a sense of awe and gratitude to God in the person who proclaims it. And it is good to linger here awhile, moved by breathtaking descriptions of the night sky; of cool waters and green pastures; of the living things on the earth, in the skies, and in the paths of the deep. It is very good to be reminded that we are only a small part of an incredibly diverse and rich universe of amoebas and black holes, warblers and white dead nettles, planets and composers like Gustav Holst who write music about them.

So it is sobering to glimpse just how profound and out of proportion to our size is God's care for us humans in comparison to such an incredibly vast and still-expanding universe. To read that we have been made "little lower than God, and crowned . . . with glory and honor," that God has given us dominion over the works of God's hands, and has put all things under our feet—it's almost baffling!

How do we respond? Surely not as teacher's pet, thinking of ourselves as invincible, untouchable favorites who need show no accountability to God or the rest of creation. Surely not just basking in the knowledge of being so loved that God gave and gave and gave. But surely, secure in that love, we respond by giving. We give praise; we give by the lives we lead, generously and abundantly so that everything and everyone can continue to prosper—in warbling or bringing refreshment, in warming the earth or plowing it, in swimming the paths of the deep or fishing them.

PRAYER: O Lord, our Sovereign, how majestic is your name in all the earth! Amen.

"When the Spirit of truth comes, he will guide you into all the truth."

Like so many eager young people, we told Roberta we intended to write our own individualized wedding vows. Wise woman that she is, our professor, friend, and pastor, instead of pouring cold water on the idea, simply asked us this: What precisely did we want to communicate that wasn't covered by the familiar "to love and to cherish, in sickness and in health, for richer for-poorer, as long as we both shall live" vows? Good question.

The common task of the Spirit of truth and of wisdom is quite simply to lead us into the truth. Some ask whether Jesus didn't in fact mean us to expect ongoing revelation, new and exciting individualized words from God. After all, new ethical, social, and political situations arise constantly in our lives. We view them through the lens of Jesus' teachings or words, certainly, but perhaps more than anything through the lens of his behavior, how he lived what he professed.

Individualized designer wedding vows are all very well, but the proof of our intentions relative to any vows we may make is in how we live out those promises over the long haul. When our spouse suffers from depression or Alzheimer's, when passions wane and job layoffs or retirement strain our finances, how then do we love and cherish our spouse? How do we speak to our child the day he really disappoints us? How do we work toward good relations with a neighbor who took us aback with her rudeness on our first day in the neighborhood? Or how do we share a pew, let alone "one Lord," with those Christians who won't embrace the new hymnal or pass the peace with our lesbian daughter, who can't imagine a woman in the pulpit or can't imagine not having one there or those who show up for worship but never to help with Saturday church cleanup?

PRAYER: Come Holy Spirit, guide us and keep us living stead-fastly in the truth. Amen.

SUNDAY, JUNE 3 • Read Romans 5:1-5

Ahead of us, none of the many children has received Communion on this first visit of ours to St. Mary's in England. A notice in the bulletin that all confirmed persons are welcome at the Table seems like the explanation. I hold my breath as we kneel at the altar rail, all four of us with palms outstretched, hungry to be fed. As Episcopalians, our children have shared the weekly meal since their baptism as infants. In this house of God, would they be denied the nourishment shared by God's household?

This week's readings depict various godly guides playing different but interconnected parts to guide us to the same end. It is through Jesus, we read in Romans, that we have peace with God. It is through the Spirit that we have God's love in our hearts. It is God who creates.

Couldn't God have gone it alone? Did God need Jesus and the Holy Spirit? The better question might be whether God wanted to go it alone.

Our reading from Proverbs reminds us that God craves company. Wisdom learned at God's side. And for her part, Wisdom rejoices in God and in humans. The psalmist comments on God's care for mortals. This kind of mutual appreciation and need sounds good to me.

It also models how we might relate to one another as the household of God. We're complementary in our responsibilities, in our gifts (as Paul will say about the body, the church).

So how do we live out this calling to Christian formation in our lives—at church, at home, at work? How do we live it out as global citizens and stewards of creation? And how as coworkers, as parents, as community and world leaders? For we all come with outstretched hands, and everyone needs to be fed.

PRAYER: O God, may we live out our Christian calling in the days that lie ahead. In the name of the Creator, the Redeemer, and the Sustainer, we pray. Amen.

Rise to New Life

June 4–10, 2007 • Melanie Lee Carey[‡]

MONDAY, JUNE 4 • Read Luke 7:11-17

Her only son has died. Being a widow with no male in her family, she will now be dependent on others for care. She can only hope that others will provide for her. Relying on charity, she faces the burial of her child. She must feel hopeless and grief-stricken, as she walks along with the funeral procession.

Then something extraordinary happens. Jesus comes to the bier, lays hands on it, and tells the young man to "rise." Suddenly, what has been a march of death becomes a celebration of new life and hope for a new future.

After Easter Sunday has passed, we may forget about the Resurrection message. But God's work of bringing life from death continues throughout the year and throughout our lives. This scripture passage reminds us that resurrection, bringing life out of death, is God's work. Whether we think of resurrection or resuscitation with regard to the widow's son, new life happens. New life comes in the midst of our despair and hopelessness in surprising and wonderful ways.

God does not promise a life free from pain, sorrow, or death. Our faith *does* promise us that death is not the final word. God's final word is resurrection, and God invites us to rise. New life awaits us.

PRAYER: God, help me to remember your resurrection power and to see when and where you are meeting me with new life and renewed hope. Amen.

[‡]Senior pastor, Ypsilanti First United Methodist Church, Ypsilanti, Michigan.

TUESDAY, JUNE 5 • Read 1 Kings 17:8-16

Our local church has hosted several benefit dinners for church and community members in need. One single woman, out of work due to an extended illness, faced the loss of her apartment. Another family without documents was forced to leave our country but had no resources to begin a new life in their homeland. Our church council decided that we would share a meal and economic resources with one another. Not only were funds raised and lives changed, but our church also grew in love and strength for mission. Both the woman in need of rent money and the undocumented family made food from family recipes for members of the congregation. Like the widow in today's text, these persons were sharing the last bit of food they had available.

Many biblical commands speak of caring for widows and orphans and for the powerless ones and the most vulnerable members of the community. Often widows struggled to survive on meager handouts from others. The story of the widow of Zarephath reverses the usual experience: Here a widow shares goods with a man—the one who ordinarily would have been expected to provide economic resources. But these are not ordinary times. Elijah had earlier spoken the word of God to Ahab concerning a drought. In the midst of that drought, Elijah seeks hospitality from the widow. Elijah receives new life in the willingness of a poor widow who shares her last handful of meal with him. Notice that the widow of Zarephath practices hospitality despite economic uncertainty and the threat of famine. To underscore this radical hospitality, the Bible notes: "The jar of meal was not emptied, neither did the jug of oil fail."

God's power to create new life becomes most evident when we practice hospitality in the face of our own scarcity, want, and uncertainty. In the process of extending hospitality to others and out of love for God, our communities may experience new life.

PRAYER: God, may I practice hospitality in the face of fear and scarcity. Lead me to seek help when I need it and to extend myself to others. Amen.

When we read today's passage in conjunction with this week's Luke text, we discover Luke's literary use of the Hebrew Scriptures. Both stories concern widows whose only sons are dead or dying. Both stories tell about a person of God who brings life out of death. No doubt Luke's listeners knew the story about Elijah. No doubt that as Jesus laid hands on the dead boy's bier to bring the boy back to life, those in attendance would have recalled Elijah's story as well.

Recalling the ancient story of Elijah in the face of Jesus' bringing new life to this boy bears powerful witness to the importance of placing such stories together and calling upon them as testimony to God's continual acts of new life. Storytelling has great power to instill hope and new life for those who have lost their way.

In the practice of ministry, I have often gathered friends and family together with a loved one who faces surgery or some great difficulty. I have encouraged the friends and families to tell that person of times when they felt sure of their own faith. As we go around the circle and share faith stories and testimonies, the stories themselves become a powerful tool of resurrection and new life for the one facing difficulties. The telling of the story reveals and affirms God's resurrection power.

SUGGESTION FOR MEDITATION: Read a verse from the First Kings passage and then a verse from the Luke passage. Continue this practice until you have finished both passages. Notice the similarities and differences in the passages, and let the common message of new life wash over you.

Thursday, June 7 • Read Psalm 146

My father used to wake us on Easter by singing the refrain of "Up from the Grave He Arose," and then we would go to an Easter sunrise service. My siblings and I would protest that it was too dark to go anywhere. My father responded, "Easter begins in the dark; God's promises of new life begin in the midst of the darkness."

Psalm 146 celebrates the faithfulness of God in the midst of our all-too-human unfaithfulness. After beginning in praise, the psalmist tells us not to put our trust in princes or in governments. The history of Israel shows us rulers who demonstrated unfaithfulness to God and to the people under their care. These kings often forgot to act as if their help was in the name of God. No, we are right to remember the wisdom of the psalmist who contrasts our human weakness with the fidelity of God.

The text continues beyond the warning about rulers and reminds us that the power of God comes to those who are in the midst of darkness and distress. Verses 7-9 sweep us away with their brevity even as they speak to a long history of liberation: God "executes justice for the oppressed and gives food to the hungry; sets prisoners free; opens the eyes of the blind; lifts up those who are bowed down." After each one of these phrases we may be able to complete the story by filling in details of a time when we saw or experienced justice and when we saw the hungry given food and when we witnessed the setting free of prisoners.

Again the psalmist points to the practice of hospitality with the simple declaration that God watches over strangers and upholds orphans and widows. The Israelites understood the truth of this text; may we also rise to the challenge of this psalm.

SUGGESTION FOR MEDITATION: **Sing or hum a hymn of praise and then read this psalm again. At the end of each line, reflect upon the ways in which you have experienced these words and remember the faithfulness of God.**

Psalm 146 reminds us to put our trust in God, who remains faithful. During the preparation of these meditations, Hurricane Katrina devastated the Gulf coast of the United States. In the months after the hurricane, the human structures created to respond to natural disasters failed, compounding the suffering of those who survived the winds, rain, and floods. Because of this crisis, the face of poverty, long glossed over, came into focus.

We saw and heard powerless people, and we knew that God's love sustained them. In response to the images on television and computer screens and to the stories, people around the world were moved with compassion—offering money, help, and even their homes. Many people from the affected areas relocated to the portion of southeast Michigan where I live. The outpouring of love and support offered to those who had lost so much touched me deeply. The stories told by the survivors of this disaster gave me new understandings of compassionate witness.

Behind the disaster (and every disaster—not forgetting the December 26 tsunami in Asia in 2005) comes this truth from Psalm 146: human systems may fail, but God's love does not fail. It remains constant, inspiring us to act in love and charity toward our neighbors and seeking ways to extend hospitality to others. God's love invites us to discover new ways to rise to the occasion.

When the next natural disaster comes, how will we respond? This psalm of praise reminds us that God gives justice to the oppressed and brings the way of the wicked to ruin. Praise God—the one who lifts up those who are bowed down by natural disasters, who gives refuge to strangers whose lives are disrupted and uprooted, who sustains orphans and widows and gives power to the powerless! Praise this God who reigns forever!

SUGGESTION FOR PRAYER: **Pray Psalm 146 throughout the day. Let this biblical witness inspire your words and actions of praise and thanksgiving.**

SATURDAY, JUNE 9 • Read Galatians 1:11-24

Paul offers us a small glimpse into his spiritual journey as he describes his own personal coming to new life. He was transformed by the love of Christ and died to his old self and rose a new person. God often works in people's lives bringing about transformation. This passage offers eloquent testimony to the ways in which God brings this change to our lives. Paul, the former destroyer, proclaims the faith that he once tried to destroy.

How have you been transformed? What is new in you? How have you experienced the new life that we share in Jesus Christ? How has God been working in your life?

In the church that I pastor, members of our Latino community share personal testimonies during worship. These testimonies often describe the gift of new life in the transformation brought by Christ. These personal and powerful stories often move the congregation to tears. While different in details, these contemporary stories echo the witness of the apostle Paul in describing the way in which the living Christ gives us new life.

As people in our church share testimonies that concern trusting God to see them through a difficulty or freedom from addictions or the gentle encouragement of the Spirit in the midst of discouraging times, I remember how God works in each of our lives. As we know from the life of Paul, God's love changes us, reshapes and reforms us; we become new creatures in Christ.

SUGGESTION FOR MEDITATION: Think about your personal life story. How has God been working in your life? Tell someone your faith story and listen to his or her story.

God does not call us to raise people from the dead; the act of resurrection is God's job. God does, however, call us to share the word about resurrection with others. As Christian believers we tell others about the power of God to bring new life in the midst of the old.

According to Luke 7, many bystanders see the dead man sit up and begin to speak after Jesus touches the funeral bier. These bystanders realize that something special and mysterious is happening, and they know God is at work in the situation. They begin to worship and to cheer and to celebrate. They glorify God and tell others what has happened. The story about Jesus and the widow's son spreads throughout the region. The words "God has looked favorably on his people!" indicate the joy with which they told the story.

As we consider the crowd's reaction, we need also to think about our calling or vocation as Christian disciples. While we do not have the power to resurrect, we can work with God to help others receive new life. Our vocation calls us to offer new life in God's name to all those who, like the widow in Nain, have lost hope. Each day we have the opportunity to speak words of hope and new life to others. Every day we have the opportunity to share with others God's resurrection power. The opportunities are limitless: phone conversations, e-mails, visits, cards, gestures of compassion and care. As people tell us of their struggles, we can offer the love that we know in God's gift of Jesus Christ. Like the bystanders, we can tell others with great joy what we have witnessed and experienced. We can say that God has looked favorably on all humanity.

SUGGESTION FOR MEDITATION: Read the text from Luke and put yourself in the crowd of bystanders. Think of ways in which you can witness to others about this new life. Pray and listen for God's direction. With whom will you share this good news?

Temptations and Consequences

June 11–17, 2007 • Luis F. Reyes[‡]

MONDAY, JUNE 11 • Read 1 Kings 21:1-10

How easy would it be to give up your heritage? If someone in a position of power asked you to give up a personal possession, how would you respond? In our story Naboth answers King Ahab's request for his vineyard by saying that "the LORD forbid that I should give you my ancestral inheritance." We should never be asked to give up our heritage, which includes our cultures and traditions.

The vineyard is not for sale or trade. Naboth will not give up what his ancestors have entrusted to him because the Lord forbids it. Naboth is being faithful to God, and his response is in tune with his values. He acts with integrity, protecting what generations to come may need to see and receive. The vineyard is not as important as Naboth's moral character. Who we are does not reside in our possessions so much as in the values, character, traditions, and beliefs we have adopted on the journey.

In our society temptations will come, moments when our values and identity will be put to the test. How will we respond? It is easy to go with the flow; it makes us feel accepted and supported. But what about that part of us that we modify for the sake of feeling good?

God created us and gave us a heritage. The promises we have made to our God are not to be dismissed. From Naboth we receive an example of faithfulness to God and a sense of honor for family. Let us be like Naboth in faithfulness and moral character.

SUGGESTION FOR MEDITATION: **Pause and thank God for your character. Consider ways to affirm the heritage you have received. Celebrate and praise God for who God is in your life.**

[‡]Pastor, First United Methodist Church, Bensonville, Illinois; native of Puerto Rico.

The story has shifted; no longer is it about the vineyard but about the ways God's children harm others. Jezebel, the one closest to the king, uses her power to set the scene for what is about to happen. The elders and nobles follow through with Jezebel's plan. False charges are brought against Naboth, and the people stone him to death. Ahab now moves to possess the vineyard. Elijah, God's prophet, comes onto the scene with a clear message: Ahab's actions will bring God's consequences. As Elijah says when speaking for God, "I will consume your descendants and cut off from Ahab every last male in Israel—slave or free" (NIV).

Our actions have consequences. We have the freedom to do the right thing. It may not be what we want to do, but the choice is up to us. We may find ourselves swayed by others to choose a way that leads to death. At times, we may let our greed overcome our God-given sense of righteousness. We can delude ourselves into thinking that someone else made us do this or that when we should be willing to take responsibility for our actions.

We know how the story ends for King Ahab. However, we still have time. Our Creator has endowed us with the ability to discern consequences of the actions we take, actions that may lead us to death instead of life. The questions we must answer are these: Why don't we do the right thing? What do we want to prove to ourselves by doing otherwise?

Contemporary culture promotes new temptations each day. Remaining open to God through discernment offers us hope-filled choices.

PRAYER: Gracious God, thanks for your love and understanding. Help me be faithful to you. May I always recognize that what I say must be followed by what I do. Guide me to act in ways that glorify your name. Amen.

Wednesday, June 13 • Read Psalm 5:1-8

Phrases such as "Give ear to my words" (NIV); "Listen to my cry for help" (NIV); and "In the morning, O Lord, you hear my voice" (NIV) make up this special prayer in Psalm 5. In each of these phrases, we experience the psalmist's desire to be heard in different ways.

As people of faith, we pray daily in varying circumstances. Our morning prayer may thank God for a new day; we pray at mealtimes for our food; we pray in our time of need and so on, until we lie down to rest and thank God for the day's activities. We may also take time to examine the day's deeds, seeking forgiveness and grace. We have a unique, personal, and valuable relationship with God.

What happens when we read, "Lead me, LORD, in your righteousness" (NIV)? Do we follow that request in how we pray? Do we keep our promises to God? Do we willingly follow wherever God may lead us? Often we are not ready to go that far.

We know that God hears us. God listens to our cries in difficult times. Not only in the morning but all day long God hears us. But what about the part that is up to us? God truly listens to us, but are we listening to God?

It seems to me that the sounds of this world overwhelm us. In the midst of chaos, destruction, and war, we may find it hard to listen to God. Or perhaps the answer we receive is not the one for which we prayed. In the midst of all the conflicting noise, we sometimes struggle to hear God's still small voice. We seek the way that, in the words of the psalmist, is straight. Let us listen to God, as God readily listens to us every time we pray.

SUGGESTION FOR MEDITATION: **Where do you hear God's voice clearly? What places in your daily routine cause you to face temptation? How do you walk in righteousness?**

PRAYER: **God, I give honor and glory to you. Please tune my ear so I can hear your voice in the midst of the world's sounds. Help me to listen to others' cries, to others' voices. In responding may I find you. Amen.**

Our Galatian brothers and sisters experience Paul's affirmation that the observance of the law is not the basis of a right relationship with God; the right relationship comes "through faith in Jesus Christ." Paul takes this radical approach in opposition to those who sought to convert Gentiles to Judaism as a condition of Christian discipleship. This was one of the first church fights. Will the first-century church affirm Paul's belief or will two separate churches emerge?

Paul argues that if observation of the law brings justification, then Jesus died "for nothing" (better translated as "gratuitously"). Instead, writes Paul, all are saved by grace. The cross is not a one-time occurrence but a reality that points toward and shapes the future. The truth of the gospel extends God's love and grace to all people. The early church seemed to accept this simple proclamation about grace and faith, but the church continues to face or ignore the consequences of Paul's argument. Are *all* people saved by grace? Or must some standard of belief (or membership) exist?

Paul writes that Jesus' crucifixion establishes our relationship with God. Our challenge is to respond daily to the love we know in Christ. We may read the Bible. We may sit expectantly in prayer. Our daily practice may include thirty minutes of silence that end with the gentle beep of a telephone alarm. We may enter a fast for the sake of service and growth. Every day we seek new ways to grow in our relationship with God. Like the Galatians, we learn through perseverance. Growing spiritually and faithfully takes time. While our culture demands instant gratification in all things, spiritual maturity cannot happen overnight. Consistency and perseverance matter!

PRAYER: **God help me day by day, step by step, to remain faithful to you. Guide me, lead me; my trust is in you. Amen.**

Jesus related to those whom society had set apart or tried to cast away. Because of his openness to God, Jesus comforted all persons, no matter their cultural status. While associating with those who were oppressed, Jesus also addressed those in power and challenged them to see God at work in their midst.

Jesus' host can too easily label this woman with the alabaster jar of ointment. Simon the Pharisee judges her as an unclean sinner. Because someone may not look, speak, or act like us is no reason to judge and exclude any person created by God. That seems to be the thought behind Jesus' response to Simon's grumbling, but Jesus does not preach.

Instead Jesus tells a story about a moneylender. The story seems intended to help Simon understand something about compassion, forgiveness, and joy. We read that the Pharisee replies that the one with the greater debt expresses more love to the one who offers forgiveness. From Simon's speech we sense that the answer comes grudgingly.

In response to Simon's answer, Jesus offers another lesson. He contrasts the behavior of the unnamed woman with that of his host. While Simon did invite Jesus to eat in his home, Simon offered no basic hospitality. Perhaps he thinks that he has done enough by inviting Jesus. In some ways the church today may be more like Simon than like the woman. At times we think that the church is hospitable, but we may be looking at our hospitality from the vantage point of a Simon and not that of Jesus. How can we insure that our hospitality is genuine and loving? How can we practice the openness that Jesus practiced?

PRAYER: Loving God, you sent Jesus into the world to proclaim good news to all people. Help us to see Jesus in all the persons who come into our lives. Amen.

The story of the woman with the alabaster jar causes us to pause as we reflect on our journey this week. She goes without a name. All odds are against her; she is a woman labeled as a sinner by those at the house. However, before Jesus forgives her, he calls Simon to accountability for not following the laws of hospitality. Jesus says to Simon, "You did not give me any water for my feet"; "you didn't kiss me"; and "you didn't put oil on my head." It is this anonymous woman who wets Jesus' feet with her tears and who kisses Jesus' feet and puts oil on them. She is the one who has extended hospitality and love against all odds, despite her being labeled a sinner by those who consider themselves righteous. How easy it is to label someone or blame others for what we have *not* done.

As I watch my kids, I have learned about a ghost in the household. No one knows what happened. No one takes responsibility for what is misplaced or missing or for not doing his or her "home task." My children blame one another for different reasons. The blame game reflects on our society and on our places of ministry. It is easy to blame others for our lack of responsibility, and yet we want to grow personally and as a church. To grow implies our acceptance of personal responsibility. If we want our prayer life to flourish, we become responsible for daily practice. If we want to become more hospitable people, we practice hospitality.

PRAYER: God, like the woman with the alabaster jar, make us hospitable people. Help us avoid the blame game and accept responsibility to become the people you would have us be. Lead us into a life of compassion and justice, for we are learning to follow you. Amen.

Jesus extends his ministry of hospitality far beyond our wildest imagination. As he travels from place to place, many decide to follow him. Some experience healing from different illnesses; others experience the freedom of a new life. In all circumstances, those who decide to follow Jesus experience a change in heart. They cannot remain the same. Something beautiful happens, and they know it. The text may not explain in detail about all those who follow Jesus, but their stories are as important as those we have had the privilege to know. In this case, these women have experienced change in their lives and have chosen to follow Jesus. The text names three specific women: Mary called Magdalene, Joanna, and Susanna.

These women are not mere followers; they help and provide from their resources to follow him. As we live out our beliefs in communities of faith, we receive an invitation to collaborate in that ministry. The text says that these women help to support Jesus. How are we helping?

We tend to criticize, complain, or simply not see things clearly when we are not the ones in charge. Instead of rejoicing in the goodness of God and the opportunity to be in ministry, we blame others or whine. Christ Jesus calls us to embrace with joy all opportunities that God offers because we are in partnership with the One who redeems us. We are called to serve and serve well, with gratitude in our heart.

PRAYER: God, in our journey to be faithful, we thank you and seek your grace and mercy. Help us to grow as disciples so that we can continue our part in proclaiming the good news. Amen.

When Life Is Tough

June 18–24, 2007 • F. Belton Joyner Jr.[‡]

MONDAY, JUNE 18 • Read 1 Kings 19:1-15a

Elijah did not exactly get it right, did he? God gives him a great victory over four hundred-fifty prophets of Baal in a face-to-face encounter, but Elijah runs scared from the threat of one person, Jezebel, who is miles away. God sends a messenger to make sure that Elijah eats, but the prophet has to be told a second time to take on nourishment. Elijah complains that he is left alone as the only faithful one in Israel, but God points out that seven thousand others have not bowed to Baal (v. 18).

Been there. Done that. Fear has a way of making us feel that we are alone. Fear has a way of throwing our view of reality out of kilter. Fear has a way of shutting down the ways we usually care for ourselves. But the final score here is God 1, Fear 0.

Of course, God does not show up exactly as Elijah (or me . . .you?) might have expected. I'm ready to say, "Let's hear it for the God who is loud and clear! Let's hear it for the God who thunders what we ought to do! Let's hear it for the God who appears in the power of earthquake and fire!" But am I quite so ready to recognize the God of "sheer silence"? Am I eager to follow God when the voice of silence is the answer to the plea, "My God, my God, why have you forsaken me?"

I take heart from the realization that after Elijah has had such a roller-coaster ride with God and after Elijah has been ready to quit in despair and after Elijah has been immobilized by fear, today's lesson ends with God still sending Elijah on a mission. Even with my own unevenness of trust, what does God have for me to do?

PRAYER: What I can offer, O God, is a frail beginning (and even that beginning has come from you), but send me on a God-sized mission. Amen.

[‡]Retired United Methodist clergy; living in Bahama, North Carolina.

The psalmist knew what it was to live in the desert. Life itself depended on finding water that kept flowing, even in the midst of the summer's driest heat. That's the kind of relationship we seek with God: a fountain that flows when our souls are thirsty, a presence that is real even when we do not feel it.

If God's love is like an ever-flowing river, sometimes it seems that the flow is an underground stream, not visible to the eye of our experience. "Where is your God?" is the mocking call, not only of the unbeliever (see Matthew 27:43) but also the cry of one who has sought to be faithful (see Matthew 27:46). To wonder why God is not more evident is a question from the human journey. We ponder that issue each time there is a hurricane or tornado or tsunami or bombing or some other disaster beyond our grasp.

For the writer of the psalm, Jordan and Hermon are a long way from the familiar joys and festivals of Jerusalem. Those lands (those experiences) are a long way from the place where he remembers God's active presence. But remember he does, for in the remembering he finds hope—hope even in the far places, even in the dry places. Because the God he remembers is a living God, he has hope. In the language of the Old Testament, the word translated "living" is the same word that describes fresh water. That's a good hope for a dusty day!

PRAYER: O God, our help in ages past, our hope for years to come, bring the freshness of your presence in such a way that I can celebrate you even when I do not see you, praise you even when I do not feel you, thank you even when I do not hear you. Amen.

One thing you can say for the psalmist: he does not hide his true feelings from God. "Why have you forgotten me?" "Why must I walk about mournfully because the enemy oppresses me?" One of God's gracious gifts is that when we state our honest emotions before God, it does not scare God off.

Have you ever tried to act a certain way to make an impact on someone you wanted to impress? Perhaps you smiled when you really wanted to grit your teeth. Perhaps you laughed at a joke you really didn't understand. Perhaps you left a huge tip so you would appear to be supergenerous.

Not so the psalmist. He tells it like it is. And his forthrightness in stating his loneliness and misery lends a sound of truth and believability when he proclaims with equal passion, "I shall again praise him, my help and my God." This proclamation is no slippery smile from someone trying to make believe that everything in life is wonderful. This is no fake happiness from someone attempting a kind of self-hypnosis about how grand the daily grind is. Rather, in the very context of distress, the psalmist—not denying the hurting places—lifts up the good news that God is still in charge, a helper worthy of praise.

When I tell God where I hurt or that I am angry, I express my trust in God. It is a way of saying, "You know me as I really am and still you love me." After all, the word for "help" can also be translated "savior."

PRAYER: God of all mercies, hear me tell what you already know: my life has good moments and hard moments, and I thank you for the hope planted in my heart in both. Amen.

Thursday, June 21 • Read Galatians 3:23-29

Imagine this scene: young Zenas dawdles as he walks to school, the hot early morning sun in first-century Rome makes him wish more for playtime than classroom time. Walking with him a family servant encourages, chastises, insists as he makes certain that the boy gets to his first class on time.

Imagine this scene: Zenas is having fun running races with other lads from the neighborhood. Just as it appears that another boy will be the first to reach the goal at the end of the dusty street, Zenas reaches out his foot and trips the would-be winner. As the fallen youth writhes in anger, the family servant moves to Zenas and exhorts him to better sportsmanship, challenging him to run a fair race.

Imagine this scene: Zenas has carried a burning stick from the family home, pretending to be a soldier with a torch. The flame licks the side of a merchant's tent and begins to burn the awning. Zenas is trapped by the fire, but the family servant reaches through the blaze and pulls Zenas to safety.

Imagine this scene: Zenas, his father, and the family servant sit under a shade tree. To the servant, the father says, "Zenas is now a man. You no longer have to protect him, watch over him, and discipline him. Zenas is free."

The New Testament word for that servant is *paidagogos*. Paul uses this word in verses 24 and 25 in today's text: "disciplinarian." Until we are free in Christ, the law—rules and regulations— serve as our *paidagogos*. Now, we are justified (made right with God) not by law but by faith in Christ.

PRAYER: Thanks be to you, O God, for freedom in Jesus Christ. In him, I am your child, set free from shackles of law but free to be obedient in thanksgiving. Amen.

What makes one person more valued than another? In some places, it is how much money someone has. In another place, it might be the color of skin. In school, it could be the person with the highest grades. In some cultures, the politician has the greatest influence.

In first-century Galatia—part of present-day Turkey—certain qualities set people apart from one another: a free man was more valued than a slave; a male had more authority than a female; and even in the church, members argued about who had more value in the eyes of God: Greek or Jew.

Paul sends ripples through the Galatian Christian community when he writes, in effect, "Baptismal waters have washed away those differences and clothed all the believers in one garment: Jesus Christ." (In early baptisms, the newly baptized literally had their old clothes taken away and new baptismal clothing put on.) Of course, you are still male. Of course, you are still female. You are slave. You are free. You are Jew. You are Greek. But in Jesus Christ, you all have the same family inheritance!

I ask myself: which Christians have I made into second-class believers? How about those with whom I disagree theologically? How about those who feel God leading them to a social issue conclusion different than mine? How about those who are new to the faith or those who seem stuck at the same spiritual spot for fifty years?

This Christian family is a mixed bag! But as a friend of mine said, "I have been blessed by my blood family and by my water family." Thanks be to God that in baptism we have become water family!

PRAYER: Lord Jesus Christ, you have clothed me in the family robe. Amen.

Whom have you known who has broken an addiction to alcohol? Do you know a person who was released from an unhealthy obsession with sex? Has anyone you've met been able to leave behind racist attitudes? Who has moved beyond violence and war as the best way to resolve differences? What about persons who no longer need gambling to make their lives complete? Which acquaintance of yours understands the social and economic patterns that create poverty? (Do any of these questions describe you?)

There is a wonderful "before and after" quality to someone whose demons have been cast out. In this text, a man goes from insane to sane, from unclothed to clothed, from antisocial to social. Jesus does good work!

In Luke's account of this healing, Jesus asks for the man's name. (To name the demon is the first step in overcoming the demon. That is why Twelve Step groups begin their introductions with a statement such as "My name is John; I am addicted to pornography.") The man's answer is "Legion." In Roman military terms, a legion represents thousands of soldiers. In this naming, it means that this man is pulled in many directions all at once. Can you imagine a Roman legion in which each soldier demands control? That is what comprises this man's life: forces pull him in every direction all at one time, each one wanting to be in control.

If anything or anyone other than Jesus Christ is shaping my life and forming my priorities, I need the healing, unifying gift of our Lord. Can I name the demons he needs to send from me?

PRAYER: Dare I look within, O Lord, to see what tugs me away from the fullness of your presence? Amen.

Although this text is about a healing and about the restoration of a man to a full life, on three occasions fear is the dominating presence. First, the man possessed by demons so frightens the public that he is kept under guard and in shackles. Second, when folks see this man whom they have long feared now in his right mind, it scares them. Third, as the word spreads about what Jesus has done, the fear becomes contagious and people from the surrounding countryside ask Jesus to leave; "they were seized with great fear."

Why does so much alarm arise when something so good happens? Fear of the unknown? Fear of change? Fear of outsiders? The trepidation could be made up of any or all of these factors. One aspect is clear: even though we Christians often say that Jesus brings perfect peace, we have an account here in which the presence and actions of Jesus upset the way the people have life put together; the result is not peaceful.

I have experienced this unbalanced feeling (fear) when someone I thought to be mean-spirited does me a favor. I have experienced this uncertainty (fear) when an idea I had always assumed to be wrong, even evil, begins to emerge as God's truth, God's will. I have experienced this apprehension (fear) when I recognize that God has called me to a ministry that is not comfortable, to a tomorrow that is not like today.

Although fear can sometimes immobilize us or deplete us, it is not necessarily a bad thing. It might even signal our Lord's presence with us, accomplishing life-changing work!

PRAYER: Lord of all—Lord over my demons, Lord over my fears, Lord over my tomorrows—grant me peace. Amen.

The Still Small Voice May Be Your Own

June 25–July 1, 2007 • Darlene Saunders Ousley[‡]

MONDAY, JUNE 25 • Read 2 Kings 2:1-2, 6-14

My mom likes to tell the story about my request for an extra seat at the table for my invisible friend (Jesus) when I was four or five years old. She honored my request—even though our dinner table already had ten places set. During dinner I regularly conversed with "my friend," being sure to ask if he wanted peas or chicken. She never questioned my behavior.

God's presence overwhelms Elijah. It comes not in the wind and fire but in the stunning silence from which the Lord beckons Elijah to anoint Elisha "as prophet in your place" (1 Kings 19:16). Many scholars justifiably credit Elisha's unwavering loyalty to Elijah and his undying commitment to the God of Israel in his refusing three times Elijah's request to "stay here." In Elisha I also see a young man who honors his own voice as a source of wisdom. He relies on the strength of his own spiritual insights to guide his decisions and actions.

Rather than emphasizing Elisha's willingness to follow Elijah mindlessly, the writer records the strength of Elisha's decision to accompany Elijah. In refusing Elijah's request to tarry, Elisha clearly stands his ground for what he believes is a better avenue of action. He has spent enough time observing Elijah's relationship with God to have developed the same presence of mind and confidence in his own connection to God. By following rather than tarrying, Elisha receives the mantle. Trusting in one's spiritual intuition is honored by God.

PRAYER: God of the prophets, God of the dinner table, restore our courage and confidence to stand our ground. Help us understand that the young learn by following. Amen.

[‡]United Methodist layperson; active in Native American worship throughout the Southeast; living in Waynesville, North Carolina.

As a young Christian woman, full of faith but lacking an experienced relationship with God, I found myself at age twenty-three lying in a hospital bed eighty-five miles from home in a strange town about to give birth to twins. Until that spring I hadn't needed to depend on God for anything much more than general conversation.

Twenty weeks pregnant with twins is not the time to honor the voice of premature fetuses who want to come into the world ahead of schedule. I interceded with my own weak and frightened voice and sought the comfort and wisdom of God during my first dark night of the soul. As the psalmist proclaims, "I cried aloud to God, that he may hear me. . . . In the day of my trouble I seek the LORD . . . ; my soul refuses to be comforted."

During the night God revealed things to me in my discomfort and brought me great joy: that I would have a boy and a girl—and eight weeks later I did. In my naiveté, I only sought comfort without fully realizing the power of my one-on-one encounter with God. As I focused solely on what I needed, I failed to rise above my situation and be awed by what transpired.

Often I have reflected on the purity of my faith in my twenties. Even with more life experience, that long dark night became the pivotal moment when God became very real and personal for me. We cry aloud to God in our need with hands outstretched, and God answers.

PRAYER: Creator God, there is the moment when we accept your saving presence—then come the endless nights of the soul when we seek truly to experience salvation. Father, let us hold tightly to the hope we say we have, for we can trust you to keep your promises. Amen.

WEDNESDAY, JUNE 27 • Read Galatians 5:1, 13-25

A lot of folks these days talk about wanting to live in balance and harmony. It isn't easy to do in today's culture. Apparently it wasn't easy in the days of the early church either. Paul gently chides the Galatians to be wary of walking out of balance as they follow the teachings of Jesus Christ. He warns his readers to be careful about misunderstanding the role of the traditional law (religious effort by the outer self) and the importance of keeping balance within the inner self.

Native Americans refer to this balance that Paul endorses as "living on the Red Road." The Red Road is a metaphor for treating all of creation with respect, dignity, and compassion, while fully living your truth as a spiritual being. It holds each living creature accountable to every other living creature. For Paul, knowing the Christ leads naturally to reflecting the Christ. As we practice alignment with love, joy, peace, patience, kindness, generosity, faithfulness, gentleness, and self-control, our spirit merges with—comes into harmony and balance with—the Christ Spirit.

The absence of walking in balance is equally apparent. A total disregard of others leads to quarrels and factionalism. Paul hopes that both we and the Galatians can learn from his experience of imbalance; he encourages growth into a deeper wisdom and affirms the value of nurturing balance daily in our lives. We must shift the concept from head to heart and soul.

SUGGESTION FOR MEDITATION: **Many Native Americans intuitively understand the balance that Paul requests. We understand the interconnectedness of all living things. In loving neighbor as self, the Christ love is fully proclaimed. In helping others, we help the whole. In hurting others, we hurt the whole. In loving this spiritually natural way, we all are set free, and none of us is a slave to the other. Paul's path may have been Jewish and Roman, but his wisdom also reflects Red Road medicine. How does your life reflect this intuitive care and balance?**

As I write this, news has broken that twelve coal miners have died in a West Virginia mining explosion. Though I am now a North Carolinian, West Virginia is and always will be home. I grieve a loss beyond twelve husbands and fathers—my grief is much deeper in my soul. The community proclaimed they were lied to; and one member has declared a loss of faith in God.

Although I have not lived in West Virginia in over twenty years, my heart resides there with people and families who mine coal for a living. These families are knit together in ways that cannot be described. These deaths call to mind my own loss of family members to that industry—my father (when I was sixteen) of complications from emphysema and black lung; my brother-in-law, tragically crushed at age thirty in a mining accident; my brother at age fifty-two, recovering from a lung transplant—after dedicating his life to mining coal. All three were Christians; all three deaths shook my faith.

Understanding this community's pain, I can't describe the grief that I feel and hold for this coal camp. The psalmist's words have been a healing balm in these last few days. The psalmist searches for meaning through his remembrance of God's redeeming action. During his darkest days even the heavens, the earth, and the seas remind him that God is God. "What god is so great as our God?" Sometimes in the chaos we can seek that which is beyond ourselves and discover what endures.

SUGGESTION FOR MEDITATION: When we experience no stability, nature can and does rescue us, helping us recall more stable times. God's still small voice may speak from nature when we're unable to sing, shout, or even speak for ourselves.

FRIDAY, JUNE 29 • Read Galatians 5:13-25

Maya Angelou says that when you know better, you do better. Paul's letter teaches us to be on guard for conflictual desires that prevent us from doing what we should—to be watchful of behaviors when necessary. Watch out for the difficult times and draw upon the banked reserves of the Spirit.

Down times can bring opportunity for spiritual growth. As I write this, I am awaiting spring. It's the dead of winter, and I have the winter blues. After fifty years of living in a four-season region of the country, I still have not adjusted to approaching winter. I have never mastered the depression that spills over me each November and gradually begins to lift late March.

My spiritual reality check tells me that my own negative thoughts weigh me down. Especially now, I have to remind myself that life exists in ebbs and flows. The earth needs the winter rest to prepare for spring. When I meditate and apply Paul's teachings to my current moodiness, they remind me that I am as dependent upon God to get me through the down days as the earth is to get us all through winter.

At Paul's insistence, I can choose to alter my perception of reality: "For you were called to freedom, brothers and sisters; only do not use your freedom as an opportunity for self-indulgence." I can choose to view things either from the winter blues or from the winter rest perspective.

Throughout our winters, if we store self-defeating thoughts that are less than our spiritual best, then that is the light-deprived, cold bank our reserves have to draw upon. But a seasonal shift helps us see that the down times also reflect an opportunity for a deeper dependence upon God. And the fallow time prepares us for growth.

SUGGESTION FOR MEDITATION: **Like a gentle parent, Paul awaits the blossoming of the Galatian Christians and reminds them of the potential outcome of patiently practicing the spiritual journey. In what ways do your down days provide opportunity to wait and depend more fully upon God?**

For three days, a robin has tried to find a way to build a nest flush against my sliding glass doors. The glass bears the marks of her feathers where she has thrashed and fluttered against it. She persistently pursues this activity. Nothing has distracted her except the threat on her life by my cat.

The robin's tenacity helped clarify for me the meaning of today's passage. Using my normal means of approaching scripture, I read between the lines. As with the robin, my tried-and-true method is failing. In my first pass at the sliding door of the text, I am distracted by the outlying themes, unable to approach the central theme. Pass two, I only see the theme of hospitality. Jesus is rejected, boldly rejected. So I run with that thread for a bit. But, no, that's not quite it.

I read the passage again, and I'm distracted by the disciples' frustration at the reception their master receives. I follow that thread for a while, getting caught up in the emotion, their fire-and-brimstone mentality. Then Jesus sets his face toward Jerusalem and addresses several would-be followers. I find myself unsettled by the multifaceted passage.

I'm making excuses for not understanding this passage. It dawns on me that this passage is a like a metaphor that uses a writer's ploy to place a "scene within a scene"—often used when a character needs to be dramatically revealed.

I am struck by the robin's struggle at my door and my own struggle at the door to this passage. My attempt to understand parallels Jesus' journey to Jerusalem. Jesus tells us the journey will not be easy. We must stay the course, not giving way to the distractions of comfort or family responsibility. We face forward, not looking back; following Jesus requires a focused effort.

SUGGESTION FOR MEDITATION: **Consider the cost of discipleship as set forth by Jesus in this passage. God's work takes priority over distractions. Jesus showed us the way. Will you follow?**

The still small voice may not be very still or very small at all, particularly if it is the voice of the Lord. But many times we fail to hear that voice.

Imagine the frustration of realizing that after years of teaching, drilling, preparing, speaking, crying, singing, rejoicing with friends and family that your prep work may have been in vain? Jesus senses that his time is drawing to a close; the urgency of the kingdom becomes all the more important. People need to get onboard.

"I will follow you Lord, but. . . ."

This is the moment; the time is now. No more time to prepare. After all the intense teaching, the intimacy, the daily exchange, can you imagine how Jesus felt when no one apparently gets it?

"I will follow you Lord, but. . . ."

I have actually pondered this thought most of my adult life: *Lord, if those who followed you most intimately struggled with the meaning of your words, how on earth are we supposed to get it?* Luke's point illustrates a scene from Jesus' past but also serves as a lesson for our present: "Lord, I will follow you, but. . . ."

First I have to get us a place to rest, prepare dinner; then I have to drop the kids off, or take the dog to the vet, or do laundry, or do research. . . . Perhaps if we cease our endless activity and quiet ourselves, we will hear Jesus call us to follow him. Two thousand years ago Jesus was physically present on this earth. He called then and he calls now, "Follow me." No more excuses.

SUGGESTION FOR MEDITATION: Jesus still has his face set toward Jerusalem. He has known his mission. Lord, slow me down so that in the silence amid the chaos, I make every attempt to get it. Amen.

It's Not about Us

July 2–8, 2007 • *Carolyn M. Anderson*[‡]

MONDAY, JULY 2 • Read 2 Kings 5:1-14

Just as it often is for us today, God's instructions come to Naaman from a most unlikely source. He responds just as we sometimes do, allowing his pride to get the best of him and therefore not doing exactly what the young Israelite girl has said. Rather than following the guidance God is sending, Naaman decides to go to the authority figures, hoping to get what only God can give.

Since the letter Naaman carries contains nothing about contacting the prophet, the king of Israel cannot understand why he receives this unreasonable request. Elisha hears about this mess and sends word to have Naaman come to him. But Naaman's pride gets in the way again because he has his mind made up about his treatment and the manner of his healing.

It is amazing how God offers simple instructions, and we look around for something spectacular. Rather than do as we have been told, we try to figure things out our way, rejecting God's option. Often just like Naaman we come close to missing our blessing because we have predetermined how and when God will respond to our needs. Surprisingly stubborn Naaman finally relinquishes his pride. Having listened to the pleas of his servants, he takes the necessary step himself toward the healing that God offers. Naaman has to go into the water himself; no one else, no authority figure, no prophet, no one can do it for him. God's plan for our well-being often requires little more than our willingness to step out into what God already has in place for us.

PRAYER: Eternal God, give me the wisdom to listen to you and follow with an obedient heart, mind, and will. Amen.

[‡]Deaconess, women's retreat leader, Disciple Bible Study teacher; member, Curriculum Resources Committee, General Board of Discipleship; living in Waldorf, Maryland.

Most of us have experienced an illness or accident that caused us to sink very low. Our condition may have required doctors, nurses, and other health professionals to give us pills, injections, anesthesia, bandages, food, and all that accompanies getting well. We may even know what it is like to have friends and family stand with us and pray for us in the midst of it all. Sometimes we might even be tempted to think that our recovery was related to the advances of modern medicine or the faithfulness of family and friends. In our appreciation for the physicians, family and friends, we may forget to thank God, who is really responsible.

The psalmist has obviously been through a difficult time, and he uses this occasion to give God all the credit for taking care of him and for bringing him back even while his enemies want to gloat over his circumstances. The psalmist unashamedly yells out to God for help, and God gives him another chance at life.

We can also see from this psalm that it is not enough to thank God ourselves; we must share our gratitude with enthusiasm by inviting others to join us in joyful praises of thanksgiving. Our solo voice becomes a part of a melodious choir that sings praises to the Lord, giving thanks to God with our whole heart because we all walk in God's loving care. Yes, we may sometimes anger or disappoint God, but that never lasts long; God's love lasts forever.

Our words of praise and thanksgiving encourage us to believe that the tears of our nights will give way to the joy of an entirely new day.

Prayer: Dear God, keep me ever mindful of how often and how much I need to thank you. Amen.

Because of God's covenant with us we are like a rock: unmovable. Our remembering that we cannot rest or depend on material prosperity or comfort but only rest in God keeps us solid, like a rock. At times too much self-reliance can lead us to think that we are immune to trials and troubles. We can even talk ourselves into believing we have nothing to fear because of our status, income, or education. And then something bad befalls us; we determine that God has turned away from us—perhaps in anger. Life often then becomes our worst nightmare.

Those nightmare situations change our prayer life as they did the psalmist's. Whenever our situation is bad or we are sick, our prayers become more intense and more sincere. And like the psalmist we often make the most pitiful case for why God should answer our prayers. The psalmist tries to persuade God by saying that if he dies he can no longer praise God or declare God's faithfulness to anyone. And God's healing comes, as it always does, because of God's grace, not the psalmist's pleas.

When God changes our situations it is better than getting new clothes that only alter the outer appearance. We can finally rid ourselves of the old garments of sadness, depression, and frustration and step into the newness of full, rich abundant life where our days can be full of praise to God. We never forget what God has done for us or take the healing for granted. God deserves our gratitude forever. Because of God's covenant with us we can be like a rock; unmovable in our thankfulness.

SUGGESTION FOR MEDITATION: **Call to mind the ways God has healed or delivered you. Allow the situation(s) to become pictures in your mind. Consider how different the outcome would have been without God.**

Thursday, July 5 • Read Galatians 6:1-10

What might a picture of Christian community look like? Paul gives some broad strokes in painting our life together when he writes to the Galatians. The picture includes mutual accountability and personal responsibility. Our response to wrongdoing involves less criticism and more care. Calling our neighbors to account is a way we show our love of them. We offer restoration in the community. We cannot become too high and mighty to assist those who bear burdens. Our help can lighten their load while demonstrating the behavior Christ expects. We only fool ourselves when we act as if we are too good or as if helping others is beneath our dignity.

With the guidance of the Spirit we focus on the work of Christ and not on ourselves. Our responsibility is to do the best we can, not compared to others but for Christ. For this reason self-examination becomes an important aspect of our own personal accountability. Then we can rejoice at what can be done and not point out what cannot be done.

Paul offers a pointed choice: serve the Spirit or serve the flesh. We cannot fool God. God sees our neglect even if no one else does and rewards accordingly. We will reap what we sow. In our selfishness we not only ignore the needs of others, but we ignore God.

We cannot allow ourselves to become fatigued and worn out because whether we realize it or not, the bountiful crop comes to those who don't give up. Paul encourages the Galatians and us to do good "whenever we have an opportunity," and for Paul, the opportune time is now. Our working together in mutual accountability produces an everlasting harvest beyond the limitations of our human ability. As John Wesley said, "Do all the good you can, in all the ways you can, to all the people you can, as long as ever you can."

PRAYER: Dear God, help me be and do that which will give you glory, remembering my own imperfections while depending on your good and perfect will for all of humankind. Amen.

People willingly accept traditions—until they find out they may have to change their old habits. We are also more than willing to have others follow the traditions we have approved. Persons in the church sometimes try to force others to accept particular traditions. In Galatia, a group of law-observant Jews are pressing the Gentiles to be circumcised, a Jewish rite. And yet for Paul that physical distinction has no bearing on the Gentiles' acceptance of Christ through Paul's law-free preaching. The Jews are merely demanding that the Galatians jump through another set of religious hoops, thereby giving the Jews something to boast about. Circumcised Gentiles become a trophy of the Jews' success.

Paul will only boast about the cross of Jesus. The cross—not any tradition—frees him from the need to please others, frees him from the world's and the church's expectations. The world has lost its attraction for Paul; the glamour and appeal of his former life is now fading.

The important aspect for Paul and for us hinges on God's action: God is making us new without regard for circumcision or uncircumcision, transforming us from who we are to who God envisions us to be. Being "new" is not just an improvement on the old; it is becoming someone entirely different. Rules of division fall by the wayside; peace and mercy are ours as we begin to own everything that is part of the new creation and put aside everything that is not.

PRAYER: Dear God, deliver me from those traditions that keep me from a new life in Christ. Amen.

Jesus selects workers to go where he intends to go. He has commissioned twelve and now commissions seventy more! Then as now, there is more to be done than there are workers to do it. And the sense of urgency is great. We live in a time of enormous opportunity. We pray because the need is enormous and the laborers are few. But in praying for more workers we then make ourselves available because after praying we are told to *go*! Get on our way! The work will not be easy. We will enter a hostile world that will not treat us as if we are special. We can anticipate difficulties and problems.

As disciples of Christ we cannot permit ourselves to be bogged down with a lot of stuff; personal comfort is less important than the reason for being sent. As Christ's followers we spread the good news, not gossip or chit-chat. The urgency and enormity of the mission allows no time for delay.

We accept hospitality when offered. Those who receive us favorably are people of peace; those who don't will miss out, because we will continue to spread Christ's message and mission. There is no need to impose this message on anyone. Stay with those who first offer a place, rather than appear to be comparison shopping to find out who provides the best offer. We express gratitude for whatever we have.

So the seventy set out with a threefold mission: (1) to eat what is set before them, (2) to heal the sick, (3) to proclaim the kingdom. In what ways are these still the church's mission? How has that mission changed? How do you participate in that mission?

We may be welcome; we may not be. The people who receive God's messengers will experience healing and discover the nearness of God's reign. Those who do not welcome the messengers do not realize the opportunity they miss—God's kingdom at their doorstep.

PRAYER: Gracious God, grant that I may hunger to lovingly share your message in all of the places you intend me to go. Amen.

Jesus concludes his instructions to the disciples by letting them know they act as his ambassadors. He gives us this role as well. Jesus confers on the disciples and us the rights and authorities of a legal agent. We carry the authority of the sender. Today in the world of diplomacy rejecting an ambassador is considered an affront to the head of state who commissioned and sent that person and to the country the ambassador represents. Rejecting an ambassador implies that neither the head of state nor the country are worth even a semblance of polite goodwill.

It is not possible to reject or despise those who represent Christ without rejecting or despising him also. When people do not choose to hear our testimony, they are indicating an unwillingness to know Christ himself.

The seventy return from their assignment understandably excited to report their success—even the demons are subject to their power. We too sometimes get caught up in the "success" of wholehearted response to our witness, ministry, or activity. We easily think it is *our* efforts that have made the difference. But Jesus reminds them as well as us that our greatest glory is not in what we have done but only in what God has done through us. The reward comes in knowing that our "names are written in heaven."

SUGGESTION FOR MEDITATION: **Reflect on the ways that you have been an ambassador for Christ this week. When were you tempted to see yourself as the source of your success? What honor did you bring to Jesus? What challenges did you face because of whom you represented? Write down the words that express your thanks for the opportunity to be an ambassador, no matter what the outcome.**

A New Standard

July 9–15, 2007 • Bill Lizor[‡]

MONDAY, JULY 9 • Read Amos 7:7-9

I love gadgets. Always have, always will. You can imagine my excitement when I saw the newest laser level on sale. Having just moved, I had boxes of pictures and other wall hangings just waiting to be unpacked and hung. Surely this tool would do the trick! Minutes later, I was at home shooting that little red beam on every flat surface of my house. It even curved around corners if you tilted it at just the proper angle. An hour passed and I concluded that everything in my house was level. Content with my exploration, I put the level on a shelf—where it still sits today. The boxes of pictures and wall hangings remain unhung.

In the reading from Amos, God talks about a different type of leveling tool—a plumb line. The plumb line, a piece of string with a metal weight, is hung to see if vertical lines (such as walls) are straight or "plumb." God says that a time is coming when all people will be measured according to God's standards. God is no longer content with the way the people have begun to buckle and sway over time.

Just like the people to whom Amos spoke, we now must be ready. It is time to begin to examine ourselves by a new standard—the standard that God has established through scripture and Christian tradition. God won't leave the standards on a shelf to collect dust. God is faithful; this is one project that God will see to completion. Are you plumb?

SUGGESTION FOR REFLECTION: **As you begin to think of a new standard this week, list on paper the things the world values as tools that measure worth. Now, in another column, make a list of things God values. How do you measure up?**

[‡]Director, Young Adult and Single Adult Ministries, General Board of Discipleship, The United Methodist Church, Nashville, Tennessee.

The prophets often get a bad reputation among the people to whom they are called to speak. For some reason, people don't enjoy being told how wrong they are; that they need to shape up; and that if they don't, bad times are ahead. I certainly would count myself among that crowd! At the same time, the prophets are some of the most blessed people in all of our Christian tradition. The blessing they receive is God's vision for the future—a sneak peek, if you will, of the standards to which all people will be held.

Amos, having received a vision from God, sets out to share it with God's chosen people. Needless to say, the message isn't well received. Amos is chastised for his vision and threatened with exile if he continues to speak prophetically. You see, the people are in no way excited about the idea of God's establishing God's own standard for right living. The rulers of Amos's day have no interest in being held to any standards but their own.

Perhaps people (then and now) react so strongly to such a word because of the radical difference between God's plumb standards and the world's. God doesn't expect perfection; but God does call toward action, not just personal piety in one's life but a piety that extends far beyond oneself.

It is true, especially in our world, that God's standards differ greatly from our own. Unselfish use of power, care for others, the development of the inner life, and the supporting and building up of God's people—these are God's standards. Together they create the plumb line to which we can compare ourselves. Quite a standard to live up to!

PRAYER: Creator God, enlighten our minds to see your new standard. Enable us to accomplish these radical tasks you've set before us. Help us, dear Lord, to be "plumb." Amen.

There is a currency in our world today that is more ubiquitous than money and twice as effective. People use and exploit it often but trade it only as a last resort. The leaders of the land have meeting after meeting to legislate it. Nations go to war with one another in order to gain it. It isn't a tangible thing—it can't be touched or stored, only used. No, it isn't wealth or land or possessions. This ubiquitous currency is power, and the world seems hungry for it.

Psalm 82 provides a behind-the-scenes look at a powerful group—a divine council. God serves as host to this assembly. If you want to talk about power, it surely resides with this group. Not just any power—supreme power, control of the universe as we know it. From the text we can surmise that those assembled beneath God have been using power as a means for lifting up those who are already high within the land. The powerful seem to be getting more powerful, while the poor and oppressed are ground further beneath the feet of the oppressors. The wicked continue to prosper, aided by those with power.

This group seems to be operating within the standards of our world—using power for the advancement of its own needs. However, as you may recall from Amos, God sets a new standard for all creation. God says to those assembled that the best way to use power is to give—not trade—it away. God challenges us all to side with the weak and the oppressed. We are called to use whatever power we may have not to oppress but to free, not to weaken but to build up.

SUGGESTION FOR REFLECTION: **Reflect on the areas of your life where you exhibit power and control. How do you use that power? In what ways does your power oppress or free people? How do you seek to give over power and control?**

A few years ago a person from my hometown church invited me to preach. The night before the service I sat trying to finalize my thoughts, nervous about what I would say to my church family. As I sat there I kept feeling that the stuff I had written wasn't right. I had a sense that I should go deeper and be more vulnerable about myself. I finally gave in and scrapped the entire sermon. I needed to start over if I wanted to get to something deeper. So I opened up to the congregation about my own struggles with sin and the freedom I have found through Christ.

A week later a letter arrived in my mailbox from the pastor of the church. Included with his own words of thanks was an anonymous letter from a member of the congregation. The anonymous writer said that I had shared the exact words that he needed to hear at this point in life. Apparently the person was having trouble being authentic about his trials and struggles. He needed to hear a voice of reassurance that someone else also had struggles but could see hope through Christ. I still have no clue who wrote that letter, but I know the effect it had in my life. I needed to hear those words of affirmation just as much as the anonymous letter writer needed to hear mine.

As we see in Paul's letter to the people at Colossae, speaking blessing is an important part of our calling to live by God's standards. Just like Paul, this individual acted in God's image by speaking a word of blessing into my life, and it made all the difference.

PRAYER: Lord God, for people who speak and for people who listen, we thank you. For moments to share and moments to partake, we thank you. For the blessings of our connectedness in Christ, we thank you. Amen.

Paul was dedicated to challenging others to embrace God's standards. In this instance, however, Paul doesn't leave it at just an exhortation; he fleshes out the idea into two areas that comprise living the worthy life: bearing fruit in good works and growing in knowledge. These two components, one outer and one inner, work together to become a complete and full life.

Notice that Paul first chooses bearing fruit in good works. Think of the process one must undertake in order to produce fruit. The ground must be fertilized, seeds planted, plants pruned. Growing things takes time and effort; it requires active involvement in the world.

Next Paul challenges us to also grow in knowledge of God. While action in the outer world is incredibly important to living the Christian life, attention to our own inner self has eternal significance as well. It is here, inside our own soul, that the lessons learned from our actions and the whispers of God in our heart combine to push us further toward becoming the creation God has called us to be. Out of the overflow of this learning and growing we are compelled by the Spirit to take action again. That action brings growth (both in the world and in ourselves), and the cycle continues.

So what are the by-products of living a life that is worthy? Paul promises that endurance and patience are gifts bestowed upon those devoted to action and knowledge. But even more, says Paul, that endurance will be transformed into a life of thanksgiving to God. Living a life worthy, a life in God's standards, is about living in celebration of the Spirit within us and the world around us.

PRAYER: Dear Lord, help us to be people who live worthy lives. Help us to be present in the world through action and present to ourselves through growth and knowledge. Amen.

The religious leaders of Jesus' day were famous for questioning and challenging Jesus and his ministry. In this story a scholar approaches Jesus wanting to know the way to eternal life. The scholar knows the intellectual answer, "Love the Lord your God with all your heart, and with all your soul, and with all your strength, and with all your mind; and your neighbor as yourself."

The scholar could have left well enough alone at that point, having articulated a good model for operating in God's will. Instead, he questions Jesus again as a means of justifying his own actions. It isn't enough to know the law; this man wants Jesus to say that the little he is doing is enough. The scholar wants the minimum requirement to be sufficient.

Jesus, however, turns things upside down by putting flesh onto that law through the story of the good Samaritan. It is one thing to hear words like "Love God" and "Love neighbor" but quite another to envision what that means. The scholar could easily see his peers and high religious leaders as neighbors, just as we can easily picture our friends and family. But Jesus has a different picture in mind. Essentially, Jesus says, picture the poor, the oppressed, the weak, and the beaten.

Jesus' story exposes the polar standards at work in our world. The first two passersby, both important and highly influential individuals, turn a blind eye to the wounded neighbor. They have the power to help but turn away. On the other hand, the Samaritan operates with God's standards at heart. He doesn't just stop to see that the man is OK. He goes the extra mile, not leaving until the man's every need has been met.

SUGGESTION FOR REFLECTION: As you reflect on the story Jesus tells, think back on your own journey. When have you been the one who was hurt? When have you been the priest or the Levite? When have you been the Samaritan?

A woman named Mary, one of the sweetest people I've ever met in my life, worked for my college. She has a soft voice that can calm you down, even if the world is trembling, and a heart so big you wonder if it has an end. She has never read me scripture or preached me a sermon, yet Mary's quiet confidence in God's will and her cheerful spirit shines through. Mary's life (not just her word) is her witness. She lives a life that is "plumb" before God, evidencing that quality in everything she does. She was, and continues to be, a living and breathing example of Christ in my life.

At the end of the parable of the good Samaritan, Jesus challenges the scholar and the reader to "go and do likewise." The scholar questions Jesus, trying to gain a theoretical understanding of "neighbor," and comes away with a simple commandment: "Go and do likewise." No matter how you look at it, this command requires action. The first part is to "go." That is simple enough. We are called to go into our homes, our schools, our offices, our neighborhoods, and our world. The second part is a little more of a challenge. "Do likewise." Jesus calls that man (and each of us) to live as the example we see in the scripture. Thus, as we seek to live up to God's standards, we find ourselves compelled to a life of action. The scripture doesn't say, "Go and *speak* likewise" or "Go and *think* likewise." It says, *do* likewise.

The best way we can share God's good news is not through the words of our mouth but through the actions of our life.

PRAYER: Creator God, strengthen and empower your people to "go and do likewise." Give us the tools we need that we may be your hands and feet on earth. Amen.

Christ in You, the Hope of Glory

July 16–22, 2007 • Robert Charles Leibold[‡]

MONDAY, JULY 16 • Read Amos 8:1-12

On New Year's Eve dear friends suddenly found themselves in a life-and-death crisis when their SUV went into an uncontrollable spin on black ice. With a full load of groceries and two children buckled in the rear seat, the SUV flipped over and slammed into a telephone pole, snapping it in two—a totally unexpected and frightening moment for this family of four. Sam, father of the two boys, was driving. He later told me of the utterly helpless feeling that overshadowed him, knowing his family was in danger and unable to do anything about it.

Amos 8 carries a similar feeling of crisis for the people of Israel. Surely it's difficult to read Amos's prophetic message and not be overwhelmed with heaviness of heart. Whether we speak of a personal crisis of soul or a crisis of national proportions, our feelings resonate with Amos's dark night of desolation. Amos sees "a basket of summer fruit" that appears to him in a prophetic vision. God seems to say to Amos, *You're eating your last basket of fruit—"the end has come upon my people Israel."* The totality of famine and loss is great, coming as the cost of Israel's living unjustly with no compassion for one another. In the end, the people desperately seek for a God who wants no part of them.

It would not be easy to preach this sermon to God's people. Yet, sometimes God's people need to hear hard things. On occasion (or perhaps more often than not) we need to be confronted with how we live. Amos causes us to question: Is God part of my life? Is God near when I need God? What word is God asking me to hear today?

PRAYER: Help me, O God; you alone are my strength. Amen.

[‡]Pastor, the Village Church of Bayville; Director of Wellspring Institute for Spiritual Growth; living in Bayville, New York.

TUESDAY, JULY 17 • Read Amos 8:11-12

In the days following their accident, Sam and his loving wife, Kelly, along with their two boys recovered from their injuries. Several days after their hospital release I took Sam and Kelly to retrieve the accident report and to see their demolished SUV. "It was a miracle," exclaimed Kelly, and there was no doubt that God's hand had been with them. The roof was caved in where Kelly had sat, and the doors on the driver's side were crushed in—it was a miracle that they were alive. What's more, Kelly remembered how one good Samaritan had pulled their boys from the SUV and placed them in his vehicle with his own children. The Samaritan had signed his name as a witness on the accident report. His name was Angel. Yes, God had his angel watching over this Christian family.

Whom do you call; where do you find help if God is not part of your life? In high school I distinctly remember a conversation in which several students argued about the existence of God and life after death. Though I took no philosophical stand for God, I do recall the deep awareness of God's presence in my life and the senselessness of life that simply ends in death. Sam and Kelly have a deep faith in God and are teaching their boys of Jesus' love. How devastating must be the plight of persons who desperately run to and fro, seeking the word of the Lord but never finding it. What a great emptiness: to seek God and not find God.

Amos 8 is difficult to read—what a word for a new week! It's important though to understand the depth of human darkness without God. In the days ahead we will encounter in the word of God, the One who is always with us.

SUGGESTION FOR MEDITATION: **In what ways do I seek God's presence?**

The psalms, like all scripture, need to be prayed inwardly and digested. Addressing the complexities of life with its harshness, suffering, and beauty, the psalms touch the depth of human emotion. The Hebrew title of the psalms also means hymns; musical instructions included in the psalms were originally intended for musicians who led corporate prayer in the form of song. *Selah* is one of these terms, and it appears twice in Psalm 52. It is thought that *selah* indicates an interlude in the music. At this point we stop reading, rest, and quickly meditate on the words of the psalm. A periodic *selah* throughout the scriptures might prevent spiritual indigestion. We easily forget the formational qualities of scripture when speed-reading only for content.

Pausing to reflect on the words of Psalm 52 reminded me of a conversation my father had concerning his land on a Vermont mountainside. On the corner of the property was a small sandpit. One year a local resident "borrowed" sand for his new driveway. My father had to confront the resident to stop future pilfering of our sand. Instead of a direct confrontation, Dad decided to ask the guilty neighbor to watch over his land because "someone has been trespassing and stealing from our sandpit." The resident's young son, who was standing nearby, looked up at my Dad and said, "That's not your sandpit; that's my Daddy's sandpit." At that moment, the guilty resident knew that he had been caught in a lie. Verse 3 reads, "You love evil more than good, and lying more than speaking the truth." I considered how treacherous life is when living a lie. In the concluding verses, the psalmist proclaims his trust rooted in the steadfast love of God.

PRAYER: Come Lord Jesus, help me trust in your love. Amen.

Thursday, July 19 • Read Psalm 52:8-9; Colossians 1:15-20

Mitchell is one of my star confirmation class graduates. When asked to write a short paper titled, "Who do you say I am?" (Jesus' question to the disciples in Matthew 16:13-20), Mitchell wrote about his faith in Jesus. He stated how Jesus is like his best friend, and if Mitchell ever finds himself in tough times and needs someone to look up to, Jesus is always first on his mind. Mitchell is also a star baseball player at the local high school. One day in a tough game, Mitchell prayed, "I took a minute, took a deep breath, and thought of Jesus. I said a small prayer in my head and a few minutes later my prayer was answered."

Mitchell was diagnosed with leukemia in the fall of his sophomore year at high school. It has tested his faith just as it would any reader of his story today—suffering through the side effects of chemotherapy, unable to attend school, and putting the sport of baseball on hold. Yet Mitchell, surrounded by a positive faith and family, exemplifies great courage in tough times.

Sometimes life gets overwhelming for Mitchell, and he sheds anxious tears. But whenever I pray with Mitchell and his family, I feel the presence and strength of God. Mitchell has found his strength and life source in Jesus. He is like the green olive tree deeply rooted in the steadfast love of God. Mitchell roots his trust in his friend Jesus, the image of the invisible God; and in him all the fullness of God was pleased to dwell. When we find ourselves in tough times, may we discover again our rootedness in a fertile faith the nourishes and sustains.

PRAYER: Come, Lord Jesus, help me rest in your care. Amen.

On what would have been my parents' fifty-first wedding anniversary, my father wrote a love note to my mother, sealed it in two plastic sandwich bags, and buried it at my mother's grave site. I retrieved it when my father died at the age of eighty. In his concluding words Dad wrote a simple statement of faith, "I love you with all my heart, my mind, my soul; and I'm trying to do the same with our Lord Jesus." It was no Apostles' Creed, but it was Dad's creed; and in the days of grief that followed, it was enough to assure me that Dad was safely in the hands of Jesus.

Sometimes when extending the invitation to Holy Communion, I reflect on how few would be welcome if trusting God depended on our intellectual understanding of Jesus. What if our salvation depended on our total comprehension of what biblical scholars have debated for two millennia? What about children, those new to the Christian faith, and persons with mentally challenging conditions? How many confirmed Christians find it challenging to explain the Christ? I'd rather trust my father's simple expression of faith, as well as many other earnest Christians who express their love for the Lord Jesus in heartfelt ways.

In this letter, the writer stresses the importance of understanding the person of Jesus. Neither the Colossians nor we exist in a religious vacuum. People have many ideas as to the identity of Jesus. The writer's word is clear: "[Jesus] is the image of the invisible God. . . . in him all the fullness of God was pleased to dwell." The scripture readings during the past few days have taken us from despair in God's absence to hope: "Christ in you, the hope of glory."

PRAYER: O God, help me trust you in hard times; take me from despair to hope, through Christ, the hope of glory. Amen.

SATURDAY, JULY 21 • Read Luke 10:38-42

Martha allows her many tasks to distract her. If we are observant, the holiday dinner often reveals the Marthas among us. Martha puts extra fuss into the holiday meal. I am thankful for the Marthas in my life who prepare delicious meals and unforgettable desserts. Martha too often gets a bad rap, but she displays her devotion to Jesus through her service to him. I do remember, however, a few Marthas whose tasks never seemed to end. Although I thoroughly enjoyed Martha's food, I wanted Martha at the table with me.

New Yorkers living in the metropolitan Long Island area often feel that our lifestyle is extremely stressful and hurried. I often listen to busy people who are overwhelmed with it all. The lifestyle plays to the Martha in us. Endless activities expand personal calendars to the point of excluding "Mary time." Although there is a unique New York personality, I doubt the answer completely lies in moving to Florida or elsewhere—the story of Mary and Martha is played out everywhere and in everyone! Mary and Martha are not two disconnected personality types, existing in unique persons; the tension of Mary and Martha lives in every human being.

Jesus appreciated Martha's devotion through her many tasks; the tasks were not unimportant, but she had gotten too busy *doing* for Jesus. Like Mary she also needed to be near Jesus and to listen to him. Speaking to our United Methodist Women, Anna, a missionary to Haiti, said that to serve God's people effectively you first need to listen to the people and see how they live. With good intentions, Martha hurries through her tasks; but Mary takes the moment to be with Jesus. In listening to him, she finds herself empowered to do the tasks of God.

PRAYER: O God, help the Martha and Mary in me to be at one with you. May I be empowered to do the tasks you entrust to me. Amen.

When my father retired as vice president and creative director of an advertising agency, he handed me a cartoon that had hung in his office for many years. The first frame showed a young boy, fishing beside a stream, dreaming of himself as president of his own company. In the second frame, he is a grown-up sitting at the president's desk, dreaming of himself as the small boy fishing beside the stream.

Peter, when addressing the crowd on Pentecost, quotes the prophet Joel: "Your young men shall see visions, and your old men shall dream dreams" (Acts 2:17). One of the Mary/Martha tensions that exists for each of us is that many tasks *do* distract us, resulting in little sabbath time for listening to the visions and dreams of Jesus. On summer vacation in Vermont, working on the family home, I consciously caught myself worried and distracted by many things, anxious about a to-do list far too long to accomplish. With beautiful Willoughby Lake within sight of the house, I found myself feeling weary of the work and saying to myself: *I don't have to do this; I'm on vacation, I don't have to do anything.* I then gave myself permission to sit down in the lawn chair by the lake and to do absolutely nothing. What freedom!

Busy pastors, district superintendents, and bishops who advocate sabbath time, often find themselves in the shoes of the writer of Second Corinthians: "In toil and hardship, through many a sleepless night. . . . I am under daily pressure because of my anxiety for all the churches" (11:27, 28). Even spiritual leaders easily find themselves worried and distracted by many things. Sabbath time is a spiritual practice that frees us from the endless need always to be doing something.

PRAYER: **Come, Lord Jesus, let me rest in you. Amen.**

Right Relationship with God

July 23–29, 2007 • Terry A. DeYoung[‡]

MONDAY, JULY 23 • Read Read Colossians 2:6-15

Scripture has merit when read piecemeal, isolated from its context; but new worlds of understanding and application open when we gain an appreciation for the life situation of the original author and audience.

This letter is written in response to a "Colossian heresy." Although scholars differ on specifics, certain issues are clear: Some in the Colossian church adhered to a kind of mysticism that questioned the completeness of Christ's revelation. The writer emphasizes that Jesus fully embodied God's presence. Being united to Christ by faith means we already have direct access to God's fullness. Nothing more is required. Verses 8-15 represent justification for the supremacy and sufficiency of Christ's work.

Nothing we do can add to the work of Christ; no philosophy we might adhere to can trump the revelation of Christ. So we do well to beware of tacked-on practices of Christianity—speaking in tongues or seeing visions, for example—that supposedly enhance or legitimize God's revelation in Jesus.

Perhaps the "What Would Jesus Do" (WWJD) movement can help us in this regard; namely, since Jesus manifested everything that God was and is, we do well to follow his example and make his way of life our own. God does not award extra credit for solving spiritual mysteries.

PRAYER: O God, by your Spirit help us humbly to ask for and willingly receive your wisdom, discernment, insight, and courage. Through Christ our Lord. Amen.

[‡]Managing editor, *The Church Herald*, the monthly magazine for members of the Reformed Church in America; living in Holland, Michigan.

When it comes to the assurance of resting in the sufficiency of Jesus' work on our behalf, certainly we can know of our arrival in a gracious place where God accepts us and never forsakes us. But if we also seek to live out God's call on our lives, our acts of discipleship are never-ending; there's no kicking back triumphantly and resting on our sanctified laurels, as if God were finished with us. The distinction is subtle but significant.

The writer warns the Colossian Christians not to be drawn into an extraspiritual pursuit of piety that somehow assumes we need to go the extra mile in order to arrive in God's good graces. He insists there's nothing more to be done to achieve our salvation; to suggest that there is calls into question the sufficiency of what Christ has done for us.

Such teaching underscores the "Colossian heresy," which insisted that certain spiritual gimmicks would reveal more of God than belief in the gospel of salvation through faith and trust in Christ's atoning work. The author understands the value of a deepened understanding and pursuit of a sanctified life through the power of the Holy Spirit but never as a way to merit salvation or somehow complete the work Jesus began. If Jesus "paid it all," then we owe nothing more. In Christ, our freedom has been paid for in full.

When religious communities require for membership more than faith in Christ as Savior and Lord, they must be careful not to slip into a creeping legalism that implies that God's grace requires something more. The Holy Spirit calls us to freedom from a life governed by confining rules and ultrapious standards. Through a disciplined lifestyle, we live out our faith within a community setting, but nothing overshadows God's emphasis on grace.

PRAYER: Gracious God, remind us that it is not by human strategies or cleverness that your work is done but by the grace, guidance, and gifts of your Spirit. Through Christ our Lord. Amen.

When a relationship falters or a situation turns sour, it calls for some sort of fix. With no correction, matters can go from bad to worse. Healing and restoration are needed, but sometimes they come only after we hit rock bottom.

The book of Hosea represents a dramatized prophecy, a kind of metaphor for the precarious moral-political deterioration of Israel's northern kingdom. Assyria is on the verge of annexing Israel to its burgeoning empire in spite of Israel's diplomatic maneuvers that fail to persuade Assyrian rulers. In the long run, Israel succeeds only in violating the covenant with God.

To illustrate the nature of Israel's infidelity, God instructs Hosea to marry a "wife of whoredom," Gomer, who gives birth to three children. Each child's name specifically symbolizes the consequences of Israel's unfaithfulness in its deteriorating covenant with God:

- Jezreel, meaning "God sows," portends God's judgment on Israel. The name comes to symbolize God's judgment on evil, similar to Armageddon in the New Testament.

- Lo-ruhamah, meaning "not pitied" or "not loved," symbolizes the nation that by its attitudes and actions has become God's rejected child. Without love, trust, or relationship, how can there ever be forgiveness?

- Lo-ammi, meaning "not my people," symbolizes the last straw, the complete breakdown of God's relationship with a people who no longer acknowledge God as their own.

In our relationship with God—and in relationships with one another—we maintain faithfulness by recognizing the warning signs of a strained relationship and then making midcourse corrections, preferably sooner rather than later.

PRAYER: O God, open the eyes of our hearts so we can recognize the sins and shortcomings that inhibit the lively flow of your Spirit. Through Christ our Lord. Amen.

The names God gives to the children of Hosea and Gomer—Jezreel (God sows), Lo-ruhamah (not pitied), and Lo-ammi (not my people)—represent Israel's progressive deterioration and ultimate self-destruction. But the prophet's proclamations carry a greater purpose than merely judgment; they call for repentance to renew the covenant's vitality. "Yet," begins verse 10, "the number of the people of Israel shall be like the sand of the sea," language that hearkens to God's everlasting covenant with Abraham.

God's overriding desire is not to castigate and cut off but to restore and redeem. God's expanding focus is not only on the past but also on the future; likewise, verse 10 both recalls the covenant with Abraham and anticipates the exposition of Paul. In the midst of his mind-bending explanation of God's election and rejection of Israel in Romans 9–11, Paul borrows from Hosea: "Those who were not my people I will call 'my people,' and her who was not beloved I will call 'beloved.' And in the very place where it was said to them, 'You are not my people,' there they shall be called children of the living God." These are the words of Hosea revisited and reinterpreted by Paul centuries later for our benefit.

Whether spoken to Abraham, Hosea, or Paul, it's the same divine love that never gives up on its beloved. As Hosea's hope-filled love for a wayward wife will not allow him to divorce Gomer, so God's relentless love reclaims and blesses the people Israel. All three children of Hosea and Gomer receive new life: Jezreel is reclaimed; Lo-ruhamah is forgiven; and Lo-ammi is a child of the living God.

Behind God's anger dwells mercy. Behind God's call to repent lies an invitation to reconciliation with the living God whose love never ends. We give thanks for God's judgment, knowing that God's overriding desire is to restore and redeem.

PRAYER: O God of fresh beginnings, give us minds open to your vision and hearts ready to be warmed by your Spirit. Amen.

When the disciples ask Jesus for a lesson in prayer, he gives them a template for praying—if not the exact words (though the words themselves are helpful)—and then goes on to teach them about the practice of prayer and the basis of prayer.

The amount of space the New Testament allots to Jesus' time in prayer to the Father is both moving and instructive. Jesus bases prayer on a relationship whose focus is communion, and that's where Jesus begins teaching the disciples. "When you pray, say: 'Father. . . .'" Jesus reveals his intimate relationship with his Father in heaven elsewhere in his use of "Abba," affectionately translated as Daddy. While the petitions "hallowed be your name" and "your kingdom come" acknowledge the sovereign power and majesty of God, Jesus begins with the relational aspect of prayer.

Jesus also defines in what sense it's appropriate to relate to God as Father. In the world of Gospel writer Luke, fathers wielded far-reaching, coercive power. But Luke carefully includes Jesus' instruction on how the fatherhood of God is to be experienced—not only in authoritative power but through generosity, compassion, care, and faithfulness. And so Father God is concerned about our everyday needs ("our daily bread"), our relationship with God and one another ("forgive us..., for we also forgive," NIV), and our daily encounters and struggles ("the time of trial").

Jesus' teaching shows that the purpose of our praying is not to provide information to God, as though God were not paying attention to our situation. Nor is prayer our way of giving advice so that God might make the world a better place. Prayer's ultimate purpose is to deepen our intimacy with a God who wants to be in a personal relationship—one that's akin to the healthiest, most life-giving affection between parents and children.

PRAYER: Loving and life-giving God, we welcome your presence in our lives and seek to know you in more intimate and fulfilling ways. Through Christ our Lord. Amen.

An important factor in prayer is recognizing the one to whom we pray. In providing his disciples with a template for prayer, Jesus begins with prayer's relational component, addressing God as Father, and not as an impersonal, universal force. The depth of our prayer life reflects the intimate, personal relationship that we have with the God of the universe, the one who created all that is, seen and unseen.

Luke carefully includes more about prayer than simply Jesus' template, which we know as the Lord's Prayer. Jesus also teaches his disciples about the practice of prayer (verses 5-10) and the basis for our prayers (verses 11-13).

Luke does not include the parable about getting what we want or need through sheer persistence and perseverance to teach us a lesson in how God dispenses blessings or answers the prayers of the people. Rather than picturing God as one who will respond only when pestered unceasingly, the parable illustrates the importance of regular, ongoing communion with God. Prayer is not an occasional text message sent to a virtual father but a continual sharing with the One who is always tuned into us.

How then does this God respond to those who in prayer regularly ask, search, and knock? The Holy One graciously exceeds our expectations. "If you then, who are evil, know how to give good gifts to your children, how much more will the heavenly Father give the Holy Spirit to those who ask him!" God responds to our need with the gift of the Holy Spirit—even before we know enough to ask, seek, or knock for the indwelling of God in our lives.

The Holy Spirit is the key to our praying and our persevering in prayer. Although Jesus provides the model for prayer, the Holy Spirit gives life to the model and to our communion with the Father.

PRAYER: Our Father in heaven, through your Spirit give us new life and new power; grace our lives with your love. Amen.

Sarcastic expressions have become an art form in our culture, appearing regularly on T-shirts, bumper stickers, billboards, and TV and radio. Some of us smile and file away selected expressions for future use. Others see them as a sign of a culture's cynicism, another manifestation of shock talk, and a tendency to speak in sound bites. Their frequent use makes us realize that all can benefit from an occasional refresher course in civil conversation.

We know the agonizing feeling of uttering words that we immediately wish we could inhale back into our mouths—foolish words we'll eat sooner or later, mean-spirited words that carry half-truths, blistering words that inflict permanent pain, deadly words that destroy a relationship. We bite our tongue and ask, *Why did I have to say that?*

Defining the point where a line is crossed is tricky. Wherever words are used—at home or at work, in phone conversations or in e-mails, in family gatherings or church meetings—discretion is due. We sorely need that discretion in our churches, where passions around important issues run strong, where ample time often seems in short supply, and where with painful regularity motives are misdiagnosed. To paraphrase Ecclesiastes, "There is a time to vent and a time to listen, a time to defend what you believe and a time to consider other beliefs."

Psalm 85 says it this way: "Let me hear what God the LORD will speak, for he will speak peace to his people, to his faithful, to those who turn to him in their hearts. . . . Righteousness and peace will kiss each other." Righteousness—living in right relationship with God and with one another—is God's gift or blessing to us, but it's also God's expectation for us as we continue to live in divine blessing. How we speak to one another and how we lend a listening ear and open mind are essential ingredients in bringing together righteousness and peace.

PRAYER: Loving God, in our lives may your righteousness and peace embrace and become visible through our speech and conduct. Through Christ our Lord. Amen.

God's Parenting Love without Limits

July 30–August 5, 2007 • *MarLu Primero Scott*[‡]

MONDAY, JULY 30 • **Read Hosea 11:1-7**

"I took them up in my arms" is the line that captures the theme for this coming week. Do you remember the line from Shakespeare's *Hamlet*, "I must be cruel, only to be kind"? Have you experienced a similar situation when giving your young child medicine, battling to cram it down his or her throat to treat an infection? The scripture passage for this week paints the image of God as a loving parent who cares and loves human beings with tough love. We see Hosea pleading the case of the parent God who has patiently loved the people of Israel only to be ignored and rejected. This scripture brings to mind a father whose daughter continually rejected his patient and loving counsel about her self-destructive behavior. He financed a rehab residency treatment and even provided an allowance, only to discover she had used the cash to purchase alcohol. Nevertheless, the father persisted with compassion and hope that his daughter would turn from her destructive ways.

Similarly, we as children of God continue to turn away from God when we make choices that separate us from God. The reading from Hosea invites us to reflect on ways we consistently ignore God as a loving parent. Have we taken time to simply sit still for fifteen minutes and talk to God in solitude?

May Hosea's words guide us toward God our parent. May we find strength and grace to be bound by God's cords of human kindness and bands of love.

PRAYER: All-loving God, we thank you for your love without limits. Forgive our bent to turn away from you. Give us courage to hear your call and respond to your love. We ask this in your Son's name. Amen.

[‡]Pastor, Wilbur Memorial United Methodist Church, Yakama Reservation; living in White Swan, Washington.

TUESDAY, JULY 31 • Read Hosea 11:8-11

My heart recoils within me;
my compassion grows warm and tender.

The rich texture of this verse captures God's unconditional parenting love that comes as both gift and demand. Yesterday we read Hosea's words of admonition about our tendency to turn away from God. Today we experience a text packed with images of God as loving parent who will not execute fierce anger and destruction in spite of human tendencies to turn away. Recalling an experience of parents in a small, secluded community in eastern Washington will bring this image to life.

The peace of this isolated quiet community was shattered when five young boys were charged with trespassing on school property and slaughtering pigs in the agriculture building. Feelings of shock, hate, distrust, and judgment consumed this rather laid-back band of folk. The community ostracized, judged, and blamed the parents of the boys. The overwhelming brutality manifested toward animals, especially in Native American culture, merited punitive consequences. Embarrassed and humiliated, the parents stood by their children in court but also demanded appropriate restitution. They gifted their sons with love that demanded accountability. God as loving parent gifts humanity with love and demands faithfulness.

SUGGESTION FOR MEDITATION: **Think of ways that will instill faithfulness, passion, and commitment to God, the loving parent, that will keep us from our bent of turning away from God. Pray for strength to confront subtle resistance in responding to God's call.**

PRAYER: **Loving God, our parent, thank you for your constant love. Instill in us grace to embrace your faithfulness regardless of our resistance to follow your call. Give us faith to hear your word today. Amen.**

O give thanks to the LORD, for he is good;
for his steadfast love endures forever.

Today's psalm resonates with the theme of God's unwavering love. In a society focused on looking out for number 1, thoughtfulness for others is a rarity. The psalmist expresses a selfless response to God's constant love—doxology!

A member of my congregation struggles with multiple issues. Chronic pain in her hands and legs forces her to use a wheelchair, and she was diagnosed with cancer. She depends on caregivers for chores around the house. On top of these health issues, her sons look to her for support.

One ordinary day, her doctor told her she had another growth in her mouth that needed excision. Tissues from a previous biopsy indicated cancer. Her world caved in. She could not take another diagnosis of cancer. In her distress, she cried to the Lord in the presence of our little congregation. God heard her cry for mercy. She later learned that the cancer in her mouth was fully excised, and she did not have to undergo radiation. She, along with the congregation, echoed the psalmist's response, "O give thanks to the LORD, for he is good!"

When we cry to the Lord, God will heed our plea. Consider issues we can take to God the loving parent, who responds with compassion to those who are helpless and destitute in spirit. We cried to the Lord in our trouble, and God delivered us. Thanks be to God!

PRAYER: All-powerful God, we thank you for your enduring love to those who cry to you for help. Thank you for hearing our pleas. Forgive us when we falter and fail to call upon you. We praise your name for loving us just as we are. Amen.

Thursday, August 2 • Read Colossians 3:1-4

Set your minds on things that are above, not on things on earth.

As children of the loving parent God, we are adopted into God's family through Jesus Christ. Through Christ our baptism transforms us from children of this world to children of the heavenly family. From this point on, we belong to God. A sense of belonging is a vital human need. While the feeling of being in the right place brings comfort and stability, it also entails responsibility.

For the past four years, our church has sponsored seven intense weeks of summer school as a congregational outreach to an Indian reservation. Yet, the program, which receives federal funding, restricts any religious activity. We cannot tell Bible stories, sing gospel songs, or memorize Bible verses. The absence of these acts of proclaiming the gospel appeared acceptable to the majority of the congregation. The money we received from tribal grants blurred our missional and evangelical vision.

When tribal and federal funds stopped, the financial burden of the project created a cloud of uncertainty over our ability to undertake the summer school project. Today's scripture reminds us "to seek things that are above." When our congregation took that advice to heart, the responsibility to keep our doors open for summer school became not a problem but an opportunity to carry on the task of proclaiming the gospel message to the children alongside their academic skills. Only by setting our minds on the glory of Christ were we able to move beyond our expectations.

Suggestion for meditation: Take a deep breath and allow the Holy Spirit to flow through your body. Slowly breathe out the toxic energy from every cell of your respiratory tract. Make a mental picture of those things that have prevented you from hearing the loving parent's voice.

Stripped of the old self. . . . clothed with the new.

Yesterday's encouragement to set our eyes on things above takes us to a deeper level of discipleship. Could it be that by putting to death those human urges cataloged here we will be brought to that deeper level? Simply put, being separated from the whole shuts off life-giving forces.

Gleaning orchards for fresh fruits, I noticed that the prolific branches were the ones free of dead limbs. Broken and bent branches were cut off. As followers of Christ, we must intentionally stay focused on what keeps us connected to our Source.

These words to the Colossians could just as well be sent to Christians today. Worldly urges continue to subtly seduce us. These forces do not present themselves with fangs, horns, and horrible images; they come innocuously. Countering the seduction of materialism, sex, and violence requires us to put on a new self. The lure of these commodities enters our homes daily through clever marketing strategies. A witness from a young man who was into drugs, sex, alcohol, and gambling comes to mind. These activities left a void, and when he reached rock bottom he sought out a community of faith. The people surrounded him in a way that transformed him. He became clothed in the image of Christ. He has given his life to helping teens. By telling his story, he helps direct them away from the seduction of such things as television and video games.

Reflect on those urges that keep us from being clothed fully in a new self in Christ. It may be the desire to eat sweets knowing you have diabetes. Or you may surf the Web for hours instead of taking time to pray. Search your heart for worldly desires that constrict renewal in the image of God.

SUGGESTION FOR MEDITATION: Light a candle and sit in silence. Make yourself completely transparent to God the Creator and turn over all worldly "stuff" that holds you back from being fully centered in Christ.

Take care! . . . for one's life does not consist in the abundance of possessions.

The image of the loving God grows more focused. Jesus, the visible image of the invisible God, tells us clearly to "be on your guard against all kinds of greed." He takes this opportunity to teach the crowd about possessions and how desire for "things" influences our decision making. In our relationship to God as loving parent, we depend on the underlying assumption of reliance on God to assure us of provision.

Have you encountered families who have alienated themselves from one another because of unfair inheritance distribution? Acquiring "stuff" is inherent to human nature; often when we do not get what we want, irrational behavior consumes us. Might this be the case of the brothers who come to Jesus? When have we allowed possessions to consume us to the point of sacrificing relationships?

A family member wanted a piece of furniture after the mother's death. The mother, unaware of her daughter's yearning, gave the furniture to a niece who had admired the piece for a long time. The daughter's inability to understand the situation made her avoid communicating with the family—an unfortunate situation. The niece would have relinquished the piece. Consumed by her desire to acquire the inheritance, the daughter lost objectivity, cutting herself off from sharing wonderful moments with her family.

When our drivenness to acquire material things leads us to forget the loving parent who bestows all abundance, we are cut off and in danger of perishing. Jesus warns us to guard against all kinds of desire to acquire. God knows our needs and longs for nothing but complete reliance.

SUGGESTION FOR MEDITATION: Reflect on possessions that clutter your relationships with family, friends, God. Answer the question: Are my relationships with others founded on what I possess?

Those who store up treasures for themselves . . . are not rich toward God.

The parable Jesus tells to buttress his point about possessions is poignant. I cannot resist sensing the passion of God for those adopted into the heavenly family who simply trust in God's word. If we rely on the wisdom of God as parent, we rid ourselves of unnecessary stress.

My conversation with a parishioner one beautiful autumn day brings this truth home. The crisp morning carried the slight scent of baled hay, a moment for doxology. However, filled with stress about the beach house, the garden, the church, and her own unaccomplished chores, the woman was oblivious to the gift of an extraordinary day.

We can buy material possesssions effortlessly by clicking a button on our computer and typing in a credit card number. How do Jesus' words apply to us when we are steeped in abundance and material excess? Perhaps there is no better time for us to listen seriously to this parable and respond to Christ's invitation to live simply.

How many times do we go to our closet and say, "I have nothing to wear," yet the closet is packed. Can we respond to storing up riches toward God when we are overloaded with earthly possessions? Consider making a list of ways to turn from activities that obstruct us in relying and trusting God.

PRAYER: Loving God, thank you for your boundless love. Give us strength to heed your call to trust and rely on your wisdom for our daily living. Amen.

Desiring a "Better Country"

August 6–12, 2007 • *Mary Lou Redding*[‡]

MONDAY, AUGUST 6 • Read Hebrews 11:13–16

On this midsummer Monday, we are deep into the season of the Christian year known as ordinary time—the longest season of the liturgical calendar. The festivals of Easter and Pentecost are memories, and Advent is far ahead on the planning calendar. These days bring few special observances in the church—they are "ordinary" time. For us here in the South, August can also bring long days of stifling heat—the "dog days of summer." This August landscape fits the emotional tenor of the week's lectionary readings.

Today's reading from Hebrews offers a poignant picture of a people who describe themselves as "strangers and foreigners." Like the Israelites leaving Egypt, we who follow God leave behind the familiar, holding in our hearts a dream of a better place, a dream of being more than we are. Yet we set out with no sure destination in sight, no guarantees, no place to call home.

The image that comes to mind is that of thousands of refugees who streamed out of New Orleans in the aftermath of Hurricane Katrina in 2005. That exodus was a phenomenon seldom seen in this country. And, setting their sights on a new future, many refugees chose not to go back. Following God is something like that. We have no guarantees of where we will end up or how long it will take us to arrive. Yet as Hebrews also tells us, God is "not ashamed to be called [the] God" of people who set out on the search for that better homeland.

PRAYER: O God, give us a vision of what you want for us, a vision so compelling that we willingly leave behind all that weighs us down on the journey toward the better country. Amen.

[‡]Managing editor, *The Upper Room* daily devotional guide; author of several books, most recently *The Power of a Focused Heart*, a small-group study of the Beatitudes; living in Brentwood, Tennessee.

This psalm pictures not a domesticated God tamed to our purposes but a God who is wholly Other. This is the Almighty, the one who "summons," who "shines forth." This is no sweet and gentle, meek and mild Jesus boy. This God denounces comfortable faith and lives of business as usual. This God calls out in order to judge, to "tear apart" those who forget the covenant they have made.

Many of us may shy away from such sharp-edged images of God. We prefer to talk about God's love, God's desire for healing, a God of shalom. We prefer a God who comforts the afflicted rather than one who afflicts the comfortable. Seeing God as surrounded by a mighty tempest and on the other side a "devouring fire" stretches me and unsettles me. But who else would have the power to call us out of our comfort and ask us to live in a wilderness? Would we follow a less compelling God?

The psalmist does not say that all we do to honor God—"your sacrifices . . . your burnt offerings"—is meaningless or wrong. But this God looks deep within us to our motives, saying, "Those who bring thanksgiving as their sacrifice honor me." In the movie *As Good as It Gets*, Jack Nicholson portrays a curmudgeonly writer who says to another character, "You make me want to be a better man." In a similar way, this holy God calls us forth to want to be better than we are. When we look honestly at all that God has given us, at how God has sustained us in all our ordinary days, we will see many reasons to come to God with thanksgiving.

SUGGESTION FOR MEDITATION: Consider how God sustains you on ordinary days.

PRAYER: Holy God, help us to see your holiness and to yearn to be better than we are. May our gratitude for your great love transform us from the inside out. Amen.

We hear in the prophet's words the yearning to know God and to be faithful, but we are often not quite sure how to proceed. Singer John Denver sang of "coming home to a place we've never been before." That's sort of the image I see in Isaiah's words. We know the feeling of home, so we trust that God is calling us to a place that is good; but we're not sure how to get there.

The prophet gives us direction: Cease to do evil, learn to do good; overturn injustice. These words call us to continuing unrest—and to following Jesus, who came to unseat the powerful, to topple kingdoms, to send the rich away empty, and to feed the poor. Overthrowing entrenched powers always elicits resistance. If we think of the events that followed the deposing of Saddam Hussein in Iraq, we may have an image of the magnitude of the change to which God calls us.

Who would want to join such an undertaking? In Iraq, at first many rushed to participate in rebuilding the country. But as losses mounted and fighting continued between factions, people began to pull back. Staying with the process, seeing through the change and the rebuilding is a long-term project.

When we think of all that God wants for us and for the world, it helps to remember that we're not talking about some overnight miracle. The change that God is about continues long-term, through all the ordinary days of the ordinary time in our lives. The long stretches when nothing spectacular seems to be happening form the bulk of our days—and the time of God's faithful, steady working in our lives. God is in this for the long haul. And, if we answer the call of the prophet, so are we.

PRAYER: O God, help us to be the change you want to see in the world. Make our hands your hands as we work to overthrow injustice. Amen.

This probably never happens to you, but I sometimes get angry with other drivers in traffic. One morning someone cut in front of me and forced me to slam on my brakes to avoid a collision. As I was saying (okay, yelling), "You jerk!" to the other driver, I thought of my personal mission statement. At that time my statement said that I intend to "interact with each one I meet as a dearly loved child of God for whom Christ died." Yelling, "You jerk!" does not exactly meet this standard. So I determined to change my behavior. When I found myself in traffic beginning to say, "You jerk. . . ," I would add, " . . . and dearly loved child of God for whom Christ died." Each time I did this (and I had lots of opportunities), I would find myself smiling and recalling my mission statement.

After a while of reminding myself of the child-of-God status of others in these situations, I began to realize that God was calling me to self-examination. God was nudging me to see that though my words and actions are important, just changing what I say is not enough. Beyond specific words I want also to honor God and others in the attitudes of my heart. To signal this insight and increase my accountability, I changed the phrase in my mission statement from "interact with each one I meet" to "honor each one I meet." That small change in my focus caused me to pray differently and, over time, to stop (most of the time) reacting harshly in the situation that seems to push my buttons.

As this passage from Isaiah tells us, God wants to work in us not just to change our behavior but to transform the affections of our heart. God calls out to us in the familiar activities of the ordinary days of life. If we listen, we will hear God inviting us to allow ourselves to be changed.

PRAYER: O God, change my heart. Transform the attitudes from which my actions grow that I may honor you and others in my daily interactions. Amen.

Having commented yesterday about transformed attitudes, today I want to say a good word for *doing* what is right whether we want to or not, whether "our heart is in it" or not, whether our attitudes have been transformed or not.

If we were all perfect, we would always act in love. We would always be patient with our family members and coworkers, doing what is right without hesitation, joyfully. But we're not perfect. And even though we understand that, we sometimes dismiss the love that often underlies our small, imperfect, mundane acts. We might say, "I was only doing my duty" as if that were a bad thing.

Picture a sleep-deprived parent walking a fretful baby in bleary-eyed fatigue, someone explaining to a third-grader for the sixth time how to do a math problem, a customer service rep refusing to be rude to an angry and abusive customer, a tired son or daughter dealing gently with an elder whose dementia is worsening. Are these acts of less value when done automatically or wearily, simply because they are the right thing to do? Of course not. In fact, we might say that such acts become more valuable because of the patience and self-control required of the actors when they are weary and not feeling particularly loving.

Today's reading tells us that doing our duty, being found faithful "in the second or third watch" when we're tired and would rather give up is to be called "blessed" by our master. We're heading for a better country, but we're not there yet. Wherever we are today, God notices and blesses our small acts of faithfulness.

PRAYER: O God, thank you for accepting and blessing the acts that we do just because they're the right thing to do. Help us daily to notice and affirm those acts done by those around us. Amen.

"Come now, let us argue it out," says the Lord. This invitation would perplex those who see God as having planned every detail of each human life. Reasoning together—even arguing, as the NRSV translates the verb in verse 18—shows a give-and-take relationship with God. People in this sort of relationship are in process, not finished yet. And this God knows our weaknesses and inconsistencies. The passage continues, "Though your sins are like scarlet. . . ."

God does not ignore the reality that we fail. As writer Rubem Alves has said, humans have the capacity to create both gardens and concentration camps—and God knows we have done both. Isaiah points us to the reality that we have a choice between obedience to God and rebellion. On days when we live with awareness of our citizenship in the better country of God's realm, we are able to choose wisely. We follow God on the way that leads to life. On other days, we may not choose as well. Still, as with the wandering Israelites in the book of Numbers, God journeys with us, continually giving us second chances—and third and fourth and fifth chances.

We are imperfect; God calls us on it. But as always, there is a word of hope: God forgives us when we forget who we are and whose we are. Though our sins and forgetfulness and fatigue and failures are "like scarlet," within God's mercy they shall be "like snow." God wipes them all away and helps us stand up to resume the journey toward that better country.

PRAYER: God of second chances, call us back to you when we forget to live as your children. Help us to forgive ourselves and others and to continue the journey—running or stumbling or edging toward the better country you offer us. Amen.

This passage from Hebrews gives us another image of living in the in-between times, before we reach the better country toward which we journey. The heroes of Hebrews remind us that journeying with the faithful often requires obeying without seeing results and trusting that God has prepared the way ahead.

The journey is not always exciting, and we are not given a clear map. God calls us to an open-ended relationship that changes and grows. You may have learned as I have that times of growth in the spiritual life may at times look remarkably like upheaval.

As I learned when my daughter was young, this process has a parallel in physical growth. My daughter would seem for a while to be fairly calm and settled but then would change and become restless, pushing the limits. I learned that developmental experts sometimes speak of children's development as a cycle of equilibrium and disequilibrium. That is, children grow to a certain point and become comfortable with a set of skills; they reach a place of emotional, physical, and mental equilibrium. Then with growth, the brain begins to change and the child stretches out to learn new things—and moves again into disequilibrium. In this unsettled time, the child may seem irritable; sleeping and eating patterns may change as rapid physical, mental, or emotional growth drains the child's energy. Moving forward, though good and necessary, is demanding.

Moving to a new spiritual "country" is also demanding. We live between this country and the better country that we desire in our moments of clarity and commitment. In this open-ended relationship with God, we learn and relearn one of the basic lessons of the spiritual life: God asks us to trust—and God is trustworthy.

PRAYER: God of the journey, help us to trust you today and every day and to believe that we are making progress, even when it is not apparent or spectacular. Amen.

Reaping What We Sow

August 13–19, 2007 • *Marshall Gilmore*[‡]

MONDAY, AUGUST 13 • Read Isaiah 5:1-7

Isaiah 5:1-7 is a parable that makes one point, which Isaiah takes a roundabout route to reach. He starts with a wedding scene. As friend of the bridegroom, he says, "Let me sing for my beloved [my friend] my love song concerning his vineyard: My beloved had a vineyard on a very fertile hill." The bridegroom has done everything for the vineyard, the bride, to be fruitful. He gave it a prime location. Plus, he selected "choice vines." He built a watchtower for protection and "hewed out a wine vat in it." The disappointment comes when the vineyard "yielded wild grapes."

A courtroom scene (Isa. 5:3-6) replaces the wedding scene. Isaiah owns the vineyard; he is also the prosecutor. As judge and jury, the people of Jerusalem and Judah must consider two questions. One, "What more was there to do for my vineyard that I have not done for it?" And, two, "Why did it yield wild grapes?"

The rhetorical technique Isaiah uses in the two questions implicates Jerusalem and Judah. The people find themselves in the same guilty place where David was when Nathan said to him, "You are the man" (2 Sam. 12:1-7). They, like David, condemn themselves by their own words.

A judgment scene follows: God the ultimate owner of the vineyard, Jerusalem and Judah, will remove the hedge of protection; outside foes may now enter the vineyard and devour it. The point of the parable is restated by the apostle Paul: "Do not be deceived; God is not mocked, for you reap whatever you sow" (Gal. 6:7).

PRAYER: As your people, O Lord, give us grace to live circumspectly. Amen.

[‡]Retired bishop, the Christian Methodist Episcopal (C.M.E.) Church; living in Dallas, Texas.

The God of the Bible is One of relationships. Having made humankind in the divine image and likeness, God bestows on them the capacity for fellowship. They long to be personally known by God and to know God in return.

The God of the Bible is One of *covenant* relationships. Hearing the groanings of the Israelites as slaves in Egypt, God "remembered his covenant with Abraham, with Isaac and with Jacob" (Exod. 2:24, NIV). God delivered them from Pharaoh's Egypt with the promise, "I will take you as my own people, and I will be your God" (Exod. 6:7, NIV).

At Mount Sinai, Moses dashed blood on the Israelites and announced what he had done as "the blood of the covenant that the LORD has made with you" (Exod. 24:8). God initiated the covenant and remained faithful to it. God expected obedience from the people; they were to keep the commandments.

The historical well-being of the Israelites serves as a barometer of their obedience to the covenant. Psalm 80, a psalm of lament, signals in its opening verses that all is not well. The opening petitions, "Give ear, . . . Stir up your might, and come to save us" give evidence of a down time.

In spite of their historical circumstance, the Israelites continue to hold to their faith. Their sense of God does not change. They address their petition to the "Shepherd of Israel." Despite their adversity, they use the royal title "Shepherd." Things are not well with them, yet they affirm the Lord as their shepherd who provides and protects them.

Israel's situation appears to contradict God's sovereignty, and yet the people attest to God's reign, saying, "You who are enthroned upon the cherubim." With faith in God, they pray, "Stir up your might, and come to save us."

PRAYER: God of all, grant us faith to maintain our faith, even when your hand we cannot see. Amen.

The Israelites are not shy about questioning God, particularly if God appears to be slacking off on fully supporting them. Beginning with Moses at Mount Sinai (Exod. 32:1-14) and continuing with Gideon at the oak of Ophrah (Judg. 6:11-18), the people of God ask, "Why?"

Verses 8-11 recite the history of the Israelites. The Lord brought them as "a vine out of Egypt" and led them to the land promised their ancestors. God drove out the nations in Canaan and planted his "vine," Israel, preparing the ground for it. "It took deep root and filled the land," stretching from the Mediterranean Sea to the Euphrates River. The people attribute all their success to God's planning, leading, support, and care.

Psalm 80:12 challenges the Lord, asking, "Why then have you broken down its walls, so that all who pass along the way pluck its fruit?" The vine is fruitful, but the owner has exposed it to destructive forces from the outside.

God does not answer. What happens next? The Israelites continue to seek God. This time they call upon God to "turn again," that is, "repent, O God"—change your mind and cease punishing us for our sins.

Why haven't the people confessed and changed? Their restoration and continuity depend upon God. Should God favor them with divine grace, they promise, "We will never turn back from you." Remembering their former relationship with God, they offer their final plea for salvation: "Restore us, O LORD God of hosts."

PRAYER: Lord, we wait for you to restore us. Grant it. Amen.

The Israelites: God's people who await their deliverance. Isaiah 5:1-7 depicts them as vulnerable. In Psalm 80, they lament their plight, yet they keep faith with hope.

Hebrews 11:29-39 records the faith history of God's people. The author relates the story as the acts of faith of men and women. Yet these acts bear witness to the deeds of God far more than to those achievements by humanity.

Verse 29 begins the recounting of three events of "faith," events that draw sharp contrasts between those who triumph in faith as opposed to the unbelieving. The Israelites pass through the Red Sea by faith and the Egyptians drown. Next, "by faith the walls of Jericho fell." The prostitute Rahab, who hides spies, does not perish with the disobedient.

The writer of Hebrews then offers two portraits of faith. The first bears witness to great, miraculous, and courageous acts: kingdoms conquered, justice administered, promises obtained, lions' mouths shut, raging fires quenched. The Israelites escaped the edge of the sword, won strength out of weakness, became mighty in war, put foreign armies to flight. These things they did through faith in God.

The second, and equally valid, portrait of a life of faith involves torture, mocking and flogging, chains and imprisonment, death by stoning. These victims suffer neglect and go without the basics of life, finding themselves relegated to lives of destitution, persecution, and torment.

This honor roll of faith consists of those "of whom the world was not worthy" and those who "did not receive what was promised." We must take our place on the continuum somewhere between the two. Apart from us, they will not be made perfect. The story of faith is a long one; God is patient.

PRAYER: Gracious God, give us grace that we not disappoint those who depend upon us for their perfection. Amen.

Even as we dive into Hebrews 12 and the cloud of witnesses, take time today to read Hebrews 11. That chapter begins with the words, "Now faith is the assurance of things hoped for, the conviction of things not seen" (11:1). Then the writer identifies a number of individuals who act by faith and offer a witness to God's magnificent deeds. Each person named takes part in God's drama of redemption. Each person on that list is part of the cloud of witnesses. The list of heroes of the faith stretches to our time. It includes well known and unknown, those who have statues in their honor and those whose graves are unmarked.

Every generation owes much to those who preceded it. We offer prayers of gratitude for those who walked faithfully before us. The seeds of faith that they planted and nurtured grow within us. Our gratitude sows and plants and nurtures seeds of faith in generations to come.

Along with the gratitude that undergirds Hebrews 11 and 12, we also receive direction to "lay aside every weight and the sin that clings so closely." G. K. Chesterton wrote: "Angels can fly because they take themselves so lightly." Perhaps Chesterton's comment about angels can teach us something about the spiritual journey and the race that is set before us. We carry much baggage with us. That baggage may take the form of old wounds from childhood that remain unhealed. The load of weight may come from the protective work of the ego, defending us against something new that threatens our old way of doing and being. The baggage and weight may cling to us as the remains of a fifty-year-old tradition. As we put off the excess baggage, we run the race with stamina and diligence, guided by Jesus Christ the pioneer and perfecter of our faith. Perhaps we fly!

PRAYER: Give us stamina, God, and sustain us as we persevere in joyful faith. Amen.

The heavenly host praising God on the "silent night, holy night" of Jesus' birth, announced, "On earth peace among those whom he favors" (Luke 2:14). But Jesus as adult Son of God says, "Do you think that I have come to bring peace to the earth? No, I tell you, but rather division."

Division will affect the cohesion of families, dividing parents and children and causing friction between in-laws. We cannot conclude, however, that Jesus intentionally causes the division. His death, which he refers to as his "baptism"(some scholars believe the term refers to coming events in Jerusalem), not only causes him "stress" but is also the crisis of life.

Jesus' willingness to die a shameful death by crucifixion creates a crisis for humankind. At some point in our lives, individuals through their decisions choose either life or death. Those who choose Christ choose life, and that choice can set the stage for division. Households and families may divide along the lines of belief or unbelief.

Jesus teaches that commitment to him has its price. The price affects relationships with even closest family members as we make his values, goals, and priorities ours. In spite of opposition, not only are the committed forewarned but empowered to live courageously in the world through Christ who has conquered it (John 16:33).

PRAYER: Lord, we know that in the world we will face trouble. Thank you for your assurance that we can live with good cheer, for you have overcome the world. Amen.

Jesus tells the people on one occasion that they are knowledgeable about reading daily weather signs. They can see "a cloud rising in the west" and say with confidence, "It is going to rain." Also, they will "see the south wind blowing," and say, "There will be scorching heat." Without the service of Doppler radar, they get the weather right. Being weatherwise is nothing new for Jews of Palestine. Elijah the Tishbite from Tishbe in Gilead comes to mind. From Mount Carmel his servant sees a small cloud over the Mediterranean Sea, about the size of the palm of a man's hand. When he reports the sighting to Elijah, the prophet knows the cloud's size signals the coming of rain (1 Kings 18:41-46).

The people of Jesus' time know how to read weather signs, but they do not "know how to interpret the present time." They can look at a wisp of cloud in the sky and make determinations. The direction of the wind relays information.

So why then does Jesus call the people hypocrites? While frittering away time with wisps of cloud, the kingdom is dawning before their eyes, and they do not see it. Jesus stands among them with signs of messiah and the in-breaking of the new age, yet they refuse to believe. They refuse to see him as the source of grace for believers and the sign of judgment for unbelievers.

How do we interpret our present time? This question challenges us to remain aware of what captures our attention and what we casually pass by. On what do we focus our attention? Among the many bushes do we see the one that burns without being consumed? Or do we miss the one among the many?

PRAYER: God, grant us grace to read the signs of your reign in our world. Amen.

Coming to Comfort

August 20–26, 2007 • Dave Brauer-Rieke[‡]

MONDAY, AUGUST 20 • Read Jeremiah 1:4-10

God comes to comfort. God comes to heal, to disturb, to reorganize, to destroy and overthrow, to build up and plant. Ours is an active and involved God with plans, hopes, dreams, and visions. Cover to cover the Bible gives testimony to this fact.

Some of the most spiritually influential people in my life have been those who teach me to see or watch. Some days I wake up wondering what *I* have to do this day—what I have to achieve or endure. I call this my Day-Timer® mentality. I allow that little calendar on my handheld device to control my life. On other days—better days, days of faith—I waken and wonder what *God* will do today. I look up and out. I watch with expectation and joy mixed, perhaps, with a touch of apprehension and fear. I know that God will cause the wheat to grow, the sun to shine, and children to learn. I also know that God might call to me, the Involved to the watcher, and say, "I appoint you a prophet to the nations."

"This is my Father's world" we sing in church. Indeed, this is God's world, full of singing birds and awesome galactic spheres. The Creator shapes and speaks wonder into reality. The Holy One heals and hopes. God destroys, overthrows, builds, and plants. I would rather live my days in humble appreciation of this truth than under the arrogant weight of my own self-importance. So I try to remember that before I was born God loved me, and after I die God will continue to come, bringing joy and comfort to our world.

SUGGESTION FOR MEDITATION: Spend a few minutes watching the world around you. Let life happen apart from your efforts. Try to trace the footsteps of God.

[‡]Pastor, Atonement Lutheran Church (ELCA), Newport, Oregon.

Coming to serve

God comes to comfort. God comes to serve. And in this coming the faithful are often enlisted in God's cause.

God drafts Jeremiah in this way, calling him to be a prophet, to be the hands and heart of God speaking out, tearing down, rebuilding, and revisioning. Jeremiah's reservations about his abilities don't impress God in the least.

"Do not say, 'I am only a boy.'" I have made you a man.

"Do not be afraid," for I shall deliver you, says the Lord.

I imagine that I would like to be a prophet. I can just see myself speaking fiery words, uncovering the lies of government, and opening people's eyes to truth. Of course, the truth I might speak would probably be mine, not necessarily God's. That could be a problem. So God in divine wisdom has made me a father, a husband, a pastor, and a friend—not a prophet.

My hands do not tear down corporate lies; they simply shred bank statements. My wisdom does not awe the masses. It more often elicits "Give me a break" from my children. My sermons may occasionally inspire, but generally my presence with a friend in pain receives the greater thank you.

Can you be at peace where God has called you? Can you serve in the ways God needs? Sometimes I wish my calling were grander—sometimes more showy. Yet, it is what God needs, so what have I to fear? You have been touched, empowered, and appointed. Rejoice!

PRAYER: Gracious God, this day let me hear your call, serve your people, do my part, and rejoice in your presence. Amen.

Coming for refuge

Yes, yes, yes! Whether you're the prophet Jeremiah set to over-throw the world or a parent with a car full of six-year-old soc-cer players, you know this feeling. "Lord, I'm coming. Open the gates. Chaos and crisis are on my heels!"

I don't know where the lines between laziness, unwarranted self-pity, and real persecution fall, but I know they're there some-where. What do you do when you're unjustly pursued? Where do you go when life is cruel and uncaring? What if you're just feeling sorry for yourself?

"Come unto me, all ye who labour and are heavy laden" (Matt. 11:28, KJV), the Lord whispers. (Funny that I should know that in the King James translation!) For me this means taking the telephone off the hook or getting on my bike and hitting the road. Because my demons are mostly psychological rather than physical, I find my refuge in quiet or isolation. The walls I need shut out rings, buzzers, and beepers. Were people actually shoot-ing at me I might want a stone fortress, but you know the rock and refuge of which the psalmist speaks. You know what it looks like for you.

So, is it wrong to go there? Must we always be out in the field, or is it okay to crawl in a hole and hide sometimes? "Lord, take care of me right now—just me!"

Yes, yes, yes. We've all been there. We've all prayed this prayer. Personally I think it's okay. "Ask, and it will be given you; search, and you will find; knock, and the door will be opened for you" (Matt. 7:7). The world will wait for you—and you will return. I know you will. You will return.

SUGGESTION FOR MEDITATION: Enter God's fortress for a while today. Make yourself unavailable. God has you covered.

Coming from the womb

Our life begins in a warm, watery refuge; we finish our course in the arms of God. In between times we come and go. Sometimes we need God's armor around us, and other times we soar freely in the air of privilege and productivity.

"Upon you I have leaned from my birth; it was you who took me from my mother's womb." We all have a history. Our life stories differ immensely, but they all begin in the same place. Somebody, our mother, gave us shelter and protection. A woman we may not even know nurtured our unformed being. She gave of her life, her freedom, and her hope.

I have an adopted child. His birth mother knew she would be unable to parent him and so gave him up to us. She is not an active part of his life today. She has not taken him to school or picked him up when he has fallen. Yet a bond exists between them. I cannot explain how it exists, but that it exists is obvious.

We all have a history. Whether we've been parented well or not; whether the world has treated us fairly or not; whether we have honored the gift of life or not, one thing is certain. God has always been there. The psalmist knows this. Along life's way there is always one we can count on. Let our praise be continually of this midwifing one.

PRAYER: **Hands of hope, I praise you because you know me.**
I know you because you are near me.
You are near me because I need you.
And I need you because I cannot
give birth to myself. Amen.

FRIDAY, AUGUST 24 • Read Hebrews 12:18-29

Coming to the city

I live on the central Oregon coast, having recently moved from the drier, high plains portion of the state. Even after a full year I look out at the great expanse of the Pacific Ocean, unable to comprehend its reach and majesty. Or I might walk through nearby forests replete with fern-saturated fir trees, weaving my way around nurse logs, newt-infested marshes, and find myself overawed by the cacophony of life. Dryness I know. Sagebrush, jack rabbits, and river trout I have seen. Open land—but not great expanses of water—I have learned to navigate.

Hebrews 12 invites us to contemplate a grand contrast. The old order of rules, death, dryness, expectations—this we know. The acid of our own sin has burned our hands time and time again. We know the Temple. We know the darkness we drag into its sacred halls, and we've fashioned an uneasy peace with the gloom we find outside.

Yet, in Christ, a reality lies before our eyes that our souls cannot even begin to grasp. We see the colors of love and hear the sounds of acceptance, but our minds cannot touch them. We have no frame of reference for the astounding love of God in Christ Jesus our Lord. We have come to a city with skyscrapers of care when all we have known are hovels of hope. "Innumerable angels in festal gathering" (Heb. 12:22) fill the halls of tomorrow. What can we say to this?

Sometimes I think silence is called for.

PRAYER: Lord God, since we are receiving a kingdom that cannot be shaken, teach us to give thanks. Let awe and reverence seize our hearts. Amen.

Coming to worship

It is amazing how many of Jesus' healings and confrontations take place in a synagogue—and on the sabbath to boot. The sanctuary of a special time and place, a God place, a God time, is as important to us today as it was to Jesus' first-century contemporaries. Things should simply be different in church. We may dispute how things are to differ, but we all understand that things should be different in this sacred place.

In Luke 13 a woman appears before Jesus with a crippling spirit. Why has she come? How might her pain be understood against the backdrop of the sacred? Nothing indicates that the woman comes for healing. She has simply come to worship. Jesus, however, considers her infirmity and the truth of sabbath to be at odds. So he calls her to him, and the joy of sacred rest and renewal becomes her physical and spiritual reality.

Unfortunately the story ends in conflict. Jesus' view of sacred time and space clashes with that of the elders. Have the rules changed? No. It will not do for us to make new rules about the sacred. This time, this day, this sanctuary is still God's. It continues to be a place of mystery, hope, and wholeness. New rules are no better than the old if they seek to circumscribe what is beyond our comprehension.

Prayer: Lord God, when I gather with the faithful for worship and praise, let my heart be open to the freeing power of your spirit. Amen.

Coming to freedom

I find this story's language interesting: "A spirit that had crippled her. . . . Set free from her ailment. . . . Set free from this bondage." We would say the woman was healed. Jesus says she has escaped a prison.

Do you ever feel like the walls are closing in around you? I do. It may be a growing awareness of my own personal limitations or a deadline looming on the horizon. Friends share with me a sense of being trapped in marriages without love. Some are confined to wheelchairs with legs that refuse to support their weight. The language of bondage or spiritual and physical imprisonment gives me a different take on life. "I am still here behind these bars. Who will set me free?"

For eighteen years this "daughter of Abraham" (slave to no one) has been bound by a crippling spirit. The evil is not part of who she is to be. A spiritual pariah fights to define her identity. For eighteen years she keeps coming to synagogue because there is a counter claim being made in the sacredness of sabbath joy.

The battle has gone on long enough. The daughter of Abraham that she has always been needs to be set free. "Stand up straight, sister. Embrace your true self. Slough off the evil accretion of your past. God sees the real you behind those bars, and it is that sparkling spirit called to life this day."

SUGGESTION FOR MEDITATION:

> **Behind the bars of broken hearts,**
> **of banishment and pain,**
> **lives a spirit crying out for freedom from the shame.**
> **"Long enough!" is Jesus' cry,**
> **"Stand up straight with spirit spry.**
> **This is the day the Lord hath made;**
> **let love be known and bondage fade."**

Service Well-Pleasing to God

August 27–September 2, 2007 • Linda Sutton[‡]

MONDAY, AUGUST 27 • Read Luke 14:7-14

Have you ever attended a function or a special occasion at church and, having arrived late, found that the only vacant seats in the house are up at the front, reserved for special guests? It's funny though. The front seats in the house are not always the most sought after.

The one chartered accountant in our small country town offered a secretarial position to our daughter, Beth, on certain conditions. She would start at the bottom of the heap and be first at the office each working day to sweep the front and back steps. The kettle must be on the boil, just in time for the boss's cup of tea after his arrival. As the lowliest junior, she would be expected to fetch and carry for the rest of the staff, run errands, collect and post the mail, and answer the telephone. At the end of the day, she would have made countless cups of tea and coffee, brought the front doormat in, turned off the lights, and have been the last to leave. She accepted the job.

Although unaware of this fact at the time, Beth lived out the parable of the last becoming the first. Eventually the company invited her to "move up higher." They entrusted her with more responsibility and soon a new junior fetched and carried for her! True Christian discipleship calls for leaders who do not, in the words of Paul, think too highly of themselves. Seeking God's guidance ensures that our "calling" is from God and not from selfish ambition.

PRAYER: Let me be content, Lord, to serve humbly. Encourage my willingness to work enthusiastically as a member of a committee, when I would rather run the show. And if you call me to lead, let it be as a playing coach. Amen.

[‡]Lay minister, Uniting Church in Australia; freelance writer; living in Kadina, South Australia.

God's people did two things to anger and disappoint. They forsook God, the fountain of living water, and dug for themselves "cracked cisterns that held no water." They gave lip service to God while making room for the worship of the pagan god Baal. Their unfaithfulness did no service that was pleasing to God.

Like the people of Palestine, I live in a low-rainfall area. In Jerusalem, the inhabitants built the cisterns within the city walls, so that under siege, they would have no need to go outside the fortified walls for water. The cisterns were cut into rock to hold the rainwater that fell between October and the middle of May.

Householders in our area are encouraged to install tanks to catch every precious drop from gutters and downspouts of houses and outbuildings. Soon after my family moved in to our present home, our tank began to leak ever so slowly; gradually the pinpricks in its outer shell widened. We were unable to save any precious rainwater, except for a trickle diverted to a garden patch.

Our family had relied heavily upon the supply of water in that tank. After the installation of a new tank, we had to rely much more on God. It would take a good downpour of rain to fill it, and that happened infrequently.

In the process of installing the tank, we also reviewed our priorities of dependency. The rain tumbled down in God's own good time, and we had a good supply of drinking water to sustain us in the coming, drier months.

SUGGESTION FOR MEDITATION: **Think of the kind of insurance you hold against want. Think of a time when you let your independence get in the way of relying upon God, the Living Water.**

Quite frankly I don't have the gift of hospitality. I can readily offer coffee and cake to callers; but when it comes to organizing a dinner party, I'm a nervous wreck and quite unable to enjoy the company of my guests in my anxiety about the presentation of the meal. I worry if it will cook in time or be overcooked—and will there be enough for everyone?

I resignedly accept that my gifts lie in a different direction and settle for some take-out from a restaurant. I admire those people to whom hospitality is second nature, or perhaps I should say, those who are gifted with it: the couple who readily invite visitors home for a potluck lunch after morning worship; my aunt, whose children issue casual meal invitations to friends and strangers—her battered, renowned soup pot can be topped up at a moment's notice to feed one or two extra mouths on a Sunday evening; Jo, who understands the elderly's preference for cups and saucers instead of coffee mugs.

The writer of Hebrews advises in favor of entertaining strangers; they might be angels in disguise! Much of Jesus' teaching occurred at the meal table. He enjoyed the hospitality of many people, including some Pharisees to whom he was a mysterious stranger. Jesus was a stranger to Zacchaeus, the short tax collector. Did Zacchaeus really know whom he entertained at dinner that day in Jericho? What about Peter's mother-in-law who bustled about in her kitchen after Jesus had healed her sickness? She didn't know this stranger—only that he was a friend of Peter's; yet she served him gladly. Hospitality toward strangers gives us an opportunity to serve the Christ who comes incognito.

SUGGESTION FOR MEDITATION: **Where might you be alert for the stranger today or when you worship on Sunday? Seize an opportunity to entertain an angel unawares.**

"Be content with what you have," says the writer of Hebrews. This statement became the topic of a recent mealtime conversation. "Progress is based on discontent," declared one participant, dipping a spoon into the sugar bowl. Others joined in with their ideas of how discontent with poverty and deprivation had inspired social justice reform in the Western world. How medical science had progressed to the point of eradicating most childhood diseases because some people were not content with the high rate of infant mortality.

The lively and imaginative conversation progressed far enough to explore the way discontentment becomes the root of greed and the accumulation of wealth for its own sake. Discontent comes from wanting more than we have of things that we don't really need, said one. Love of money and not wealth itself creates its own discontent.

The debate caused me to reflect more deeply upon the true meaning of contentment as understood by the writer of Hebrews. The world must have been an uncomfortable place in which Christians lived back then. The calming message of God's faithfulness would be timely, as it is for us in our world, with media-generated fear of terror and violence. God was all they needed; God is all we need.

To be content with what we have is to live the Christian life in total reliance upon God, who has promised never to leave or forsake us, even in the worst of circumstances.

PRAYER: Be with me today, Lord, through all the events and experiences, seen and unforeseen, happy and disturbing; fill me with the calm contentment of your enduring presence. Amen.

"O that my people would listen to me" expresses a poignant longing. God does not want to punish the Israelites but to bless them, to show them the way forward—if only they will listen! Through the voice of the psalmist, God expresses disappointment and exasperation because of Israel's unfaithfulness and deliberate forgetfulness. God has provided for them in their greatest hour of need, but good times have masked that memory. They turn their backs on the One who has rescued them. Although they are undeserving, God longs for a return to the former relationship.

Like the Israelites, we need a reminder to listen to God and to recognize our sin and our need for forgiveness. Being able to listen properly to others requires a certain skill, but it doesn't seem to come naturally. We want to tell our own story, follow our own agenda, pursue our own self-satisfying ways. Yet clearly, listening to God and following God's counsel bring a protective intimacy: God will subdue our enemies, feed us with wheat and honey from the rock.

In our chaotic work, opportunities to listen seem to come infrequently but may turn up unexpectedly. On a picnic in the bush one summer, I found myself away from the distraction of traffic. I could—when I chose to listen—hear the sounds of God's creation: God's voice in the chirp of a small bird, the bubble of creek water, and the soft sigh of the wind in the trees. Being attentive to God requires the discipline of listening in silence when we would rather fill the vacuum with our own complaints or petitions. Listening to God allows us to move forward in a way that is pleasing to God, and God will satisfy us.

SUGGESTION FOR MEDITATION: **Be still; be silent, for no words can best articulate praise or lament. Be still; wait to hear nothing but that which is of God. Be still; wait in the silence not for your future to be foretold but to hear the voice of One who says, "Receive my grace, then be who you are, for my sake."**

Paul Giardina, a sixteen-year-old with Down syndrome, was a victim of the 2005 tsunami. He died in Phuket when the fierce tidal wave of water plucked him from his parents' arms. At his funeral, one of his teachers spoke of the way Paul taught others to love unconditionally. His greatest success, she said, was to influence those around him.

God is pleased when we obey the commandment to love as Christ loved: inclusively and mutually. Henry Drummond believed that love is the greatest thing in the world: "You will give yourself to many things; give yourself first to love." My copy of his little book *The Greatest Thing in the World*, with its profound testimony to the power of love, is well-thumbed and marked up. Many of its passages have made their imprint on my soul.

The author of First John says that we love because God first loved us (4:19). I am called to be part of the great and original love triangle of God: you, me, and God. Sometimes I fail to fulfill this commandment.

I'm not alone in backsliding when it comes to loving mutually, but that doesn't excuse me from excluding those I consider unlovely from the love triangle. It's a human failing to be drawn only to those we find attractive, those who openly admire us, or even those sycophants who use flattery for their own purposes.

I may have unintentionally hurt someone, or I may have felt wounded by another person. I may harbor harsh feelings toward that person, but God calls us to let mutual love continue. Such love may mean that we do the work of reconciliation and restoration. Sometimes mutual love translates into a ministry of encouragement or taking time to process difficult situations—to be honest and real and to seek God's healing love in the midst of brokenness.

PRAYER: You ask a hard thing of me, O Lord of my life, to love and forgive as you do. To forgive, not just for me but for you. Help me in Jesus' name. Amen.

"They were watching him closely," Luke tells us. It's difficult to read the subtext in this narrative of Jesus' attendance at a dinner party at the home of the leader of the Pharisees. The Pharisees, hostile to his mission, constantly look for some infringement of the law; yet this leader invites Jesus as a guest! Is this another trap?

What those watching aren't prepared for is that Jesus watches them closely also! He sees the pecking order in force at the dinner table. Guests chose places of honor reserved for the most important officials, according to the customs of the day. We wonder who else is there. If the disciples are among the other guests, they would be expected to sit at the lower end of the table—uncouth characters who don't even wash their hands before eating!

Some social habits are so ingrained that we seldom stop to wonder why we do them in a certain way or at all. Jesus constantly reverses the expected behavior of his time—even the social conventions of his time. In fact, we might call the gospel of Jesus Christ the gospel of reversal. The way things are always done and have always been done is not necessarily the best way to do things.

Service pleasing to God is devoid of class-consciousness, free from prejudice of any kind toward those served in Christ's name. Becoming a disciple means to watch Jesus, to learn from him, and to imitate him in service well-pleasing to God.

PRAYER: Teach me, O God, the way to look afresh at how I do things. If the reasons are not of you, show me the way to reverse them. Curb my impatience for change with time to watch and listen and learn from you. Amen.

Being a Disciple

September 3–9, 2007 • *R. Charles Perry*[‡]

MONDAY, SEPTEMBER 3 • Read Jeremiah 18:1-11

I occasionally have the opportunity to observe someone making a vase or some other vessel out of clay. I find fascinating the care with which the person molds the clay. The potter or craftsperson is seldom pleased with the initial article and reworks the clay until satisfied.

In the parable of the potter Jeremiah sees God taking similar care in molding the people of Judah. The parable depicts God's patient and persistent love for the people. God wants them to be different people. "Turn now, all of you from your evil way, and amend your ways and your doings." We witness God's love through the disciplining of the people; God eventually brings them out of exile to the promised land. Even when the people stray from the path, God continues to love them. God will continue to mold the nation.

While made in the image of God, we are not always Godlike people. Sin creeps in, making us less than the people God wants us to be. When that happens we are not true and whole vessels, but the Creator will continue to work with us. The potter's hands do not let loose the clay.

As we yield ourselves, God molds us. At times we may have sought our own way; followed our own plans in life rather than God's way, like the Israelites of old. But as we cooperate with God in the molding process, our future can change. We become useful vessels in God's work.

PRAYER: Lord of life, mold me into the person you would have me be, and may I cooperate with you in the molding process. Amen.

[‡]Retired minister, the Methodist Church of Southern Africa; living in Wilro Park, South Africa.

Most people are familiar with examinations. They take various forms: physical, mental—even spiritual. Many churches offer worshipers an opportunity during the Holy Communion service to examine themselves inwardly and spiritually.

The psalmist reminds us of God's examination of us: "Lord, you have examined me and you know me" (REB). The Lord knows where we go and what we say. The psalmist is aware of the omniscience of God, the infinite knowledge that God has of people and creation. The psalmist also has a keen awareness of God's support of us and presence with us. "You keep close guard behind and before me and place your hand upon me" (REB).

It is spiritually meaningful for us to open our lives to examination by God. In a time of quietness let God speak to us and renew us inwardly. A time of silence in an atmosphere of worship is a good time for us to look at our lives in the light of God's word, especially the Word made flesh in Jesus.

It is also spiritually meaningful for us to be aware of God's presence with us in the Spirit of Christ day by day. Our busyness with so many things makes us less aware of God's presence. Life is a flurry of activities; there is so much to do.

In the rush of life we need to remember that God knows us. "You know me at rest and in action" (REB). Nothing about us escapes God's attention.

PRAYER: Lord, in the midst of the day's activities, help me remember that you know all about me and still love me. Amen.

When I was engaged in full-time ministry I got to know some people very well. I came to know something of their backgrounds, family relationships, and the state of their spiritual and physical health. Such knowledge helped me more adequately minister to them.

The psalmist reminds us that God knows us even better than that. "You know me through and through" (REB). Our Lord knows us intimately and, because of that knowledge, can relate more personally with us.

The psalmist expresses gratitude for the understanding that God has of him. "I praise you, for you fill me with awe; wonderful you are, and wonderful your works" (REB). We are also grateful because God's knowledge of us enables a closer connection to our Creator.

God's intimate knowing of us means that we are more adequately ministered to by the One who loves and cares for us. That God has taken the trouble to know us this well indicates a concern for our well-being. As Christians we affirm that God's care and love have been supremely expressed in the person of Jesus, one who came to live among us in the midst of our human foibles. Jesus' ministry to people brings God's intimate perceptions of humanity to the fore.

God's understanding of us is as incomprehensible to us as it was to the psalmist. "How mysterious, God, are your thoughts to me" (REB). Mysterious though God's thoughts may be, we are grateful for God's knowledge of us and love for us.

SUGGESTION FOR MEDITATION: **Think about your life and God's hand in your life. Give thanks to God for love and blessings received.**

Sending messages via electronic means has to a large extent replaced letter writing. Text messaging and e-mails have taken the place of personal letters.

This letter written by the apostle Paul to Philemon is personal, although some scholars have suggested that Paul also intends it for the whole church at Colossae. In this personal letter the apostle asks a favor of a "dear friend." He appeals to Philemon to receive Onesimus back "no longer as a slave but more than a slave, a beloved brother."

The apostle is confident that Philemon will grant this favor because Philemon is a friend and a brother in Christ. His certainty about Philemon's response also rests on the fact that his request is based upon the love and faith of a follower of Jesus.

People ask us for favors—sometimes personal, sometimes general. We also make requests of other people—at times simple and straightforward, at other times more profound. Our bidding, especially when it involves matters of faith, needs to be based upon love and faith. Our love for the other person and for God serves as the foundation of the request. Our petitions to God of also need to be based upon faith and love.

When we base our asking upon love we acknowledge our part in the request we make. The part we play will depend upon our request. In all instances, the expectation is that we will use all within our power to bring that request to fruition; we take action. The apostle Paul actively engages himself in helping both Philemon and Onesimus find each other.

PRAYER: Lord, help me to remember in all my requests to love you and those around me. Amen.

In an area where I once served, a large house on a sizable piece of ground was offered to a group who ministered to people who came out of prison on parole. The group renovated the property and established a place where people on parole could live. That group of concerned Christians went the extra mile in seeking to help those who otherwise would have been homeless.

The apostle Paul expects Philemon to go the extra mile: "I know that you will in fact do more than I ask" (REB). He echoes Jesus' words in the Sermon on the Mount: "There must be no limit to your goodness" (Matt. 5:48, REB).

We may react in various ways when asked to do something for another person or undertake some service in the church. We may say no and later regret that decision. We may say yes and do it halfheartedly, or we may tackle it with a smile and enthusiasm. While in active ministry I appreciated positive reactions to a request for service in the church.

But so often we discover that even a halfhearted commitment leads to a renewing and refreshing experience of service. Helping someone else or being of service in the church benefits us. It builds us up, and we grow as God's people. How much more might our compassionate service extend if we approach each request with a yes, knowing that we will in fact do more than is asked. With love of God as our basis for service to others, we can go the extra mile. That is what God's love flowing through us is all about.

PRAYER: God of compassion, may we go the extra distance in service to others. Amen.

Many people find themselves in a conflict situation when it comes to the demands of work and family. The long hours engaged in work and travel leave little time for the family. I found that to be true at times during my years of ministry. Trying to meet the demands of the congregation and also those of my wife and daughters was not always easy.

In what has been described as a "hard saying," Jesus seemingly gives people a choice by requiring any follower to choose between family and him. He goes on to mention cross bearing in the next verse as a condition of discipleship.

These verses and the next two parables illustrate Jesus' desire that people know up front the demands of discipleship. It will be costly to follow him. Jesus asks, "Is this a life you can willingly embrace?" We may shake our heads, for how can we know? It sounds so hard. Scripture recounts a number of times in which disciples, citing the hardship of the journey, turn back. They leave the cause.

How often have we made commitments and been unable to follow through? Following Jesus is costly, and he wants us to know that before we choose to follow. For some people it may mean leaving family and going where God leads. That has happened throughout the history of the church. For most people the costliness will come in other ways. It may mean standing up for the truth in a family or work situation. Our voluntary cross bearing in commitment to Jesus will bring consequences.

In our lives we remember that we are kingdom people. Whether within our family life or work situation or recreation or church life or wherever we find ourselves, we live under the reign or rule of God. Such living can be costly.

PRAYER: Lord of life, help us always to live as kingdom people, seeking within all of life to put you first. Amen.

Occasionally in driving around my home city or through the rural areas, I have come across an unfinished building. Usually it has not been completed because either the owner or the contractor has run out of money.

A friend came to me with beautiful color drawings of a house he wanted to build. Then he began telling me about the financing for the building of his new house. He had counted the cost of embarking on this building project.

Jesus warns his followers to count the cost of following him. We are called into a relationship with God in Christ Jesus. Sometimes we are called into a specific service within that relationship. We need to count the cost of that service before we embark upon it. Sometimes we measure the cost in financial resources. Jesus has mentioned the costs related to family and cross bearing. Now he warns his would-be followers, "If you are not prepared to leave all your possessions behind, you cannot be my disciples" (REB). Hard, hard sayings.

Other costs of discipleship may include the emotional and physical toll on ourselves, the cost in terms of relationships. All these and perhaps other costs need to be borne in mind if we are faithfully going to follow Jesus. It is no good putting our hand to the plow, says Jesus, and then looking back. We count the cost and press on to possess the kingdom.

We cannot always count the cost beforehand, but we need some idea of where we are going and what following Jesus will mean for us. He lays it out for us; the urgency of the kingdom requires total commitment; disciple wannabes won't have the stamina. Part-time disciples need not apply. Committing ourselves to go with him, we follow with steadfast resolve.

PRAYER: Lord, give me the courage to follow where you lead. Amen.

Surpassingly Overabounding!

September 10–16, 2007 • Rebekah Miles[‡] and Len Delony[‡‡]

MONDAY, SEPTEMBER 10 • Read Jeremiah 4:11-12, 22-28

This week's reading from Jeremiah describes the people of Judah as they await imminent destruction by an invading army. The prophet's vision of the near future is grim. The coming destruction seems to undo the very act of creation itself—making the earth "waste and void" and robbing the heavens of their light. "The whole land shall be a desolation." "The earth mourns."

The coming destruction signals God's judgment on the sins of the people of Judah who are "skilled at doing evil." Although some of us may find it hard to believe that God would will the destruction of a people, we can easily understand the feelings and realities in the face of destruction and desolation. We see our own lives and plans fall apart. We watch those we love most in the world suffer. We see images of people across our globe who grieve and die. Sometimes human sin seems to play a hand in bringing about the destruction and sometimes, as in the case of many natural disasters, it seems to be out of our hands altogether. Whatever the cause, when we hit those times of desolation and darkness, it is difficult to believe that the heavens still hold light.

It is tempting to advise desolate, grieving people to accentuate the positive and look for the silver lining in the clouds. But often we need simply to acknowledge the depth of the destruction and the total darkness of the clouds.

PRAYER: Holy One, we pray for those who today suffer and face desolation. May they and we feel the power of your grace. Amen.

[‡]Associate professor of ethics, Perkins School of Theology, Southern Methodist University; clergy member of the Arkansas Conference, The United Methodist Church; living in Fort Worth, Texas.

[‡‡]Spiritual director and former hospital chaplain, active in First United Methodist Church; living with Rebekah and daughters Anna and Katherine in Fort Worth, Texas.

The bleakness of this Jeremiah text is undeniable. Bad things are going to happen. The heavens will darken, and the earth will mourn. Every line heralds bad news—except for one. Verse 27 reads, "Thus says the LORD: The whole land shall be a desolation; yet I will not make a full end." Even in this bleakest of moments, the prophet offers a word of hope. The desolation, however ominous, will not be the final end of the people and their land.

Some scholars think that this hopeful line was added later to soften the otherwise harsh picture offered by the prophet. Other scholars believe that this line makes sense when viewed in relation to other parts of the book. Jeremiah 31:31, for example, speaks of a new covenant that God will make with Israel and Judah. And in the early verses of chapter 32, God orders the prophet to do something ludicrous—to buy a field in the very land that is being destroyed.

When real-estate agents advise buyers to remember that it is all about "location, location, location," they are recommending good locations, not ones that face imminent and sure devastation by an invading army. God's real-estate advice makes no sense by real-estate standards, but it makes all the sense in the world within the larger view of God's providential dealings in human history. God's instruction to purchase a field in a land about to be destroyed is a kind of promissory note. God sees the possibility and hope in seemingly impossible and hopeless situations.

Whether we face devastation at the hands of enemies, destruction by the forces of nature seen in hurricane or flood, or loss from any other cause, we look to God's hope in the midst of pain. We remember that God "will not make a full end."

PRAYER: God of hope, be with those today who face desolation and sorrow. Help them—and us—to find the hope that comes only from you. Amen.

Psalm 14 begins with a word of judgment on fools who "say in their hearts, 'There is no God.'" But the next verses do not limit this judgment to a few. When God looks from heaven to see if there are any who are wise and seek after God, God finds that "they have all gone astray . . . there is no one who does good, no, not one."

In this verse and other places in the Hebrew Scriptures (including this week's reading from Jeremiah), wisdom and foolishness are not linked with knowledge (or a lack of knowledge) but with righteous or evil living. The fools live as if there were no God. These evildoers do not do the right, but instead they "eat up [God's] people as they eat bread." They fail to "call upon the LORD."

Few of us reading these paragraphs would agree with the fool who says, "There is no God." Yet how many of us live as if there were no God? Our atheism is not so much a claim of the intellect as it is a state of our heart. The Cistercian monk Thomas Keating writes that a central problem of the Christian life is that we often live as if God were absent. No matter how loudly we proclaim our belief in God, if our hearts and lives are not transformed by the awareness of God's immediate presence, then our lives echo the shout of the fool, "There is no God."

Psalm 14 reminds us that believing in God entails more than intellectual assent. We must allow our hearts to be converted and seek to live through our identity and calling as children of God.

PRAYER: You who are nearer than our own breath, help us today and all days to live as if you were present—because you are. May your gracious love transform our lives so that they shout of your presence in every act and word. Amen.

Thursday, September 13 • Read Luke 15:1-10

In the movie *Saving Private Ryan*, a captain leads seven men on a fool's mission to bring back a soldier from the front lines. Private Ryan's three brothers have been killed in the war, and an order has come down the chain of command to go and get the last brother so that his mother will be saved the heartbreak of losing all her sons. The captain, reflecting on the dangers, observes, "This Ryan better be worth it. He better go home and cure a disease or invent a longer-lasting lightbulb or something."

The good news of the gospel is that each of us, as a child of God, is "worth it"—even if we never cure a disease or invent a longer-lasting lightbulb. In this week's Gospel lesson, Jesus responds to those who grumble because he eats with sinners. He tells the story of a shepherd who has lost a sheep and who leaves the ninety-nine to search for the one.

It's easy to think of the lost only as those in dire trouble or those who do not know God, but a part of every person is "lost." God sees the smallest lost parts within each of us and seeks to return us to wholeness.

We humans sometimes pride ourselves on seeing the big picture. God, however, deals in the little pictures: the lost sheep, the lost coin, the tax collector, the sinner, the lowliest army private, you, and me. When we are found, God joins our smallness to the infinite and incomprehensible big picture of God's perfect love that connects and heals all. We give thanks to a God who seeks out the one among the many and whose transforming love makes each of us "worth it."

PRAYER: God of the lost, help us remember that you love and seek after each one of us as we are. May we remember that through your grace and love we are all "worth it." Amen.

When our daughter Katherine was three, she lost her beloved purple teddy bear. We searched under every bed, behind every chair, and in every closet. Len and I tried to reason with her and offered substitute bears. All our efforts failed. Purple teddy was gone, and Katherine was not to be consoled. Katherine continued the search. Then one Sunday when visiting her grandparents' church, there in a classroom, high on a bookcase, sat the beloved bear. Katherine rejoiced.

Two summers later, Katherine participated in *The Way of the Child*, a program that helps children experience God. The leader, after telling the stories of the lost sheep and coin, asked the children if they had ever lost something they loved. Did they know what that was like? Katherine raised her hand. "I know all about that, because once I lost my purple teddy."

Both Katherine's distress in the face of loss and her extreme joy in the face of the recovery of purple teddy bear did not make complete sense. Indeed, at times the strength of her reaction seemed irrational. It was, after all, only a stuffed bear.

Likewise, this week's stories from Luke have an irrational side. The shepherd leaves the ninety-nine to find the one. Would it not have made more sense to be on the safe side and stay around to protect the ninety-nine? And the woman who loses and finds her coin certainly makes a big deal of it.

God cares for us in a way that may seem irrational, but it makes perfect sense in the divine scheme of things. When one of us is lost—when even the smallest parts of ourselves are lost—God drops everything and begins the search. The lost is found; the rejoicing begins; and we witness an opening to God's love and grace.

PRAYER: God, help us help you as you seek out those who are lost. And when parts of ourselves are lost, help us to be willing to be found by you. Amen.

Len and I both go through most days and weeks without entertaining even one thought about our doctor. He is simply not on our radar. Then one of us wakes up one morning miserable with the flu, and our physician suddenly becomes a central figure. The sicker we are, the more we think about him, the more we need him, the more we want to see him and receive his healing touch.

Sometimes we behave the same way toward God. The sicker we are, the more we think about God; the more we need God, the more we want to see God and to receive God's healing touch. Our awareness of our sickness and need prompts our desire for the healer.

This passage from First Timothy sounds grim at first reading. We hear that Paul was a former "blasphemer, persecutor, and a man of violence" and the "foremost sinner"—not a pleasant description. Even so, this passage offers the best news we can hope for. Precisely because of our sickness we have a healer. Today's reading reminds us, "Christ Jesus came into the world to save sinners."

Augustine wrote about this verse, "There was no reason for Christ the Lord to come, except to save sinners." Eliminate diseases, eliminate wounds, and there is no call for medicine. If a great doctor has come down from heaven, a great invalid must have been lying very sick throughout the whole wide world. This invalid is the entire human race.

Facing our own sin and sickness may be difficult. But hitting bottom and acknowledging our wounds can drive us toward Christ the healer. In the life of faith, a bad diagnosis is often the forerunner of good news.

PRAYER: Great physician, help us to see our sickness. Give us grace to run to you for healing. Help us join in your saving work in the world. Amen.

Our little girls, like most children, are known not for moderation but for excess. When they pour their juice or milk in the morning, we hover nervously, clutching a roll of paper towels. Our daughters appear to believe that if an almost-full glass is good, then an overflowing glass must be better. We use a lot of paper towels in our household.

If we take today's reading seriously, we see that God and little children bear a striking resemblance. In this text, the story of Paul, "foremost sinner" and "man of violence," is held up as a model. Why is Paul's story a model? It is a model not because of Paul's character but because of God's excessive grace.

In verse 14 we see that God offered to the foremost sinner a great abundance of grace. In the NRSV translation we read that "the grace of our Lord overflowed." Other versions translate this word *overflowed* as " poured out abundantly," "abounded exceedingly," and "surpassingly overabounded." If grace abounds, we rejoice. And if it not only abounds but "surpassingly overabounds," what can we do but give double and triple thanks to God and open ourselves wide to that excessive grace.

The word used in verse 14 is similar to the word used to describe a person who is greedy. But in this case, the emphasis is on God's greediness on our behalf, God's excessive eagerness to shower us with grace?

We worship a God who is excessive when it comes to love and grace. As we are transformed by that surpassingly overabounded grace, we too can become greedy on behalf of others, loving them to excess. And as we allow that grace to continually shape us, its power can change everything.

PRAYER: Precious Lord, give us and others grace to accept your abundant, excessive grace. Help us to open ourselves to your overflowing grace and to share it with the world. Amen.

A Passion for God

September 17–23, 2007 • Harry C. Kiely[‡]

MONDAY, SEPTEMBER 17 • Read Jeremiah 8:18–9:1

The prophet Jeremiah is the model of the true patriot. Out of his passionate devotion to God, he sees all too clearly how his beloved Judah has forsaken God. He hears God speak: "Why have they provoked me to anger with their images, with their worthless foreign idols?" Jeremiah's heart breaks because of Judah's wickedness and his commitment to his country's well-being. "Since my people are crushed, I am crushed," he mourns.

Jeremiah bases his loyalty to Judah on his passion for God. God has given him clarity of vision to see the disaster that an arrogant nation is bringing upon itself. The prophet speaks out in the desperate hope that Judah will come to itself and return to God, thereby averting the impending calamity.

When a nation fails to distinguish between loyalty to the nation and obedience to God, it is toying with idolatry. Jeremiah's outspokenness about Judah's determination to have things on its own terms earns him the rage of the king who attempts to silence the prophet by putting him in jail. But this act only moves Jeremiah to speak out more boldly.

The faithful context for national loyalty lies within the bounds of obedience to God *first*. Only witin those bounds can we judge honestly the actions and commitments of our nation. The conflict of loyalties that we observe in ancient Judah continues to insinuate itself into the affairs of all nations today. As Abraham Lincoln wisely observed, "We pray, not that God will be on our side, but that we shall be on God's side."

PRAYER: God, grant us the vision to see you at work in the affairs of nations and the courage to hold our country and its leaders accountable to your dominion. Amen.

[‡]Retired United Methodist pastor, active member of Dumbarton United Methodist Church; living in Silver Spring, Maryland.

One student of the New Testament has said that Jesus talked more about money than he did about prayer! Considering what a forbidden subject money is in many churches, such a discovery is disconcerting. Do we not expect Jesus to focus his attention on higher things than cash?

But just as Jesus chased the money changer from the Temple, he seems determined to intervene in our personal lives to free us from unhealthy and unholy obsessions. The endless barrage of advertising, the constant flow of new gadgets, even the political exaltation of capitalism—all these reflect the preoccupation with materialism that characterizes much of our culture. For many people, the symbols of economic prosperity help define a successful person. We even talk about wealthy individuals by saying how much they are "worth" financially.

We do not have to be rich to get caught up in what Jesus would call idolatry. This is what he is talking about when he says, "You cannot serve both God and Money" (NIV). No one, he insists, can be obedient to two masters. Who of us would readily admit that money is our master? Our usual approach to the subject is not to approach the subject. Maybe that's why Jesus talked so much about money—he knew the topic required honest examination.

Of course Jesus knows that money, like food, is a necessity of life and that involuntary poverty is not a virtue. He leads the disciples in the practice of sharing food and clothing and shelter so that all are cared for, and no one has more than is needed.

So, by repeatedly confronting us with the money question, Jesus does not attempt to humiliate us but to liberate us from a value system that can take over our lives. Moving beyond the temptations of wealth to a total trust in the sufficiency of God's grace will open us to the joys of sharing in community, so that no one has too much and no one has too little.

SUGGESTION FOR REFLECTION: **When I reflect on my personal stewardship, what assumptions do I make about who is the source of my wealth?**

The heartache of tragic loss is an experience common to most of us. A severe family crisis related to job loss, the sudden death of a loved one, the revelation of infidelity, a devastating flood—these kinds of trials push us to the wall and make us cry out. In those circumstances, how shall we pray? Dare we come to God and bare our true feelings, even feelings that God has in some way let us down?

This psalm teaches us that we live our lives entirely in God. In all events, whether trivial or momentous, God, though hidden, is nevertheless present. So it is entirely appropriate to lament before God our severest distresses, as this psalmist does after an enemy has invaded the Holy City, wrecked the Temple, killed the priests, and even the king. He even holds God accountable for these events: "How long, O LORD? Will you be angry forever?"

Can we imagine praying this way in Sunday worship? Unfortunately in much of our praying we mistake politeness for reverence and thus withhold our honest feelings from our private and corporate prayer life. We pray as if God were a stranger who lives only on the periphery of our lives.

For this psalmist, however, the God-relationship is deep and enduring. Bringing his hurt, disillusionment, and anger to God reflects a total trust in divine grace. Thus his praying leads through the desert of rage and despair to the oasis of supplication:

> Help us, O God our Savior, for the glory of your name;
> Deliver us and forgive our sins for your name's sake.

In this prayer he comes to the point of accepting in Israel's name the responsibility the nation bears for the present devastation. Such honest prayer becomes the foundation for Israel humbly to accept God's judgment and to set out on a new future bonded to the One who brought Israel into being.

PRAYER: Lord, you know my deepest distress. Lead me to repentance and to trust in your deliverance. Amen.

This pastoral epistle was written at a time when the early Christian movement existed in a complex relationship with the secular rulers. The book of Acts records many incidents in which the followers of Jesus were arrested, jailed, and even executed. Being a follower of Jesus in those perilous times was risky business.

Living in such circumstances doubtless created Christian animosity toward the ruling monarch. The writer of this letter to Timothy reflects apparent concern that Christians not cause unnecessary conflict with the civic authorities. He urges his readers to include in their prayers everyone, even "kings and all those in authority." But maybe his concern goes even deeper: he wants Christians to remember how Jesus' love included everyone.

Being Christians should make us different sorts of citizens than we would be otherwise. Our first allegiance is to God, not to the state; at times crucial issues will test us. The nonviolent civil rights movement led people like Martin Luther King Jr. into breaking the unjust laws of racial segregation. Ultimately he obeyed the gospel of truth as exhibited in the life of Jesus.

Yet, as the writer of the letter to Timothy might say, those who fight for racial justice in the name of Christ are also obliged to pray for the political authorities who enforce evil laws and practices. Expecting such behavior of anyone runs so contrary to human nature that only God can temper our inner rage and convert our hearts.

This letter implies our need for inner transformation. This can occur when we firmly take our moral stand while also viewing and praying for our adversaries. While uncommon, such behavior in our tension-filled world provides the sacred witness that people of faith are called to practice.

SUGGESTION FOR REFLECTION: **Think of one example of someone who has taken a risky stand for justice while also respecting and praying for the adversary. What empowered that person to make such a witness?**

Hurricane Katrina of 2005 was one of the most devastating storms to hit this nation in recorded history. The storm brought significant loss of life, separation of families, and permanent destruction of thousands of homes and businesses. Untold numbers of people were hurried into athletic stadiums, church halls, and other buildings that had withstood the storm. But in some of these shelters, the lack of food, bedding, showers, and sanitation facilities made life in them "hell on earth" as one person described it.

Personal stories came out of this experience that will be passed down for generations. Many of the stories speak of heartache and tragedy. But there are also some different stories—stories of surprising generosity, stories of hope.

One such story, as related by writer Lily Koppel in the *New York Times*, portrays an eleven-year-old girl named A'Jenne (pronounced ah-zhe-NAY) Williams. Over a period of days, A'Jenne's family was moved to three different shelters after losing their apartment and all their possessions in Slidell, Louisiana.

Wherever the family found lodging, A'Jenne became a kind of social director, working to bring cheer to other people in the shelter. At one place she carried around a plate of pretzels topped with peanut butter and jelly from the Red Cross food table. "Would you like a treat?" she would ask.

A'Jenne carried out her self-appointed mission after school and on weekends, all the while living in a shelter. "I've been washing cars, shining shoes, doing manicures," she said. "Everybody's all doubtful, but I really want to pick up their spirits."

Jesus says, "Whoever can be trusted with very little can also be trusted with much." The surprise of A'Jenne's story is how little this child had to share, yet how it multiplied in value many times as she generously extended herself to bring joy to others.

PRAYER: Open our eyes, God, to the abundant riches that are ours to share with a desperately needy world. Amen.

Vulnerability is the price we pay when we care deeply for someone. Sad or tragic events in others' lives can tear at our hearts. Jeremiah is a classic example of such caring. Some call him "the weeping prophet" because he was often driven to tears in his concern for the sins of his homeland and the inevitable tragic consequences. Jesus reflects such deep devotion when, according to Luke, he weeps over Jerusalem because its leaders ignore or, even worse, stone the prophets. The refusal to hear the warnings of those who come to the city as emissaries of God often brings widespread suffering, mostly among the poor.

New Testament scholar Walter Wink has written that Jesus reveals to us the humanity of God. God, like Jesus and even Jeremiah, weeps for us when we suffer or when we become headstrong in our determination to go our own way. Considering the widespread human suffering in our world today—hunger, homelessness, plagues, war—God must spend a great deal of time "weeping with those who weep."

American culture frowns on male vulnerability, regarding it as a sign of weakness. Someone has wisely observed that, considering our high esteem for Jesus, it is surprising that our male heroes depicted in movies are typically men noted for toughness and readiness to fight and even kill. Could this be a clue to the reason we find peacemaking so elusive? Our culture considers toughness and revenge honorable, while regarding the model of Jesus—the man who refused to take the sword—weak or out of touch with reality. And God's tears continue to flow.

SUGGESTION FOR REFLECTION: **What does it take to move us to tears? In what ways do our tears lead us to examine our lives, opening us to hearing and obeying God's word? In this examination, what yearnings for reconciliation and readiness for vulnerability do we discover?**

Yesterday we reflected on vulnerability as a divine trait and a human possibility. We can imagine that Jeremiah's broken heart mirrored God's pain. Yet his desperate prayer hints that he wonders whether God is paying attention: "Is there no balm in Gilead? Is there no physician there?"

"You formed us as a people," the prophet says. "So how can you abandon us now? Am I to be the only one who weeps for Judah in your name?" This courageous prayer is forthright and fraught with spiritual wisdom.

A young woman pregnant with her second child had high hopes for the arrival of a sibling for her daughter. Because of an earlier miscarriage, the mother feared that history might repeat itself. Sadly, a second miscarriage did occur, and she was devastated. For several weeks she isolated herself at home with her husband and daughter and refused to answer any calls, even from family and close friends.

"I was full of grief, tears, anger," she later wrote in the church newsletter. "I was overwhelmed with depression. All I could see was darkness and despair. I was angry. Why take a child that was so wanted and loved? Why couldn't God give me a miracle? *Why? Why? Why?*"

Fortunately the woman confided her sorrow and her feelings to a Christian therapist who told her it was okay to be angry with God, that her anger would never scare God away! This assurance is grounded in a deep faith.

More importantly, the woman's anger at God gives voice to the prayer of a true believer. She trusted that God's love, though hidden to her then, was nevertheless sustaining her. As with Jeremiah, her deep faith in the steadfastness of God enabled her to bear an unspeakable loss. As she opened her heart to God, she discovered there is a balm in Gilead to heal the wounded soul.

PRAYER: Thank you, O God, for the healing power of your love that is at work in us now. Amen.

Presence and Protection

September 24–30, 2007 • Ike (Isaac) Matshidisho Moloabi[‡]

MONDAY, SEPTEMBER 24 • Read Psalm 91:1-6

At the time of this psalm's writing, God's servants are passing through times of sorrow and sadness. They wish the situation could be different or that a way of escape existed. Even today many people wish that life could be different, that there might be a way to escape the major calamities of the day: HIV/AIDS, unemployment, poverty, hunger, war . . . the list is endless.

Yet the psalmist expresses hope and trust in God. In God's hands he feels safe, secure, and protected. God cares for him in the same way that a hen watches over her chicks. The hen's wings protect like an umbrella. Her protection begins at their birth and continues by creating an atmosphere of strength and assurance. Under her outstretched wings, the chicks can live in freedom and with confidence.

We need to settle under the knowledge and assurance that at all times God reigns—at all times God is in control and, therefore, we can completely trust God. This is what the psalmist portrays in verse 4: "and under his wings you will find refuge." If we trust in God, we can look away from daily fear and anxiety to the God who is trustworthy. The people, settings, and situations that cause fear and anxiety may and will continue to be part of daily existence, but God's promise of love, care, and protection far outweigh these trials. We affirm our confidence in God by our continued expression of trust, "The LORD is my shepherd, I shall not want" (Ps. 23:1), as we face the future with the knowledge and confidence that God is in control.

PRAYER: Lord, teach us to hold on to the truth so that our trust in you may be an everyday pillar of hope and assurance. Amen.

[‡]Leader of a group of supernumerary ministers that markets, promotes, and distributes *The Upper Room* daily devotional guide in South Africa; living in Johannesburg, South Africa.

According to the psalmist, the God of love promises deliverance in return for our response of love. Consider these six actions that God promises:

1. "I will deliver." God was and will always be a God of deliverance. God delivered Israel from the pain of slavery into a new land flowing with milk and honey—a land of new experiences, new beginnings. God will continue this action into generations of those who love God.

2. "I will protect." Protection is the response toward those "who know my name." We know who God really is and acknowledge God in acts of hallowing the Holy One's name.

3. "I will answer them." God answers when we call upon the name of the Lord; the Lord will act for us.

4. "I will be with them." Presence, always an important aspect, confirms God's involvement in our lives; we will experience God in our actions each moment but more so in times of need. God's presence gives confidence and strength.

5. "I will rescue them." God will save us. "Even though I walk through the darkest valley, I fear no evil" (Ps 23:4).

6. "I will satisfy them." The people of God will receive personal fulfillment—not simply a spiritual experience with no relation to everyday life. They will have a sense of fulfillment and satisfaction, of looking back and saying *Yes!*

PRAYER: God, we come before you this day with a sure hope that your promises are forever. We pray that your mighty hand and your unchanging love will continue to remind us that we belong to you and that your ever-guiding hand will always lead us. Amen.

The land, by understanding and law, is God's own possession, committed to a given family or clan by God. It constitutes part of the past, present, and future of an individual, his or her family and community. Hanamel knows this technicality of the land and how it can be sold. Hanamel proposes therefore to sell his land at Anathoth to Jeremiah who, as a relative, has the right to buy the land. But the Babylonians are on their way; certainly they will capture the land and take it from the owner. So even if Jeremiah has the right of ownership, the land will be lost.

Amazingly, Jeremiah is ready to buy the land even though he knows of the impending doom. How does a person choose to invest in property that will soon be lost? Jeremiah finally agrees to the deal because he knows and believes that God wills this and that the transactions (formalities) that follow are enacted as the Israelite law of the land demands. Jeremiah bases his actions on his trust and complete faith in God. In other words, he invests in the future. When the God of the future tells Jeremiah to "buy the land," Jeremiah knows there is a future in that land.

God's promises are true and can be trusted. Jeremiah's trust in God creates confidence in the future. With the Holy One by our side and within our lives, any investment in the future will yield abundant harvest. Excluding God and fellow human beings paints a bleak future. The God of Israel promises protection and presence. Faith and hope in the future is the best investment.

PRAYER: Lord, we pray that you will give us this day the wisdom to learn how to trust in you against all odds. Amen.

With God's people the Lord will make "poverty history." Paul who has written to Timothy about being content with life and not setting his mind on worldly riches, now says to him: "But as for you, man of God, shun all this; pursue righteousness, godliness, faith, love, endurance, gentleness. . . . take hold of the eternal life." He then leaves a "commandment" for Timothy and therefore to our world that includes the following: "to do good, to be rich in good works, generous, and ready to share."

Truthfully, the resources of our day are such that each person in the world could have enough; poverty could become history. But we all know that everywhere in the world those who have more than enough desire to possess even more. We may acknowledge the concern of sharing the abundant resources of the world among God's children, but our need to live above others and to control their destiny—to keep others as our tools—makes us unwilling to share. We have given up stewardship and taken possession of God's world and of God's wealth.

Paul does not condemn money itself. However, he does speak of the love of money as the root of all evil. The love of money leads to all sorts of selfish acts on the part of those who love it. In a world in which the rich are becoming richer and the poor poorer, we need to hear these words. If we become generous and share our riches, we store up for ourselves the treasure of a good foundation for the future. Only then may we take hold of the life that is *really* worth living.

PRAYER: Lord, prepare us to listen to and to hear those whom you send to us. May we hear their words of challenge as we learn to share of our wealth and ourselves. Amen.

Not only are people and nations not content with their life personally and generally, many people feel discontent with their everyday life most of the time—especially with regard to their financial standing. The poor are not content because the life of the wealthy lived out in the face of their poverty raises questions of justice and fair play. The wealthy are not content with their riches; they plan, work, and wish for more.

Paul says in his letter to Timothy that there is a "great gain in godliness combined with contentment." For Paul, gain in life comes from relationship with God the Creator who, in effect, possesses all that the world contains. We may choose to pursue our greed, selfishness, and love of money; but in the end money becomes a hindrance to the promotion of God's kingdom if it rules our lives and determines our response to other people, especially the poor in our midst.

Paul reminds us that money is not a god to be worshiped. What we do with our wealth and how we view it, our attitude toward God and other people, and our commitment and preparedness to listen to God's command determine whether or not money has become a god in our lives. When money blinds us to the needs of others and perhaps even blinds us to God, Paul says we have wandered away from the faith and will be pierced with many pains. Wealth, if we are not careful, can turn our lives into a hell on earth. Paul challenges us to put our faith in God.

PRAYER: God, help us place our faith in you, and let our dependence on you challenge us to put our wealth into your hands for the world's use. Amen.

"And at his gate lay a poor man named Lazarus, covered with sores, who longed to satisfy his hunger with what fell from the rich man's table; even the dogs would come and lick his wounds." This man is not only poor but also sick. His ill health becomes even more obvious when we discover that soon he dies. Poverty that ultimately leads to death constitutes a serious poverty.

It is one thing to be hungry; hunger is painful. It is another thing to also carry painful sores—a double tragedy. Yet the man's woes go even further. He experiences a longing as he waits at the gate, a wish to have his hunger alleviated by the scraps of the rich man's table. This man is one we pass on the street corner next to our beautifully decorated churches—the Lazaruses of our day—those who live with HIV/AIDS, who are unemployed, who are hungry and poor, who are crippled emotionally by family events. As Jesus implies in this parable, if you have not been aware, begin now.

The church will pray for Lazarus. The church will have its feasts, because the church needs to be in fellowship. The world will convene large conferences on hunger with millions of dollars spent to accommodate delegates. And the dogs will lick the wounds of the poor and sick. Lazarus will continue to long for the salvation of his body, mind, and soul. The poverty statistics will grow and, in this way, Christ will continue to be crucified by what the church and the world are *not* doing about people at the gate.

PRAYER: Creator of all things, giver of all gifts, we pray that you will lead us to see the truth. May our lives be lived in relation to the lives of others, especially the sick and the poor. Amen.

Jesus reminds us that this world is a place where we must respond to God's command to care for others spiritually and materially. God uses people and situations to challenge our greed and apathy, and we must respond in the here and now.

The rich man pleads for his brothers still living in ignorance and greed to be sent a heavenly messenger to warn them of the dangers of greed. Unfortunately for those brothers, they cannot be treated as special people. God approaches them in and through those already sent, called, and commissioned. As Abraham tells the rich man, "If they do not listen to Moses and the prophets, neither will they be convinced even if someone rises from the dead."

This parable does not condemn riches. It does not suggest that there is something wrong in having wealth. The major problem here is that the rich man ignores the needs and suffering of the poor man. He lives his life as if the only thing that matters is himself and his wealth. He lives as if Lazarus does not exist.

This parable challenges the greed and apathy of our time. Jesus says, "Go." Be actively involved. Do not just give Lazarus a meal; "Go to Lazarus." He longs for someone to make him feel human, to make him feel loved. The rich man in the parable becomes *aware* too late. Now is the time to act and be Christ to the world who "though he was rich, yet for your sakes he became poor" (2 Cor. 8:9), who took human form and died on the cross.

Prayer: Christ our Redeemer, on this day of resurrection challenge us afresh; call us to serve you by serving others. Amen.

Now is the time to order your copy of

The Upper Room
Disciplines
2008

Published for over 45 years, *Disciplines* continues to grow in its appeal to Christians who, like you, desire a more disciplined spiritual life based on scripture.

Enlarged-print edition available

THE UPPER ROOM DISCIPLINES 2008

Regular edition (product #9900):
Enlarged-print edition (product #9901):

QUANTITY DISCOUNT AVAILABLE!

TO ORDER, CALL:
1-800-972-0433
Tell the customer service representative your source code is 2008D.

OR WRITE:
Customer Service Dept.
The Upper Room
P.O. Box 340004
Nashville, TN 37203-0004

SHIPPING CHARGES:
Actual shipping charges will be added to your invoice.

We accept Visa, Mastercard, checks, and money orders.

VISIT OUR WEB SITE:
www.upperroom.org/bookstore

THE UPPER ROOM DISCIPLINES 2008
is also available at Christian bookstores.

Generations of the Faithful

October 1–7, 2007 • Janet S. Helme[‡]

MONDAY, OCTOBER 1 • Read Lamentations 1:1-6

The book of Lamentations, often ascribed to the prophet Jeremiah, contains five poems of mourning that make up the five chapters. Written at the time of the Babylonian capture and takeover of Judah, these poems describe the sorrow and suffering the Jews felt and experienced during this national tragedy.

Many Hebrew lamentations began with the Hebrew word for "how"—*ekhah*. In verse 1, the word *how* begins the first sentences, so in the Hebrew canon, this book is named Ekhah.

This first week in October is the week when Christians around the world celebrate World Communion Sunday, a special time to recognize the solidarity of our union in Jesus Christ, Savior of all humankind.

Perhaps it is also a time—as we partake of the bread and the cup instituted by Jesus—to lift up in prayer those persons who live in captivity. We pray for refugees in camps, far from their homes; refugees who have "resettled" into another culture or country, who dream of going home; children, youth, and adults living in war zones of terror, death, and destruction; people held captive by economic, social, and political systems; and, sometimes, even ourselves. This is the time to pray our own sentences of "how" as we empathize with those present generations of the faithful who continue to worship God despite their bondage.

SUGGESTION FOR PRAYER: **Using a current newspaper, radio or television newscast write on an index card several areas in the world where people live in captivity of one kind or another. As you go through this day and the days this week, say a sentence prayer for these people and these places, asking God to bless them in special ways.**

[‡]Ordained minister, Christian Church,(Disciples of Christ), served congregations in Ohio and Texas; living in San Antonio, Texas.

Psalm 137 gives voice to the faithfulness of the Jewish captives. Their grief and longing for their home in Judah causes them to weep, preventing them from singing the national songs. The tears they shed indicate their ongoing loyalty to God and their homeland. In the midst of tormenting captors, these faithful Jews choose not to sing—for singing songs to God would be a farce in present circumstances. These faithful Jews teach their beliefs to the generations born into captivity. Remaining faithful in their tears and their remembering, they also turn their revenge over to God. Perhaps they realize that voicing their feelings of revenge to God will rid their system of these poisonous feelings, and God's justice will prevail.

How faithful are we in teaching our sacred God-songs, stories, and beliefs to our children, our grandchildren, and those children who surround us in our faith communities? Being part of the faithful generations of the people of God, we have the divine responsibility to share our stories and journeys and to take the time to listen to and encourage the sharing of the faith stories of others.

When I share the children's moment during our weekly worship, I can often tell which children have heard the stories of faith from their parents. Lydia and Adrianna are always ready to answer my questions. Their answers confirm that someone at home has been talking with and listening to them. They receive encouragement to become a part of the present generation of the faithful.

SUGGESTION FOR MEDITATION: **In a similar manner to the psalmist, name your enemies. Write their names on a piece of paper, then picture these people as you pray for them. At the end of this time, turn them and your feelings over to God as you tear the paper into small pieces and dispose of them.**

Recently I received a card of encouragement from one of the older women in my congregation. She knew the long hours I had spent each week trying to inspire people to help jump-start a couple of new and much-needed ministries. Her card let me know how much she appreciated what God and I were doing together. Her words stimulated me to seek a couple of additional parishioners who would keep these new ministries in their prayers as I sought to recruit and train the needed lay leaders.

Ministry always involves hard work and lots of prayer. However, it becomes much easier when many people share the load. Paul, one of our most astute apostles, knows that discouragement and ministry can go hand-in-hand, especially when the minister is young and/or inexperienced. Paul wants Timothy, his young protege, to know that even though imprisoned, Paul continues to pray—both day and night—for Timothy and his ministry.

Our own ministry of intercessory prayer may serve to indicate how we shall become a part of the "generations of the faithful." Keeping a prayer journal is one way to stay faithful to those people who need our prayers and to whom we have made a commitment. It is especially important to pray for our church leaders, both clergy and laypersons. Some of my best prayer intercessors during my twenty years of ministry have been the homebound members of my congregations! In three of the congregations I have served, I encouraged our adults to sign up to become prayer mentors for each of our children and youth. The apostle Paul knew the impact that prayer could and should make in the life of the church.

SUGGESTION FOR MEDITATION: How can you become more effective in your intercessory prayer time? How does your church mediate the prayer needs of others? Ask God to guide you in answering these questions.

In Paul's letter to the young minister Timothy, he tells him, "I am reminded of your sincere faith, a faith that lived first in your grandmother Lois and your mother Eunice and now, I am sure, lives in you." Timothy is the product of at least two generations of faithful believers who shared who they were and what they believed with this young man.

During a day of spiritual retreat with my sister, she and I wondered aloud where we had gotten a common behavior. Both of us tend to treat all persons with respect, regardless of education, economic status, employment, skin color, gender, or other separating traits. As we talked, we remembered our mother's large family of origin and how some of her relatives had worked in the coal mines of southern Illinois. One brother was mentally challenged and much loved by the entire family. My sister said, "Mother accepted everyone, regardless of who they were." I reminded her that our father, a well-educated man, often tended to look out for the underdog—the person who was lowest according to society's measurements. Somehow our parents, by their examples, had instilled in us the importance of accepting each person as an important part of God's family.

Paul knew the truth and the importance of passing on the faith. He recognized that generations of the faithful always have had and will have a hand in forming the next generation of faithful followers.

If Paul could speak to us today he might ask, "What legacy are you passing on to tomorrow's Christians?"

SUGGESTION FOR MEDITATION: If you are not already a prayer mentor for one of the children or youth in your congregation, decide today to begin praying for someone in your church. Perhaps one of your adult groups might take on prayer mentoring as a special ministry.

I was living a very good life—wife of a professional, mother of two sons, and part-time employee. But I had felt the tug of something that wouldn't let go, even though I struggled against it for several years. As organist and choir director, writer of curriculum materials for our denomination, and leader of workshops for teachers in the Christian Church Michigan Region, I kept busy and fulfilled. Finally, the Spirit had its way. I entered ministry as assistant minister, a holy calling filled with God's purpose and grace, but it was not without some suffering. Helping to raise two sons, serving full-time on a church staff, and going to seminary became part of that mix. I, however, have never been ashamed to name myself as a Christian minister.

This is not necessarily the case with young Timothy in today's scripture. He lives in a world that cannot quite accept that the "promised savior" of the Jewish nation has died as a criminal, crucified by Romans between two other criminals. Timothy does have reason to feel shame. And his mentor, the apostle Paul, writes to him from prison where he too is charged as a criminal by the Roman government. But if Timothy has any doubts at all about the power of the gospel of Jesus Christ, Paul's words in verses 8 to14 should make them disappear. Instead of self-pity and fear, Paul continues to be God's faithful herald to all who will listen: Our "Savior Christ Jesus . . . abolished death and brought life and immortality to light through the gospel." Paul continues to encourage Timothy to hold fast to his faith.

What a sterling example of one of God's faithful!

PRAYER: Gracious God, even when we suffer for your sake, we know that you are with us and that your son Jesus has led us in the way through suffering and into eternal life with you. Praise be to you and to the good news we share with the world! Amen.

These six verses in Luke teach us about faithfulness and obedience. When the disciples ask Jesus to increase their faith, he first uses the example of having enough faith to make a mulberry tree obey their commandment. Then he tells a short parable of a master asking obedience from his slave. The slave must obey the master's commands, even to the point of working all day in the fields and, being tired and hungry, serving the master before he, the slave, eats and rests. The master makes demands upon the slave, and the slave willingly obeys the master. The point? God asks obedience from the generations of the faithful, and we obey willingly and joyfully. God expects nothing less than obedience, and we give our utmost to carry out God's will.

Sometimes it truly works in this way. I remember Judy, the diminutive wife of an interim minister who served one of our churches many years ago. Judy gave all she was and all she had to every church her husband served. In the years I knew them, I never once heard Judy say, "Well, I've served my time. Someone else needs to teach the children . . . or sing in the choir . . . or play the piano . . . or serve the men's breakfast." Whenever there was work to be done, Judy willingly and graciously gave her time, her energy, and her talents as a senior member of the generations of the faithful. No job was beneath her when she was serving God through serving the congregation.

What a different response from those people who refuse to take on any and all church responsibilities by saying, "I've served my time."

PRAYER: I am your willing servant, O God. Equip me with your Spirit and lead me into the service you would have me perform as one of the generations of the faithful. Amen.

Sometimes we need the "whole story" in order to understand what's happening. The first four verses of Luke 17 shed some additional light on the disciples and us as generations of the faithful. Jesus has just given the disciples some "hard" teachings: (1) you better not cause another to stumble in his or her faith journey; (2) you will need to rebuke other disciples if they sin; and (3) you must forgive those who repent and ask forgiveness, even if it's seven times a day! In light of these teachings, the disciples beg Jesus to "increase our faith!" They acknowledge the difficulty of following through on these mandates.

Jesus' response, "If you had faith . . . ," is a conditional clause. In the Greek language, this states a condition of fact: "If you had faith—and of course you do." Jesus might have been telling the disciples that while their faith is small, God will help it grow as they continue in their faith journey. Perhaps he is encouraging them by what they might do as their faith increases.

One of my joys in ministry has come in encouraging church members to be all that God wants them to be. One woman, in particular, had little confidence in what she could do for God. Asked to be an elder, she hesitated to accept and came to me. I assured her that I would pray with and for her as she made her decision and, also, if she served at the Communion table. That was ten years ago. Her increasing faith in God and in herself has been a blessing to behold!

PRAYER: How am I, gracious God, like the disciples in this scripture—wanting to increase my faith during those difficult times in my life? How am I like Jesus—striving to encourage others who seek to be the persons you would have them be? Be with me, Compassionate Friend, and show me your way. Amen.

Abject Weakness and Unquenchable Power

October 8–14, 2007 • Brian W. Grant[‡]

MONDAY, OCTOBER 8 • Read Jeremiah 29:1, 4-7

Most of us remember what we were doing September 11, 2001. Our country's place as the unassailable center of international power was shattered. Jeremiah writes his letter to the exiles from an even deeper, though similar, darkness. Jerusalem is devastated. King and nobles, priests and Levites, landowners and merchants, are herded off to Babylon. Thousands lie dead and the Jewish state has ceased to be.

How could God allow this to happen? When would God bring the people back to Zion? Revolt in other provinces has weakened Babylon. The royal family is experiencing division. Perhaps God will choose that moment to return them to power and privilege in Judah.

In the face of these hopes, Jeremiah writes a shocking word: "Thus says the LORD of hosts, to all the exiles whom I have sent into exile from Jerusalem to Babylon." I did it, says the Lord, and I did it for a reason. God knows that a harsh dose of humility can be a sanctifying grace for the people; God knows that their illusions of power and godliness have produced an idolatrous pride.

Might this be true in this century as well? Could God have used the perpetrators of 9/11 as God used Nebuchadnezzar? Could the destruction of our twin temples and our exile from the center of the world be God's way of leading us into a new land? Could the realm of God be more blessed than any nation-state we could imagine?

PRAYER: Holy God, help us see the hope you reveal in national humility and find the peace Jeremiah found in his belief in your power over all the nations, even our own. Amen.

[‡]Executive director, Counseling Center; Lois and Dale Bright Professor of Christian Ministries, Christian Theological Seminary, Indianapolis, Indiana.

Jesus has set off on his journey to Jerusalem and Golgotha and stumbled upon the most stigmatized people of his time. In this borderland, where Jews and Samaritans live across invisible boundaries on the same streets, he meets ten lepers. Any of today's healers would find it challenging to redeem the lives of a handful of undocumented HIV-positive immigrants with the wrong religion. It's a daily dilemma to parcel out our finite healing power among the world's desperate poor.

For Jesus it seems easy. He utters the healing words, and the story gets really interesting. The lepers go off to their priests as instructed; one man looks down and notices that his lesions have vanished. Unlike the nine who continue to the priests, he turns back, praises God, and thanks Jesus profusely. Then we learn that he is Samaritan, a foreigner, who has allowed Jesus to add a saving relationship to the gift of healing.

We don't know what happened after the story, but we see possibilities. The man who returned makes himself available for a life-changing personal encounter. Jesus, through his gift, has created an opening to extend the scope of his love into a community his fellow Jews consider inferior and accursed.

When we have healing gifts to offer, is it always those most like us who respond with gratitude and transforming relationship? Or perhaps more importantly, when we have received the offer of release from our diseases, can we allow ourselves the grace of a grateful response, uniting us with the divine Giver, even if that Giver comes with a foreign face? a different religion? a different set of political loyalties?

PRAYER: God of all peoples, save us from the easy assumption that those who share our citizenship, our race, our faith, are those most likely to bear your love for us. Keep us building bridges. Amen.

Remember! That's the key word for the writer of Timothy. And there is much to remember: Jesus Christ, Paul's earlier preaching, the author's bondage in a Roman prison, the elect for whom all this is suffered, and the baptismal hymn: "If we have died with him, we shall also live with him" (RSV).

Timothy served at Ephesus, where the church faced persecution. He appears overwhelmed, in need of courage and support. Paul invites him to call up the memory of Jesus' Davidic heritage and of the liturgy with which he was baptized.

We have our sacred memories too, memories of individuals who strengthen our nerve and remind us of our sources of power. Each of us calls to mind different people: Pope John XXIII, Martin Luther King Jr., Reinhold Niebuhr, Mother Teresa, Dorothy Day, Dag Hammarskjöld, Cesar Chavez.

The epistle urges Timothy on for the sake of the elect, reminding him that though the author is fettered, the faith itself is free and powerful. We long to deliver our freeing memories to our children of the flesh and of the faith: new congregations, mission churches around the world, students and parishioners, the poor and the sick.

The passage contains a final word of hope, a reminder of God's fidelity. After the parallels, "If we have died . . . we shall also live; if we endure, we shall also reign . . . if we deny, he will also deny" (RSV): comes the unexpected gift of verse 13. "If we are faithless, he remains faithful—for he cannot deny himself." In that day's persecution or this day's apathy, the consistency of the Divine identity will not allow God to give us up, even when we fail God. This is grace not works, because God is who God is. Even our faithlessness will not lure God into forgetting us.

PRAYER: Ever-faithful God, keep us vital in our memories of those whose vision shaped our faith. Hold us in the bonds linking your Holy Self, these saints of our traditions, and our own desperate need. Amen.

Once Timothy has been urged to remember, he receives a series of passionate commands. This is no time for competition over who can best manage the language. It is a time to teach powerfully, to lay the sacred memories on the hearts of the hearers so they have strength to stand in the face of society's greed and evil.

The apostle knows that "wrangling over words" is death to those desperate for teachings with saving power. The time demands urgency and plain speech that lays out the example of the faithful for a community that needs strength to endure a present emergency.

We are urged to present our best: the straightforward heart of what we know of God, of life, of Christian hope. We present ourselves to God and to those who listen as ones who want their witness seen and heard at its honest core. It requires no finesse of speech but a rightness that comes from our very center.

In times of great decision, everything depends on the clarity with which persons of faith become transparent bearers of God's hope, mercy, and justice. Attention focuses on the basic truths in, with, and under the media of language, image, or melody—not on persons. We are called to be so full of grace that the author of that grace can be sensed in our every word and movement.

Today may be the day when someone needs a simple act of truth, a showing forth of God's mercy, a workerlike presentation of what God's woman or man can be, right where you are. Deliver what is needed with neither stinginess nor overkill, and let God be the judge of the adequacy of your witness.

PRAYER: Holy One, help us sense when we need to offer ourselves as your representatives. May we keep ourselves out of the way so those who are dying for the lack of you can see you through us. Amen.

There is a special likeness between the expressive power of music and the grandeur and might of the natural world. A particular awe overwhelms us when God seems to use that world to advance God's designs for some piece of the human family. The beauty of nature and the power of God draws forth raw outpourings of emotion in joy and hope, terror and wonder, even before we can form them into words.

Driving into the high Sierras from California's Central Valley, overlooking Lake Tahoe and the snowy peaks around it, marveling at the depths of the Grand Canyon emerging from the forests of the North Rim, relaxing into the deep green of the South Indian wetlands after coming through desert—all these amaze us with unimaginable beauty and power.

The psalmist has borrowed a piece of a sacrificial ritual, a reenactment of Israel's sacred events, making them present in a new day. The Israelites feel humbled and exult as they remember God's turning "the sea into dry land" and "they passed through the river on foot."

God surpasses all our knowing, all our imagining, all our creating. Again and again grace splashes before us the color of our dependence on God's creation of us as families and on the landscapes in which we live. In beauty and horror, in life-giving monsoons and death-dealing tsunamis, we see how our exquisite freedoms exist in a tiny space and time, cast in the midst of a cosmos that only sustains us through events we cannot compel and for which we can only give thanks and praise. These moments call joyful song from the whole earth.

PRAYER: Amazing God, grant us awe as we contemplate the beauty and tragedy of life and its physical setting. Help us sing in exultation and sorrow when transfixed by your offerings that bring hope to some and confusion to others whom you also love. Amen.

Surely we can all recall a situation where, by rights, we should have been destroyed. We were foolish enough, unlucky enough, or immoral enough to be standing on the tracks, right in front of the freight train. As the psalmist put it, "You let people ride over our heads; we went through fire and through water," yet you "have kept us among the living."

We're amazed and grateful that the truck blew its horn; the firecracker didn't explode; the police didn't come. A force far beyond our ability intervened. We walked away in one piece. A retired missionary related how two Japanese guards in a 1941 Philippine internment camp led him, with a revolver pressing into his ribs on right and left, to the food storage building. On the return trip, the revolvers were back in their holsters, and the three men—missionary and guards—were carrying milk back to camp. "Yet you have brought us out to a spacious place" on that occasion and many, many others.

It doesn't matter whether God singled us out for special favor or if we were simply nimble enough, lucky enough, interpersonally skilled enough to find the crack in the enemy's defenses. We do know that gratitude is due and that a humility that remembers our survival of war, accident, disease, or stupidity is a gift.

Such events change us. They give us a sense of life being a treasure easily lost, of the need to be good stewards in our choice of risks, and of carrying a responsibility on behalf of those who did not survive to make the future safer and more holy.

PRAYER: Divine Mystery, we humbly and gratefully receive the gift of being kept among the living. Give us conviction that this bare fact of life leaves us owing you and your world a fruitful life. Amen.

What happens when we've lost all our entitlements: the divorce settlement has taken our home, our children, our wealth; illness has forced us to live in a different future; war has destroyed property, opportunity, bodies, and life itself?

We like to think that God promised us a reward for years of study, morality, hard work, and right belief. It should lead to peace of mind, a comfortable old age, long life, prosperity, and a winning bet on the Derby.

Sometimes that's what we get. But often we discover that God has read the contract differently, and we're herded off to some contemporary Babylon: downsizing, a war zone, a child's illness, the nursing home. Experiences of that kind tempt me to become very, very angry.

Jeremiah seems to understand things differently—God offers no guarantee against exile; indeed, God often finds our good works misguided and our vision of a blessed future to be self-serving idolatry. God's vision for our future apparently differs from ours, and the prophet has advice for us: "Seek the welfare of the city where I have sent you into exile" or, in other words, "Live in the future I've given you." It's a command and a blessing, a statement that it is our duty and our hope to thrive, to build a life not based on what we believed was owed us. It's a promise that God can build hope and meaning even when what we expected is taken from us.

God's judgment is always part of God's grace; exile can be liberation; defeat can be the greatest victory; the future we had most hoped to avoid could be the source of joy beyond our imagining.

PRAYER: Holy God, remind us that faithfulness allows and requires us to give up our outrage when your rewards don't meet our expectations. Keep us mindful that grace abounds, even in this future we did not choose. Amen.

Hearts, Minds, Love

October 15–21, 2007 • Sudarshana Devadhar[‡]

MONDAY, OCTOBER 15 • Read Jeremiah 31:27-34

God speaks through the prophet Jeremiah to Judah and its neighbors during the turbulent times of its history both politically and religiously. Jeremiah comes as a prophet of comfort. Through Jeremiah God assures the people of Israel that after exile will come restoration. God will establish a new covenant. Unlike the old covenant on stone tablets, God promises a new covenant "in their minds and . . . on their hearts." God will not pass the sins of one generation on to the next or punish one group of people for the sins of another.

As I reflect on this passage, I am disturbed by the recent attitude of some so-called Christians or "religious" people who blame folks of a particular region for causing the recent natural catastrophes in Southeast Asia and in some parts of the United States because of these people's sins. God of the new covenant reminds us that we all assume responsibility for the consequences of our actions and sins; God will not pass punishment on innocent people. In order to guide and help us in our faith journeys, God will place the law in our minds and write it on our hearts. We need simply apply the law of God in our day-to-day dealings. People will know God through us or in spite of us. Our actions bear witness to the new covenant that others may see.

PRAYER: Creator God, help me, with the power of the Holy Spirit, to demonstrate your laws through my daily living. Hear my prayer, in the precious name of our Lord and Savior, Jesus Christ. Amen.

[‡]Bishop, New Jersey Area, The United Methodist Church; living in Ocean, New Jersey.

Much earlier than Jeremiah's prophecy, the psalmist's words attest to his love for the law, the law called by many names. According to the translation in the New International Version, the laws are also called "commands," "statutes," "precepts," and "word." The psalmist clearly loves all of them.

The psalmist offers several reasons for loving the law of God. One is because laws are sweet and powerful. In expressing the nature of its sweetness, the psalmist compares the law to honey. Let me hasten to say that I am not an expert on honey. However, I understand that the sugar content of honey is ideal for health, and the taste of the honey differs from place to place depending upon the kind of flowers available to the bees. Therefore, the psalmist uses the metaphor of honey to describe the nature of God's law—ideal for our health and well-being and suited to our particular needs.

When I was in graduate school, a professor used to say that students write only two kinds of papers that professors read: one is work and the other pleasure. Is God's law for us work or pleasure? Is it like tasting honey?

Second, the laws of God exert power. They make us wiser than our enemies and bless us with understanding. The psalmist does not talk about knowledge but wisdom. In this age the world supplies us with all kinds of knowledge through an abundance of sources, but wisdom is not a natural by-product of the world's knowledge. Our wisdom comes from a passionate commitment to God and living and practicing the law in our daily lives.

PRAYER: God of Wisdom, help me follow your laws so that I may become a blessing to others. Hear my prayer, in the precious name of our Lord and Savior, Jesus Christ. Amen.

Yesterday we reflected upon the love of the psalmist for God's law and the sweetness and the power of that law. When we say we love someone, we demonstrate that love not only through our words but through our actions. One of the ways in which we show our love for the law of God is by meditating upon it constantly. Meditation can be silent as well as verbal.

Biblical scholars believe that applying the law to one's daily life played an important role in postexilic spirituality. According to research done by Sara Lazar at Massachusetts General Hospital, people who meditate on a regular basis can thicken their cerebral cortex, which is central to memory. No wonder the psalmist is passionate about the divine laws and the importance of our meditating on them daily. In the prescientific society of the psalmist, meditation on the law all day long was the bastion of all wisdom. In an age without computers, meditating on the law became the school of divinity.

What is the focus of our waking hours? In what ways do we demonstrate our love of God and love for God's laws? Can we confidently state, as did the psalmist, that we have not departed from the laws of God?

If researchers believe a few hours of meditation will help us thicken our cortex and improve memory, how much would our spirits benefit by daylong meditation on the laws of God? Where is the place of meditation in our daily lives? How may we saturate this day with the wisdom of scripture?

Pastors and leaders of churches are constantly bombarded with church-growth materials and information to grow congregations. However, all the information we receive is fruitless unless we can discern the divine wisdom that comes through meditation on the divine law.

PRAYER: Creator of Order, help me to meditate constantly on your law. Hear my prayer, in the precious name of our Lord and Savior, Jesus Christ. Amen.

Even though the debate continues about the true author of this letter, whether it is Paul or not, one thing is clear. The writer expresses enthusiastic commitment to spreading the gospel of Jesus Christ. Paul speaks of the significance of Christian nurture and teaching. The first chapter of this letter refers to the importance of Lois and Eunice, grandmother and mother of Timothy. The mention of these ties reminds us of the value of Christian formation of children. Then the epistle fosters our awareness of the need for wise choices and faithfulness to our beliefs.

"Continue in what you have learned and firmly believed, knowing from whom you have learned it, and how from childhood you have known the sacred writings that are able to instruct you for salvation through faith in Christ Jesus." While Timothy learned stories of faith as a child, Paul urges him to remain steadfast in the face of present temptations. When temptations come, we often fall back on the faith stories we heard in childhood for the inspiration and motivation we need to face them. Who told you stories of faith when you were a child? Pause now and thank God for those who taught you and helped your faith to form.

Paul directs Timothy to teach, making the point that scripture is useful for teaching and for training. In a sense, Paul challenges Timothy to become the spiritual parent and grandparent to the next generations. He can communicate God's love and grace with "the utmost of patience in teaching." As you thank God for those who nurtured your early faith, also give thanks to God for those whom you nurture. In a world where child abuse and conflict seem to rule, the church offers a countercultural message of love and hope. May God nudge us to teach the stories of faith and become spiritual parents and grandparents to others.

PRAYER: Nurturing God, help me to become a spiritual mentor to others. Hear my prayer, in the precious name of our Lord and Savior, Jesus Christ. Amen.

Pause for a moment to think about people who have pastored you. How did you gauge the effectiveness of these pastors? Would the words of today's passage serve as a guide for these servants?

These verses sound like an ordination sermon, which is an appropriate way to address a young disciple, particularly in the conflict faced by the early church both within the culture at large and in the theological debates of that time. Here the voice of wisdom addresses youth. After speaking of the presence of God and the reign of Christ, Paul urges readers to proclaim the message, to persist in preaching that message by a variety of means, and to teach. Paul concludes by insisting on soberness, endurance, and witness.

Whether or not we are ordained clergy, the words of Paul find their way into our understanding of Christian discipleship because these verses speak to our common vocation to live as Christians. We proclaim the message of God's grace by our deeds—often more effectively than any sermon. When we extend ourselves in hospitality to a stranger or when we visit one in prison, we proclaim the redeeming love of Christ. When we continue each day to pray for those who persecute us or who are our enemies, we persist in the vocation to become like Christ. Our lives model or teach the love of Christ.

Some days challenge our persistence. Some situations challenge our purpose and endurance. Sometimes cultural values seemingly overcome the way of Christ. In these times we need to remember again the witness of older and wiser Christian disciples and how these remained faithful in times of challenge. As we live in the kingdom of God and anticipate the complete reign of God, the charge continues for us to witness persistently for the sake of Christ.

PRAYER: Steadfast God, help us to proclaim your love in all circumstances and seasons. In the mercy of Christ Jesus. Amen.

A New Testament professor of mine, Dr. H. K. Moulton, used to say, "Parables are earthly stories having a heavenly meaning." In this parable, Jesus tells about the need to persist in our prayers without losing heart. Prayer provides a tool by which we connect with God for ministry and mission in the world. Lifting prayer to the Lord differs from submitting a laundry list; we actually submit *ourselves* to the will of God. Prayer strengthens our faith and energizes us to participate actively in extending God's reign on earth.

Mother Teresa's unceasing activity on behalf of the poor always amazed me. One secret of her success was her dependence on prayer. She always attended morning and evening prayers at the headquarters of the Sisters of Charity in Calcutta when she was in town. Her prayer life was intensely connected to her daily life and ministry. A reporter once asked how the chapel participants did not allow the sounds from the noisy street to distract them. Mother Teresa explained that it is in the midst of all the needs of the world that we raise our voices to God.

Prayer is persistent conversation with God in the midst of daily activity. As faithful disciples of Jesus Christ, we put into action the words we use in prayer. Before the collapse of the Berlin Wall, people on both sides prayed that it would fall. Prayer is the foundation for church growth in Korea. Persistent prayer changes things in mighty ways everywhere in our world.

PRAYER: Listening God, help me to be persistent and not lose heart in my prayer life. Hear my prayer, in the precious name of our Lord and Savior, Jesus Christ. Amen.

Jesus tells this parable of the persistent widow who has a difficult place in Palestinian society. The laws of the land do not favor people like her; society tended to ignore widows, and, to some extent, they were "nobodies" in that society. When she seeks justice, the judge who hears her case has no fear of God and certainly does not care about what society thinks. Here stands a powerless widow before a powerful judge. The judge yields to her because of her persistence. In this passage the judge says, "I will see that she gets justice, so that she won't eventually wear me out with her coming" (NIV). Prayer is the tool of the powerless.

When I started my ministry in India, the church that I served wanted to install an extra pipeline to the parsonage. The local municipality officer had to give special permission because this pipeline would go under the main road in the town. The leaders of the church kept telling me that because Christians were a minority and the municipality officer was a Hindu, we would probably not get permission. During that time of petitioning, I told the church leaders to give themselves over in prayer to God so that God might convince the officer to grant permission. The day I submitted the application, the officer was so busy that he signed it without reading a word. Praise the Lord! To me it was an answer to prayer.

I am sure that, like me, you have seen God answer your prayers and do miraculous things because you asked in prayer. Prayer gives power to the powerless.

PRAYER: Responding God, help me depend on the power of prayer. Hear my prayer, in the precious name of our Lord and Savior, Jesus Christ. Amen.

In God's Own Time

October 22–28, 2007 • James C. Van Der Wall[‡]

MONDAY, OCTOBER 22 • Read Psalm 65

Psalm 65 expresses thanks for rain, which in the dry climate of the Middle East is seen as a blessing from God. People pray for rain so they can irrigate their crops, so that the harvest will be abundant, so that the community can be fed, so that neighbors can enjoy a comfortable existence side-by-side with one another. It is easier to live peacefully when the community experiences abundance rather than scarcity. The psalmist makes three assertions:

We are grateful to God for listening to our prayers. Will God hear and respond to our prayer for rain? Sometimes we feel that God simply can't respond to our needs. Can God, invisibly tucked away in heaven, do anything about the broken relationship in our life? Yes, affirms the psalmist! God does send rain to water the arid portions of our lives.

We acknowledge that God has the power to deliver us. It is an act of faith to pray for precipitation. God sends what we need when we need it. Looking at our prayer life in retrospect, we usually discover that to be the case. God listens and responds to our prayers, delivering rain to our areas of greatest need—in God's time, not on our predetermined schedule.

We celebrate God's action in our lives. Prayer is not a pious addition to events that would have happened anyway. It is a force that allows events to occur that never would have occurred without prayer. God hears our cry! God sends the rain! And for that we are thankful.

SUGGESTION FOR MEDITATION: Pray that God might water the arid portions of your life.

[‡]Senior pastor, St. Paul's United Methodist Church, Wilmington, Delaware.

Abundant harvests. Streams filled with water. Soil softened for planting by the rain. Psalm 65 describes the beauty that results when God waters the earth. For this gift of creation we all shout and sing together for joy! We moderns complain about the rain and the temporary discomfort it causes, but rain is a time for celebration. The renewing waters are essential to our survival.

Whenever I pray publicly and it is raining, I usually pray in this way: "Lord, we thank you for the rain. It reminds us that you are constantly looking out for us, caring for us, and providing what we need. For that we are grateful."

From the start, God parented us, providing what we needed. Eden, a lush garden with abundant fruit, supplied all our needs. There the Creator and the created lived together in harmony. God watered the earth, made it beautiful, and offered it to us as a gift. We destroyed this heavenly treasure and fractured the relational harmony through our sinful behaviors. For this we repent, even as we acknowledge the wonderful possibilities for life that God offers.

God does not always provide rain when we think it should fall. So we wait with patience for the rain and for the beauty of God's creation to emerge again from the ground. Waiting for God to provide the necessary resources is part of the deal of being created not Creator. We need to wait for life to reveal its meaning to us, not knowing when this meaning will become clear. We wait for rain with hope, not sure when our hope will be rewarded but unshakable in the conviction that one day our prayer for rain will be answered. Then the water will renew the earth, creating a beauty reminiscent of paradise.

SUGGESTION FOR MEDITATION: Look for a glimpse of paradise in the world today. How can you partner with God in encouraging that glimpse to grow and flourish?

For years, the Israelites lived as exiles, working as civil servants for their Babylonian captors. While sitting forlornly on the banks of the Euphrates River, they moan, "How can we sing the LORD's song in a foreign land?" Then the glorious day arrives when the captives are set free to return to Zion, their heritage and homeland. When they arrive home and see the deserted ruins of Jerusalem, they view their return as the answer to countless prayers. A little elbow grease will make their former habitat livable again.

But life back in Jerusalem is not trouble free. An invasion of locusts swarms the fields and destroys the crops. The people in discouragement say, "We received our punishment from God through years of exile. How much more of God's wrath must we experience?" With the cleansing autumn rains, a new crop emerges, locust-free. And the people are happy once again.

My wife is a postmaster. When we moved, her new commute to work was more than an hour. We hoped that she would receive a transfer closer to home, and that hope came to fruition when she was assigned to a postal facility just a few miles away. We felt certain our prayers were answered. Unfortunately that new position only lasted three months before she returned to her former office to deal with some problem issues. We were perplexed. How could this wonderful new job, which was obviously an answer to prayer, be taken away?

We may think that once we overcome a barrier, cosmic justice will not allow another obstacle to surface. But that is not necessarily so. After the exile and after the locust plague, new challenges would emerge. We can rest assured that having lived through the exile and having defeated the locusts, we can face any challenge. God's presence in our lives gives us that hope.

SUGGESTION FOR PRAYER: Pray for those experiencing setbacks in their lives.

The deliverance that Israel received from the plague of locusts assures the people that someday God will deliver the Jews from their current postexilic plight. Someday spiritual renewal will come. Someday Israel will rise up as the nation that will reveal God to the entire world. This is good news for returned exiles who need to receive strength and hope from beyond themselves.

The prophet Joel talks about the future, when "the great and terrible day of the LORD comes." The "day of the LORD" will occur when God does away with all that is contrary to the divine will and ushers in the final, permanent reign of peace, love, and justice. But that day has not yet arrived.

My son's college graduation and birthday coincided. As a gift to mark those occasions, we traveled to Ground Zero in New York City, the site of the destroyed World Trade Center. Upon our arrival, we found ourselves deeply moved by the barrenness of the site. What was once the hub of the world's commerce was now an empty lot filled with rubble. It was sobering to recall the death and destruction that a small group of people generated. As I viewed the lot, I realized that the "day of the LORD" has not yet arrived. Yet among the ruins, reminiscent of the days of Joel, the machinery of repair and renewal was at work hauling away the old and readying the site for its future.

The Bible begins with the words, "In the beginning, God ... " and concludes with the affirmation, "In the end, God." We can live confidently in the present, because we are assured of what the future holds.

Remember the future! Someday we will live in the New Jerusalem, confident that terrorists will not level our dwelling places. Someday God's spirit will be poured out freely, and the day of the Lord will arrive. In the end, God. And in the meantime, God.

SUGGESTION FOR MEDITATION: What can we do to help create a glorious future for others?

While in prison, Paul felt—rightly or wrongly—that some of his friends had deserted him. In those forlorn times he came to realize that his support, strength, and rescue was not limited to human sources. It could also come from the Lord.

The Red Bird Missionary Conference of The United Methodist Church is situated in one of the largest regions of poverty in America. Residents have minimal contact with people from the outside world—limited both by their poverty and by the inaccessible mountain terrain. My church work team spent a week there. One evening another participant related her experience with two young girls whose home had no running water. Consequently they had dirty hands and faces. The volunteer wanted to help clean them up, but the children were reluctant to let her do so. The woman had some wet towelettes, so she took them out and made up a game. She washed her hands and then invited the girls to wash their hands. The woman washed her face, and the girls followed suit. Noticing that the girls missed some dirt spots on their faces, the woman offered to clean them more thoroughly, and they agreed. As the trust level developed, the girls took off their shoes and socks and asked, "Will you wash our feet?" What a tender moment of contact.

Like Paul, many Red Bird residents feel isolated and shut off from the outside world. Missioners go to Red Bird to bring the presence of God to those who need to experience it. The church cannot forsake or forget those in need and still be the church. Paul, who didn't always feel that he received aid in times of distress, encourages Timothy to represent the power and strength of God, especially in situations of extreme need. We too hear the call to bring God's presence to those who feel isolated from it.

SUGGESTION FOR MEDITATION: **Whom do we need to visit?**

On his deathbed Paul declares that he has fought the good fight, finished the race, and kept the faith. Once a persecutor of Christians, he became the greatest of Christian missionaries. He spent much of his earthly existence making personal sacrifices in order to establish the church. God's grace, of which Paul was a recipient, assured the apostle that he would receive the "crown of righteousness" when he passed from this life to life eternal.

My grandparents departed the rural farmland of Groenegan, Holland, and arrived at Ellis Island to start a new life. They made personal sacrifices, working hard at menial jobs to provide a better future for their children and grandchildren.

When my father returned from Europe, after serving in World War II, he and Mom bought a house in suburban New Jersey. Dad worked two jobs to provide a stable life for our family. My parents reared five children whom they encouraged to become active contributors to society.

I am the person I am today because of those who preceded me. I appreciate my grandparents' leap of faith. As my siblings and I read the letters Dad sent to Mom from Europe, we understand the hopes and dreams they shared: a life together unmarred by war, a house of their own, and children who attended church with them.

At the time of his departure, Paul affirms his readiness to meet the Lord. He has established the church throughout the known world, written letters that would become scripture, and promoted the theological principle of grace.

My grandparents and parents were not perfect. They, like Paul, were people who needed God's grace. But in their own way they fought the good fight, finished the course, and kept the faith. I try to live so that someday I can declare, while acknowledging God's grace in my life: "I have fought the good fight."

SUGGESTION FOR MEDITATION: What can I do to make the world a better place?

Two men go into the Temple to pray. The Pharisee reminds God that he is better than others—not a thief, unjust, an adulterer, or even a tax collector. The Pharisee extols his virtues of fasting and tithing, yet his self-righteousness belies his claims. His religion creates a chasm between himself and others, rather than creating a bridge.

The tax collector prays, "God, be merciful to me, a sinner," a prayer that demonstrates great self-understanding. Only God can raise him out of his condition. God takes the first hint of our repentance, adds generous doses of mercy, and with that second chance creates in us the ability to become new people.

Every other weekend, one father faithfully brought his children to Sunday school, waited in his vehicle during class time, and then drove them home. I went out to talk to the parent, inviting him to participate in an adult class. He graciously replied, "You don't know me, but the people around here do. You don't really want someone with my reputation to come to your church." I knew his reputation. I also knew he could greatly benefit from the influence of the church. Church people are blessed because they receive God's forgiveness and mercy.

Sunday after Sunday, I went out to speak to him. If he wouldn't come into the church, I was determined to bring the church out to him. We struck up a relationship that finally allowed him to be comfortable enough to come inside to an adult class. Gradually he came to understand the role of God's mercy in his life, which enabled him to participate in the life of the church. The stigma of his past gave way to the power of God's amazing grace, God's second chance. God was merciful to him, a sinner, and he took advantage of God's grace. Shouldn't we do the same?

SUGGESTION FOR MEDITATION: **Pray for those who need to allow the power of God's mercy to transform their lives.**

The Tensions of Faith

October 29–November 4, 2007 • Bruce A. Mitchell[‡]

MONDAY, OCTOBER 29 • Read Habakkuk 1:1-4

It's happened to most of us at one time or another. We purchase a product or a service, try to use it, and discover it does not measure up to our expectations. We return to the supplier, asking for a refund or cancellation of a service. Customer service doesn't seem to care. Finally, in frustration, we ask, "May I speak with a supervisor, please?"

The prophet Habakkuk appears to face a similar situation involving a three-way relationship among Habakkuk, God, and the people of God. Habakkuk, a man of faith, isn't so much raising questions about his *own* relationship with God as expressing concern about the people of God. Habakkuk has probably filed all his concerns and complaints with the leaders of the land and now has decided to carry the question to the Senior Complaint Supervisor: God.

Most of us grumble about why bad things happen to good people in our world and time. We seek solutions to evil and strife—and find we can't solve the problems by ourselves.

Then, as in the case of Habakkuk, we get frustrated because God doesn't seem to step forward with an obvious solution. Perhaps we think that God isn't listening—or that God doesn't care. But the miracle of God's presence is that God *does* hear us and *does* respond—perhaps not the way we expect or within our time frame. God does respond to our prayers and concerns. Like Job, Habakkuk believes that God hears and cares.

PRAYER: Lord God, I've tried every way I can to solve the problems surrounding me; in a spirit of faith, I turn them over to you. Amen.

[‡]Retired from the Florida Conference of The United Methodist Church, serving as pastor of Whittemore United Methodist Church, Whittemore, Michigan.

Tuesday, October 30 • Read Habakkuk 2:1-4

As I was growing up, I often saw a young man in town afflicted with polio; he could not walk and got around in a wheelchair. He could have easily bemoaned his condition. However, he never let his limitations stop him; he had a deep Christian faith. I'm sure he often prayed, perhaps for release from his affliction. God didn't seem to answer immediately—or in the way this young man expected.

As time passed, the young man discovered he could coach from his wheelchair—and I'd see his wheelchair moving back and forth along the sidelines as he shouted out encouragement to the boys on his team. As he did this, his face radiated a great sense of joy.

This young man waited a significant amount of time for God's sense of direction and, though it may have taken some time for the answer to be revealed, eventually God's direction for his life became obvious and the young man responded.

This seems to be Habakkuk's experience as he seeks God's intercession for the people who, like those surrounding Moses centuries before, occasionally lose faith and begin to turn away from God's guidance. Habakkuk makes a request and then stands ready for an answer from God.

In today's world we sometimes suffer preoccupations similar to those of the people surrounding Habakkuk. God has prophets in the world today, and humanity sometimes doesn't recognize or respond to them. At times God seems to be slow in answering our prayers, and sometimes God even seems to say no. That's where patience and faith fit in—God responds in God's good time and in God's own way. The Holy One responds even when we might not recognize the fact. Those who ask and stand ready for an answer finally receive. When the final scores are totaled, the individual who remains faithful to God, like my wheelchair-bound friend, is victorious.

PRAYER: Give me faith to trust in you, O God. And give me the patience to wait for your answer. Amen.

The Bible is packed with stories of individuals tested by God — tested so severely, in fact, that you wonder why they don't turn their backs on God. What keeps them from asking, "What's the use? God doesn't hear my prayers, and maybe even doesn't care about me anymore."

One of the media world's heroes was Superman. In my early high-school years I looked forward to every Superman comic book that came along. In more recent years we came to know another "superman"—the actor, Christopher Reeve, a person who exemplified the way a human being can meet and deal with tragedy in a positive way.

We all saw Christopher Reeve as a victim of a tragic accident, who lived the last portion of his life as a quadriplegic. Yet, despite his physical limitations, Christopher Reeve set an example for many people struggling with life. He said one time that "a hero is an ordinary individual who finds the strength to persevere and endure in spite of overwhelming obstacles."

Another person who has inspired thousands is Joni Eareckson Tada who became a quadriplegic as a result of a swimming accident. She struggled with God about her disability and eventually became one of God's greatest witnesses to overcoming infirmity. I enjoy painting landscapes, yet I cannot imagine what it would be like to draw or paint holding a brush, pen, or pencil in my mouth. Yet Joni has done just that, producing incredibly beautiful works of art that testify to the greatness of God.

Though we sometimes forget it or ignore the fact, we need to be reminded from time to time that we all face challenges of varying degrees. Even in the worst of times, God offers the greatest strength to the weakest individual. God gives us "understanding that [we] may live."

PRAYER: God, give me faith and strength for the moment. Amen.

ALL SAINTS DAY

"The holy ones of the Most High shall receive the kingdom and possess the kingdom forever." Who are these holy ones, these saints? By definition a saint is a person whose life and deeds reflect the life and deeds of Jesus. Thus, those who surrounded Jesus in his immediate ministry on earth have earned sainthood.

Beyond this, who are the saints? Might it be the woman in a small church who was always there to serve and care? Might it be the person who promoted mission teams to help in hurricane-devastated communities? Could it be the persons we meet on the street who exhibit a caring and loving attitude to all they meet? Could it be the neighbor who is terminally ill but reflects consistent hope for the future? Or, might it be the person who serves Christ in various ways but never looks for recognition?

If all these persons qualify as holy ones, then we've known a few saints in our daily lives. I know I have. Time and again I have reflected on the faithful, the unselfish, the loving, the serving people I've met over the years who sought no recognition but rejoiced in simply living life to the fullest, trying their best to reflect the example of Christ.

They did not seek out sainthood; if you asked them, they would probably reply, "I believe you are thinking of someone else." Without intent but in their acceptance of the call of Christ, they have found sainthood in the eyes of God.

We may ponder the "interpretation of the matter," but the holy ones have chosen a lifestyle of servanthood, and their heartfelt and joyful commitment to Christ counts.

PRAYER: Touch my heart, Lord, that I may celebrate your call to servanthood. Amen.

A few miles beyond our northeastern Michigan retirement home, in the midst of a dense forest, stands a small church. Built in 1862, it has continually served Native Americans from the Chippewa tribe for almost 150 years.

The congregation was much larger years ago; but over time the people from the area, seeking better jobs and higher income, have migrated away from this beautiful area. Though today the church is still an Indian Mission congregation, it has opened its door in welcome to others—neighboring farmers, representatives of other ethnic groups, and folks from town who seek a peaceful place to worship God.

I'd like to think that it's the kind of congregation Paul might have corresponded with. Perhaps he would have celebrated the so-called "little" events accomplished within its walls through the outreach of that small church. I think the epistle writer would have relished hearing the joys and sorrows of that congregation. It's not a place filled with strife and conflict—it is a church that strives to maintain traditions of the past while celebrating its role in ministry in the world today. This congregation, in its own way, reflects the grace and peace mentioned in today's reading.

More often than not, pastors in our era move from church to church. Though admonished to leave church members to their successors, many pastors still receive letters from folks they have pastored before—and they often respond. Not to emphasize, influence, or dictate directions for the church but to offer encouragement and Christian love to friends.

Perhaps the New Testament epistles exist for this very reason: to remind congregations large and small that God loves them and that God's grace is theirs through Jesus Christ. These letters, without exception, express a powerful witness and love of the Father and the Son.

PRAYER: **Make me humble enough, Lord, that others will see you through me. Amen.**

We all go through times of trial as a nation, in the workplace, in our personal lives. We experience trials in the church, and that is what the writer addresses in this letter to his friends in Thessalonica. He wants them to know that he hasn't forgotten them—nor has God.

At a particular time in my life I found prayer hard to understand and even harder to do. My wife and I team-taught a lively group of sixth graders, and it usually fell my lot to present the lesson. As the class ended, I would turn to my wife and ask her to offer the closing prayer. Weeks turned into months, and it became a routine.

That seemed to work well until one of the students came up to me and asked, "Why is it you never offer the prayer?"

It took a while—longer than I like to think of—to realize that we, claiming to be Christians, might try to serve God without communicating with God. If that's the case, how do we listen for what God is trying to share with us?

The writer of this epistle not only ministers, but he prays fervently and expectantly—not simply for himself and his own interests but for the ministry of Christ and the scattered churches that have gotten started. He follows up and sounds people out, asking, "How goes it with the church in Thessalonica?"

Prayer for the total ministry of Christ is typical of the deep concern the writer has for the church. He does not pray for church survival but for an openness and response to God's call to ministry. He prays with concern but expectantly as well.

PRAYER: Dear God, we ask your power to pray not only for ourselves but for every being around us. Amen.

Over the years my wife and I have made a number of pilgrimages to the Holy Land. We departed the first time with mixed emotions related to safety, but that first trip produced a spiritual awakening in us. Every trip thereafter brought a new experience of the Bible and the people within it.

During each tour, we visited Jericho, now under Palestinian control. Our guide would point out a sycamore tree in downtown Jericho, reminding us of Jesus and Zacchaeus and how a man of short physical stature became larger than life as he chose to follow Jesus.

We've all had moments in life when we couldn't see the passing parade. Maybe someone had to lift us up high enough to see over the crowd or, as in the case of Zacchaeus, we had to climb a tree to see.

Maybe we've followed the parade or been part of the parade itself. However, has any of us ever had the parade marshal leave the parade route to take us by the hand and ask to eat at our house? Would that parade marshal have taken us by the hand if we were a known criminal or the most hateful person in town? That's what Jesus does with Zacchaeus, an unpopular man in Jericho. In today's world, we can easily insulate ourselves from those who make us feel uncomfortable or who do not fit our mold. Yet, if Jesus were walking in our town, where would we find him?

In my town Jesus might join the gathering each morning at the post office or at the grain elevator. He might be up the road a piece at a restaurant, sharing morning coffee and doughnuts. However, you might also find him at one of the bars or the homeless center. As the Gospel of Luke reminds us, "The Son of Man came to seek out and to save the lost." As Christians, do we not have the same responsibility?

PRAYER: **Help us, Lord, to accept the least of us, for that is what Jesus would do. Amen.**

God's Faithfulness

November 5–11, 2007 • Carmichael D. Crutchfield[‡]

MONDAY, NOVEMBER 5 • Read Haggai 1:15b–2:9

May 3, 2003, was a devastating day for the people of Jackson, Tennessee. A tornado completely destroyed several church edifices along with other property. As I write more than two years later, three downtown churches have not yet been completely restored. I cannot imagine the feelings of people sixty years after the destruction of the Temple. It's not surprising to hear cynicism and disappointment even though the work has begun on the rebuilding project. We can easily understand why some of the older members of the community have few good comments about the new structure they see emerging; they remember the former Temple. The prophet silences the complainers by challenging them to have confidence in what God is about to do.

Sometimes we become dissatisfied and complain. Yet we need to view our situation truthfully and look for the positive aspects. Sometimes the best we can do is encourage ourselves and others to place confidence in God.

Haggai seems to give a new resolve to the people. He uses positive exhortation with the words "take courage" and "do not fear." He employs an attitude that disregards the negative and encourages the continuance of the work at hand.

When we grow discouraged and disappointed in life, it behooves us not to dwell on the negative but to continue with the tasks before us.

PRAYER: God of faithfulness, help us be honest about our life situations and remain positive in our confidence in your promises. May we always look to you as we work for good so that we may not grow weary. Amen.

[‡]General Secretary, department of Christian education, Christian Methodist Episcopal Church; living in Jackson, Tennessee.

I still recall my then four-year-old son's response to a question addressed to a group of adults: "Ask my Daddy. He knows everything." Children often think their parents are invincible and have all knowledge. In truth, sometimes the best that parents can do is to admit to the mystery of the unknown and the limitations of our understanding.

The Sadducees, a Jewish group that does not believe in resurrection, design their question to reduce belief in resurrection to meaninglessness. However, their inquiry gives Jesus an opportunity to teach about post-resurrection relationships versus those in the present life. In typical style Jesus grounds the doctrine in the Law of Moses with which the Sadducees are familiar. Moses attests that the Lord is the God of the patriarchs Abraham, Isaac, and Jacob; therefore, "God is not of the dead, but of the living."

Yes, some questions remain a mystery to us. Job asked, "If mortals die, will they live again?" (14:14). Others have made quests to know if life exists beyond death. We cannot ignore the question, but we cannot answer either from reason or experience. It is a valid inquiry: Is there life beyond death and, if so, what will it be like?

We do not have the answer, but death takes on new meaning when we have some grasp of the doctrine of resurrection. We do not die to God but live to God. God remains the source of life for the faithful. Even in death we can trust God's faithfulness.

PRAYER: God, thank you for mystery. In the mystery and the unknown we find ourselves trusting even more in your love. Amen.

In two short verses the writer of Second Thessalonians indicates a strong movement in the early church related to those who believe that the "day of the Lord is already here." The reports of this movement shock the church, and the fallout of the shock endures.

False claims about God and the end of time have been a source of unrest for many people throughout church history. These claims continue to come by spirit, word, and letter. Probably today more than any time in the history of Christianity we hear these false claims. While present from the inception of the church, these claims travel much faster with current technology.

Some claims, although false, can do great damage and carry much weight. What makes nontruths so potent is that they sometimes masquerade in a garment of truth. We cannot always discern falsehood when it comes in the name of science or when it claims the superiority of some people and the inferiority of others. The falsehoods may even come in the name of religion and morality, from church leaders who claim to have the final answer.

How do we protect ourselves? Do not be gullible to anything that is loveless and hateful. Do not stand by for injustice practiced in the pulpit or pew. Bank on friendships that stand the test of time.

Christians are called to be bold and courageous, not "quickly shaken in mind or alarmed." At the appropriate time we will indeed be "gathered together to him."

PRAYER: God of faithfulness, may we rely on your timing to know "the day" and your vision to discern truth from nontruth. Amen.

Saudi Arabia, Vietnam, Iraq, Indonesia, Myanmar, Kazakhstan, Turkmenistan and India—just a few of the places in the world where Christians face persecution in the twenty-first century. The people of these locations bear witness to 2 Timothy 3:12: "Indeed, all who want to live a godly life in Christ Jesus will be persecuted."

When have you found yourself at the point of despair, all hope gone? In your circle of friends and acquaintances, who lives daily in an overwhelming sense of despondency? What churches or congregations seem to be on the brink of hopelessness?

How are we as individuals and faith communities to respond in desperate situations? One immediate response may be that of defeatism. We simply give up and acknowledge there is no reason to try any longer. Another response I have experienced is that of denial. This hedonistic approach may revolve around mind-altering chemicals, indulging in self-absorbing events (computer games or virtual-reality television programs) or becoming self-centered and getting sucked into materialism and consumerism.

The epistle writer sends an encouraging and assuring word to a people familiar with persecution from many fronts. He recommends a third option: looking at the big picture of God's work in the world. Advocating neither a pessimistic defeatism nor an attitude of denial, he suggests that current events will be better understood against the backdrop of God's work in the world. What we see today depicts but a small piece of God's activity. The full picture has not yet been revealed by God, but each brushstroke makes it clearer.

Prayer: O God, thank you for filling in the brushstrokes of the big picture. May we fall prey neither to defeatism nor denial. Amen.

One benefit of working in Christian education is that I often find myself in arenas where people raise interesting and much-needed questions. One concern that I often hear voiced is the seeming loss of our young people: Why do our children leave our denomination or the church altogether when they come of age? Perhaps we could ask in return why our churches fail to reach out in appropriate and creative ways to this group.

The writer of Second Thessalonians tells the people to stand firm and hold on—a great exhortation given the persecution and the evil circulating in their world. Moreover, sources that seem reputable are clothing falsehood in truth and promoting it as truth. Some teachers predict that the second coming of Christ will happen soon; others suggest that the church should wait passively for that return. Conflict built upon conflict, and the questions unsettled everyone in Thessalonica.

So how do they and we stand firm and hold on? The writer says to hold on to the traditions taught by word of mouth or by letter. The strong potential for discouragement requires that we do so. The writer stresses the faith community's commitment to truth and proclamation of the good news.

The people of our church today, young and old, have the potential of being discouraged by our conflicts. The danger is even greater if we have no firm foundation on which to stand. Maybe we have been too preoccupied with external matters at the expense of internal matters. When we fail to build a strong foundation, standing firm and holding on becomes impossible.

The church needs to teach the traditions and history of faith, which build the internal structure of our lives. This exhortation encourages comforting and strengthening the heart (the inner) rather than the external (the outer) being.

PRAYER: God of faithfulness, strengthen us internally so we can withstand the external forces that try to dissuade us from our faith. Amen.

Notice the superscription of "Praise" (NRSV) for Psalm 145, the only psalm with such designation. The word *praise* in the title sets the tone for the entire psalm.

Psalm 145 contains several literary patterns, the first one in the first five verses. Verses 1 and 2 utter announcements of praise, and verse 3 describes God's character as unsearchable greatness. Verses 4 and 5 give us a glimpse of what we understand about God's unsearchable greatness. The pattern of these verses is repeated later.

We praise God because of God's unsearchable greatness, which, according to the psalmist, is found in God's sovereignty. People connect the characteristic of greatness with God's reign. The words of verse 5, "glorious splendor of your majesty," are also associated with God's reign.

The psalmist testifies that we see God's mighty acts and wondrous works. The psalmist places all of this praise in the context of God's reign. The words *declare* and *meditate* can also connote telling.

Augustine of Hippo opened his *Confessions* with Psalm 145:3, 5. In that often-quoted opening paragraph, Augustine claims that because human beings are God's creation, we cannot experience contentment apart from praising God, "because you made us for yourself and our hearts find no peace until they rest in you."

Over my lifetime I have often wondered why my forebears spent so much time in church. I have concluded that they were seeking a deep contentment amidst all the trials and tribulations of life. To honor and adore God is our first calling, and in doing so we sense an abiding contentment. Praise the Lord!

PRAYER: God of faithfulness, teach us to praise and bless your name, thereby finding true contentment. Amen.

I grew up with a strong sense of God's protective gaze. I would often do daring things in the belief God was watching over me. I believe this feeling of God's protection came from the hymns that we sang in my church and that my grandmother sang in our home. Sunday school and worship were also faith-forming places.

As I have grown older I have come to realize that my grandmother could sing the songs of Zion because she had experienced God's compassion, grace, and love. Sunday school class helped me develop an appreciation for three words in particular. The first word is *compassion*. Throughout the Bible God sees a need and does something to alleviate the problem. In church I would hear echoes of compassion in the prayers of the church elders as they gave thanks for God's putting food on the table. I heard it in my father's prayers at meals as he thanked God for the food we were about to receive. The psalmist says, "The LORD is kind in all his doings."

The second word is *grace*. God is full of grace. I define grace as receiving what we do not deserve. Often we may think of grace as aligned with salvation, and that is true. But I think of grace as all of the places in life when I deserve something worse than I receive. A United Methodist bishop told a story about a person tipping a waiter generously when the service was less than adequate. He went on to say that God offers that kind of generosity. In the times when we least deserve it, God gives.

The last word is *love*. God's unconditional affection for us is steadfast. When the winds of life threaten, God's love sustains. "The LORD watches over all who love him."

PRAYER: God of faithfulness, "my mouth will speak the praise of the LORD, and all flesh will bless [your] holy name forever and ever." Amen.

Are We There Yet?

November 12–18, 2007 • J. Stephen Lang[‡]

MONDAY, NOVEMBER 12 • Read Isaiah 65:17-25; 11:6; 35:9

Those of us who are old enough to remember the lunar landing in 1969 may also remember the name Sea of Tranquility. I always liked this name for an area of the moon; while the moon seemed like a cold and forbidding place, Sea of Tranquility sounded like a desirable place to be—no conflict, no oppression, no violence, nothing but peace and comfort.

This week's scripture readings all have a future orientation. Thanks to human failings, there is no Sea of Tranquility on earth at present, no lasting peace and comfort. The prophet Isaiah looked forward to a time when no prey need run from predators. Instead, "the wolf and the lamb shall feed together" and no creature will "hurt or destroy" another. But such a state will not come about until God creates "new heavens and a new earth."

Isaiah's prophecies deeply moved the American artist Edward Hicks (1780–1849). A well-known Quaker preacher in his time, Hicks is remembered today for his numerous paintings with the title *The Peaceable Kingdom*, based on today's verses from Isaiah. The paintings depict animal predators in peaceful fellowship with creatures they would normally kill and devour, a sight never seen except in Hicks's imagination and in the mind of God, who keeps God's promises. Only on the "new earth" will predators—both animal and human—cease to be. Hicks's beautiful images do not reflect what *is* but what *will be*. Such promises can give us strength and hope in our troubled, violent age.

PRAYER: Eternal God, we thank you for your promises of a new world of peace and tranquility. Let your promises sustain us in this present world of turmoil and conflict. Amen.

[‡]Full-time author-editor; regular contributor to *Today's Christian*, *Christian History*, and *Discipleship Journal* magazines; living in Seminole, Florida.

"Oh, what a beautiful morning!" So opens one of the best-loved American musicals *Oklahoma!*, which has sent audiences home happy for more than fifty years. Oscar Hammerstein, who penned the lyrics for *Oklahoma!* and other theatrical classics, insisted he could not write lyrics that didn't have hope. An optimist, he focused more on the positive than on the negative. Most of us admire people with such an attitude. They seem to live sunnier lives and to be healthier in body and soul.

The Bible is, strictly speaking, an optimistic book. You won't find the word *optimism* in it, but you find the word *hope* again and again. For Christians the ultimate hope is eternity in fellowship with God and other people of faith. In the earliest days of Christianity, this proved to be a world-changing hope. Some historians believe a key reason for Christianity's triumph over pagan religions was its hope of a happy eternity, an endless hope.

In today's passage God speaks of creating new heavens and a new earth. The final verse of this passage echoes almost word for word God's promise in Isaiah 11:6-9 to a previous generation, a promise that will now come to fulfillment. The reference to the serpent takes us back to Eden and the point of disobedience.

The hope of a new creation puts everything else in perspective. We may hope for fame or riches or a beautiful spouse. Or, more modestly, we may hope for a comfortable home and a devoted spouse. But the earthly hopes seem small compared with the Grand Hope. If our earthbound hopes are deferred, and they often are, we need not suffer heartsickness permanently, for God has promised "an inheritance that is imperishable, undefiled, and unfading, kept in heaven" (1 Pet. 1:4).

PRAYER: Almighty God, you are Lord of past, present, and future. We thank you for the hope given to us in the words of your prophets, the hope for deliverance from all discord and unrighteousness. Amen.

When the twentieth century began, most people optimistically believed that human life was improving, that humankind was progressing in the right direction. The wonders related in the Bible were in doubt, but the wonders of science and technology were not. So the Bible's words about a dramatic return of Jesus to judge the earth struck many people as crude and quaint. Belief in heaven lost some of its appeal, since science seemed to promise a heaven on earth. But after two world wars and dozens of other bloody conflicts, the century became less optimistic. Humankind seemed to be taking a step backward for every step forward. Contrary to the optimists' belief, we weren't at all close to creating heaven on earth.

The twenty-first century seems no more promising. It literally began with a bang: the horrors of September 11, 2001. Persons may use science to heal disease but also to slaughter people. So perhaps the old teachings about heaven and Jesus' coming back to earth deserve another look.

The earliest believers in Jesus had a firm hope that he would return in glory—they just didn't know when. Jesus and the apostles emphasized that no one could predict the time; the writer of Second Thessalonians, like all the early believers, hoped Christ would return in his lifetime. But he scolds some of the Thessalonian Christians for becoming idlers and busybodies, apparently expecting fellow believers to support them while they wait. The message is sensible enough: keep one eye fixed on heaven, the other eye on your earthly life. Have faith in God, and keep working at your daily tasks. Since we cannot predict the time of Jesus' return, we must be ready at all moments.

PRAYER: Lord, teach us to value each moment of our earthly lives while we look forward to a greater life beyond. Amen.

Jesus' followers believe him to be the promised Messiah, the one chosen by God to bring spiritual (and perhaps political) deliverance. They assume that the "new age" will soon be ushered in, and naturally they want to know when. Jesus gives them no definite answer. The sinful world will come to an end, and the destruction of the mighty Jerusalem temple is one sign the "final age" has begun. What other signs will come? There will be prophets—false ones—claiming to be the Messiah and claiming the end is near. Jesus is not predicting the end of the world in his followers' lifetime, nor are they to heed anyone with such a message. Nor are they to be disheartened or terrified by wars, famines, earthquakes, pestilences, and other disasters.

Jesus counsels a rather tricky balancing act: know that the end time is assuredly "coming" yet not necessarily soon. Believers must wait and endure, content in the knowledge they are following Jesus' own sorrowful way of the cross. "Be patient" is hard advice to follow, especially when you don't have a definite date to focus on. But patience is easier when we rest secure in the knowledge that even when wars and other terrors occur, God is still in control and will not abandon God's people.

Almost two thousand years have elapsed since Jesus spoke these words, so we know something his original hearers did not know: the wars, terrors, false prophets, and other "signs" he spoke of are present in every age. In every century they remind the faithful that the end is coming—eventually. The end is always "near at hand"—not necessarily today or tomorrow, and yet it may happen within the lifetime of every believer. Watch, wait, and rest securely in God.

PRAYER: God, you alone are in control of this world and its destiny. Give us patience and hope as we endure the world's terrors, keeping us mindful of a better life ahead. Amen.

"All who want to live a godly life in Christ Jesus will be persecuted" (2 Tim. 3:12). These words echo those of Jesus in today's reading. Like Jesus, Christians have suffered throughout history. It begins in Acts: a mob stones to death the saintly Stephen, making him the first Christian martyr (Acts 7). The wicked ruler Herod executes James, one of the apostles with a sword, then slams the other apostles in prison (Acts 12). According to tradition, most of the apostles died for the faith.

In the pagan Roman empire, persecution was sometimes local and unofficial—mobs harassing people who shamed and infuriated them by holding to higher moral standards. Sometimes the emperors ordered the brutalities, such as the vile Nero, who had Christians crucified and torn to shreds by wild beasts.

The Roman emperor Constantine legalized Christianity in the year 312, but that did not end persecution completely. It has continued here and there throughout history. In the twentieth century, a supposedly enlightened and tolerant age, intolerance of Christians was the rule with the standard set by those who led the Russian Revolution in 1917. The new Communist regime set a goal of exterminating Christianity and all other religions. It did not succeed, but many innocent lives were lost.

Today many nations still employ anti-Christian tactics (physical abuse coupled with highly organized and efficient propaganda), but the persecuted saints of today have the same assurance as Christ's first apostles. Even if the persecutors seem to triumph in this world, God's faithful ones will survive and thrive throughout eternity. Oppressors may control the present, but the future belongs to God.

PRAYER: Lord, the path of your saints has been muddy and rough, yet you have sustained them with faith and hope. Keep us mindful of our spiritual brothers and sisters who endured persecution and are now glorified. Amen.

SATURDAY, NOVEMBER 17 • Read Isaiah 12:1-6

The book of Isaiah could be called the book of the Holy One, for Isaiah refers thirty-one times to God as "the Holy One of Israel." It first occurs in 1:14, where Isaiah contrasts his sinful nation with "the Holy One of Israel." Isaiah's famous vision in the Temple (chapter 6) is a revelation of the Holy One, making the prophet painfully aware of his own sinfulness.

According to the Bible, God is holy; and we aren't—an intimidating message, except that God still loves us and desires fellowship with us, now and forever. So today's scripture passage contains that delightful word *joy*. Religious people have a reputation—partly deserved, partly not—for being gloomy. You would never guess this from the Bible, which was conceived in joy and is a joy to read. Being in a right relationship with God and others brings joy. Persons who know where they stand with God can feel joy despite their circumstances, for they do not depend on externals.

Biblical joy differs from pleasure or amusement. It is enduring, for it is based not on the pleasant sensations of the moment but on the long view of things—enjoying the presence of God here and now but also looking forward to eternity.

Verse 4 contains the words "in that day," but Isaiah looks to the future, when no earthly worries or conflicts can take away joy. But the Bible assures us that heaven isn't just "later." Life lived in fellowship with God means that heaven already has begun. All the way to heaven is heaven.

PRAYER: Holy God, thank you for the joy we experience in this life and the promise of a greater joy in eternity. Amen.

My great-grandfather used to say, "If you want to make God laugh, tell God your plans." Human plans—so often rooted in selfishness and vanity—have a way of going awry, while God's own purposes will work themselves out according to divine plan.

Luke's Gospel correctly states that the Jerusalem temple "was adorned with beautiful stones." King Herod had built a magnificent temple, thanks to the spending (and taxing) of the people. Anyone who saw this stunning edifice would have thought it would stand for centuries—or forever. Certainly Herod assumed it would. It must have shocked Jesus' listeners to hear him prophesy that "not one stone will be left upon another." Yet this came to pass in the year 70 when the Romans quelled another Jewish rebellion. Herod passed into history, as did his monumental temple. Tyrants do not endure, nor do monuments.

Isaiah offers a sunnier prophecy. People will live long, full lives. They will make plans and not see them frustrated by oppressors. "They shall build houses and inhabit them. . . . They shall not build and another inhabit." In this future, oppression and exploitation will no longer exist. "They shall not labor in vain." Such is God's plan for the saints.

Authority and power have often attracted the lower elements of the human race. Throughout history, humankind has been bullied. People who hold power often use it to manipulate others. But Herod and his ilk pass away, while the saints who suffer in this life will thrive in eternity.

PRAYER: Eternal God, your purposes and promises stand sure. Teach us to hang our hearts upon your pledge of a brighter world. Amen.

Thanksgiving for God's Greatest Gift

November 19–25, 2007 • Eva Stimson‡

MONDAY, NOVEMBER 19 • Read Jeremiah 23:1-6

The prophet Jeremiah is not known for cheerfulness. Today we might describe him as a glass-half-empty kind of guy. The book of Jeremiah reflects the despair of a people exiled from their land and their God because of disobedience. The prophet blames the kings of Judah (the destructive "shepherds") for the plight of their people. By failing to lead the people in God's way, the kings have left the nation vulnerable to its enemies.

This passage begins with a taste of Jeremiah's usual gloom and doom: "Woe to the shepherds who destroy and scatter the sheep of my pasture! says the LORD." Yet by verse 3 the prophet begins to sound uncharacteristically upbeat. He looks beyond the exile to a time when God will return the people of Judah to their homeland and give them a wise and just leader. Today Christians recognize Jeremiah's description of the "righteous Branch" as a prophecy of the coming of Jesus Christ. Jesus, portrayed as the "good shepherd" in the Gospel of John, stands in strong contrast to the evil shepherds in Jeremiah.

This prophecy offers glimpses of God's greatest gift to the world. Jeremiah visualized this gift in concrete terms from his own experience—as a place of safety and deliverance from enemies and bad kings. We experience it as the salvation offered by Jesus Christ, who lovingly gathers us into his fold. Jeremiah's good shepherds in 23:4 resemble the God portrayed in Jesus' parable of the lost sheep in Luke 15, who is determined that none of the sheep "be missing." That is a cause for thanksgiving.

PRAYER: God, my shepherd, thank you for saving your people from the time of Jeremiah until today. Keep me in your fold forever. Amen.

---

‡Editor, *Presbyterians Today*, the magazine of the Presbyterian Church (U.S.A.); living in Louisville, Kentucky.

Zechariah has at least two good reasons to be thankful: (1) After years of childlessness, his wife, Elizabeth, has just given birth to their first son. (2) After being mute throughout Elizabeth's pregnancy, his speech has been restored.

Imagine yourself in Zechariah's situation. What would your first words be after nine months of enforced silence? Zechariah's first words are ones of praise. In loosening Zechariah's tongue, God also has opened Zechariah's eyes, giving him an even greater reason to give thanks. No longer is he the fearful doubter who wants proof that his wife can actually bear a son in her old age (Luke 1:8-20). Inspired by the Holy Spirit, he suddenly sees the events of his own life as part of a larger divine plan.

At the center of this plan is a "mighty savior" (or "horn of salvation" in the Greek text). Like the "righteous Branch" in Jeremiah 23:5, Zechariah's savior is a descendant of King David who will rescue God's people from their enemies so they "might serve [God] without fear." Both Zechariah and Jeremiah emphasize "righteousness"—just and holy living—as a by-product of the people's salvation.

While the Jeremiah prophecy is written in future tense, clearly looking toward events to come, Zechariah speaks in Luke 1 as though the events he describes have already happened. How can this be, since Jesus does not arrive on the scene until the following chapter?

This unusual choice of tenses reminds us that God is not limited by our sense of time. In God's time there is no past, present, and future. In Christ the whole world is already redeemed, even though we can't always see evidence of that reality.

PRAYER: God, give me the eyes of a prophet, so that I can see how my life fits into your unfolding plan of salvation. Give me the voice of a prophet, so I can share the good news that redemption is already here. Amen.

Preparing the way for a visiting dignitary is an important job. In today's world it means alerting the local police and press and checking the security of all public venues, as well as designing an itinerary and arranging for necessary meals and lodging.

Preparers of the way get little recognition. History rarely records their names. Their job is not to call attention to themselves but to help shine the spotlight on the one they serve.

Thanks to the Gospel of Luke, John the Baptist gets more attention than most other "advance" men. We learn his name, his parents' names, and a little bit of their stories. In Luke 1:76 Zechariah speaks almost reverently of his son, calling him "the prophet of the Most High." He charges John with giving "knowledge of salvation to his people by the forgiveness of their sins"—a heavy responsibility to lay on a newborn baby.

Yet isn't this the role all Christians are called to play? We can't save or forgive sins, but we can point people to Jesus, the Savior. We can share with others the joy of knowing that we are forgiven. Giving someone "knowledge of salvation" may move that person closer to an actual experience of God's saving power.

The Old Testament prophet Isaiah hears a call for someone to "prepare the way of the LORD" (40:3). In the poetic closing verses of his speech Zechariah echoes other passages from Isaiah. He describes salvation as the breaking dawn that chases away the shadows of night and death. His words make clear that salvation is active, not passive. The light comes not so we can sit and reach a state of enlightenment but so we can see where to step. God's light is intended to "guide our feet into the way of peace."

PRAYER: God of light, thank you for all those who have shared with me the knowledge of your salvation. Help me to prepare the way for someone else. Amen.

THANKSGIVING DAY, U.S. A.

Sometimes it's hard to be thankful, especially if you're a natural-born complainer. The Bible has its share of complainers. For example, the Hebrew people grumble constantly during their forty-year wilderness sojourn after Moses leads them out of Egypt. They have to be reminded over and over again how God has delivered them from bondage, has provided food and water for the journey, and is leading them to a promised land "flowing with milk and honey." God knew these people and their descendants would need help remembering to be thankful. So Deuteronomy 26 gives instructions for an annual "first fruits" ritual, celebrating God's deliverance and abundant provision.

The Gospel writers often portray the crowds that follow Jesus as wanting something from him: food, healing, signs, and miracles. Jesus has already fed the people described in John 6, but now they have come back for more. Instead of expressing humble gratitude for yesterday's gift of bread and fish, they confront Jesus with an attitude of entitlement with words to this effect: "Moses gave manna to our ancestors. The least you can do is give us another meal. Or even better, show us how we can 'perform the works of God' and miraculously produce food ourselves."

These folks are too busy making demands to realize that Jesus himself is the fulfillment of all their needs. He is the "true bread from heaven."

Psalm 100 and Philippians 4:4-9 suggest that thanksgiving is the biblical antidote to complaining. Both passages exhort believers to rejoice. Before bombarding God with requests, we thank God for the many gifts we have already received.

PRAYER: Thank you, O God, for all your amazing gifts, especially the gift of your presence. Amen.

Give thanks in all things. This theme runs through the Bible like a unifying thread. But it sounds way too glib to be practical.

Jesus' followers, watching the crucifixion of their Lord from the fringes, must have felt anything but thankful. Reading Luke 23:33-43 from a post-Resurrection perspective, we can hardly imagine what it must have been like for Jesus' disciples—a test of faith beyond what any of us will experience. Their whole world crumbles before them. They have left everything to follow this man, counting on him for their salvation. And now he is dying an ignominious and painful death on a cross between two criminals.

It would have been hard for the disciples to see any reason for hope in this apparent catastrophe. Christians today, on the other hand, have no difficulty finding the hope. We filter our understanding of this event through centuries of interpretation—in the New Testament writings, a succession of creeds and confessions, and the work of countless theologians.

On this side of the cross we understand the crucifixion as the ultimate example of God's ability to transform evil into good. Viewed as an isolated event, Jesus' death on the cross makes no sense; it has no redeeming value. But it stands out in the sweep of biblical history as a pivotal point in God's salvation plan.

How can we believe God is able to bring good out of the less-than-ideal circumstances of our lives? Look at the unexpected confession of faith that emerges from one of the criminals crucified next to Jesus. Unlike his colleague who taunts Jesus for being such a powerless Messiah, this man chooses to look beyond his suffering and believe in a good that can't yet be seen. Jesus rewards him with the promise of Paradise.

PRAYER: God, I choose to believe you love the world, even when I cannot see it. Thank you for accepting my halting attempts at faith. Amen.

One aspect I especially like about the congregation where I am a member is that the elders take seriously their responsibility to pray for the members. They spend a weekend at a nearby retreat center every winter, and at the end of the retreat they pray for each church member by name. Then they divide up the pages in the church directory, and each elder takes a list of people to pray for throughout the year. Every February or March my family receives a note from the elder who has us on his or her prayer list.

Knowing someone is praying for me gives my faith a boost on those days when it's hard just to get out of bed in the morning. Imagine how encouraging it must have been for the Christians in Colossae to receive the message of today's text. Paul (or, as some scholars believe, a church leader writing under Paul's name) is praying for these new believers, the letter says. And what a prayer it is!

The words ring out with confidence and authority, in keeping with the message. The writer prays for the Colossians to "be made strong" in God's "glorious power," to live boldly and joyously in the knowledge that God's power has already defeated the "power of darkness."

Looking back to the beginning of Colossians, we can see that this intercessory prayer flows out of a spirit of thanksgiving. The epistle writer reminds the Colossians, "In our prayers for you we always thank God" (v. 3). Likewise, the Colossians' strengthened faith should result in "joyfully giving thanks" to God. The principal reason for thanksgiving is God's "beloved Son," Jesus Christ.

SUGGESTION FOR PRAYER: **Colossians 1:12–14 is packed with powerful words that summarize the central themes of Christian faith: *inheritance, saints, light, rescue, redemption, forgiveness.* Choose one of these words for prayerful meditation. What concrete images does it bring to mind? What reasons for thanksgiving?**

In December 2004 an undersea earthquake triggered a tsunami that washed across coastal areas in Asia and Africa, sweeping people, animals, boats, and houses into the sea. In August 2005 Hurricane Katrina slammed into the Gulf coast, plunging New Orleans into chaos, provoking a massive exodus of displaced citizens and devastating portions of four states. And on Sept. 11, 2001, a day seared into the memory of most Americans, terrorists turned planeloads of innocent people into deadly weapons.

Catastrophes such as these cause many to wonder what kind of world we live in. Is there any kind of orderly pattern behind these seemingly random events? Is the universe good or evil?

These kinds of questions inspired the writing of Colossians 1:15–20. This eloquent affirmation of the supremacy of Christ in the universe is the centerpiece of the book of Colossians. New Testament scholars observe that the passage, structured like a hymn or confession, may have been used in early Christian worship. It is one of the first attempts to understand the life, death and resurrection of Jesus of Nazareth in terms of the cosmic Christ, in whom "all the fullness of God was pleased to dwell."

Because Christ played a role in creating the world as the "firstborn of all creation," we can trust that the universe is good. Even in frightening and chaotic times we can cling to the promise that "in him all things hold together."

Notice how many times this passage uses words like *first*, *before*, *head*, *beginning*. The message is clear: Jesus Christ has pre-eminence. But lest we begin to picture him as some amorphous deity in the clouds, verse 20 reminds us that it was Christ who lived among us as a human being, dying on a cross to redeem a broken world.

PRAYER: Reconciling God, thank you for the gift of your Son, the firstborn of all creation. Help me to put him first in my life. Amen.

Places of Holy Mystery

November 26–December 2, 2007 • *Benoni Silva-Netto*[‡]

MONDAY, NOVEMBER 26 • Read Isaiah 2:1-5

Metaphors are containers of meaning. The Bible leads our imagination to fascinating metaphors, many of which can excite our passion. The scripture passages for this week's meditations lift up for me the metaphor of "Holy Land Tour"—God's message from Jerusalem.

Many years ago I took a group of seminary students on a Holy Land tour. The meetings prior to our trip were times of keen awareness and exciting preparation. We shared our expectations, focused on scriptures related to the places we planned to visit, and became more intensely aware of current events in the Middle East.

This week's scripture passages invite us to journey through the *holy land*—not the geographical area of the Middle East but the places of holy mystery where God has a holy conversation with us through the coming of the Christ. It too is a journey that requires awareness and preparation.

In Isaiah 2 the journey takes us to the place of lasting peace. In this place we learn that God wills "to make things right" among all God's children. The swords of hate, revenge, and enmity will be transformed into shovels of productivity and creativity, "their spears into pruning hooks." God will turn hostility into hospitality, grief into grace, haunts into hopes, duels into duets, pain into gain, fear into faith, collisions into coalition, breakdowns into breakthrough.

PRAYER: O blessed Prince of Peace, may we seek and find your peace in sun and in shadow, in the darkness of the night and in the bright light of the day, in life and in death and wherever our feet and our faith take us in our journey. Amen.

[‡]Clergy member of the California-Nevada Annual Conference of The United Methodist Church; seminary faculty in the area of pastoral care and counseling; living in Hercules, California.

Many childhood memories fill the cloistered spaces of my consciousness with genuine joy and great thanksgiving. Growing up as a preacher's kid, the ritual of early Sunday mornings included my father's compelling voice saying, "It's time to go to church." For a long time I thought that my father got carried away in his religious practices. But in retrospect I realize that those invitations to "go to the house of the LORD" have directed my journey to the *holy land*, the places of sacred worship.

I became more profoundly and genuinely aware of the fact that God has over and over and in many different ways sought to converse with me. And when I enter the place of sacred worship, the meaningful conversations became occasions for significant conversions. Awareness has led to preparation. The awareness of God's presence empowers the transformation of how I prioritize my values, how I organize my relationships, how I discern my ultimate and significant concerns.

In this place of sacred worship "my heart can leap for joy," as the psalmist affirms, because God knows me more fully than I know myself. God knows the thoughts of my mind, the pains in my heart, the burdens on my shoulder, the tangled relationships I often find myself enmeshed in even before I can articulate them.

SUGGESTION FOR MEDITATION: **What attitude and feeling do you have when you prepare for worship? What do you anticipate? With whom are you bound in worship? With whom do you stand in solidarity? Before you attend worship again, consider these questions and be glad as you go in the presence of grace.**

PRAYER: **O Divine Redeemer, make the mundane places of our lives sacred, the ordinary activities holy, the common relationships occasions for holy communion through your grace and your presence. Amen.**

God through Christ comes into our lives in many ways and invites our awareness of God's coming and preparation for it. Paul (particularly in Eugene Peterson's translation of the Roman passage) presents this invitation to his readers in the most empathic and enthusiastic way.

Entering the season of Advent calls to mind once again that Christ came into our world through the birth of an infant many years ago whose birthday we celebrate annually. We use our gift of holy memory in our celebration of that event. But Christ comes to us now through the presence of the Holy Spirit working within us and around us. We use our gift of awareness in our celebration. We also hope for Christ's coming in final victory at the end of time. Even in Advent and Christmas we employ the gift of anticipation in our celebration.

Whether in the past, the present, or the future, our journey through this *holy land* tells us that God is "putting the finishing touches on the salvation work begun when we first believed" (Rom. 13:12, THE MESSAGE). It is a place of passionate work, and God wants us to be a part of it. We may be tempted to "major in the minors," lose track of time and doze off, waste and squander God's precious gift of time, or devote our physical and spiritual energies to senseless bickering about trivial matters. We overcome these temptations when, as Paul admonishes, we "dress [our]selves in Christ, and be up and about!" (THE MESSAGE)

PRAYER: You fashioned us, O God, to reflect the image of your Spirit, and we know that your Spirit moved and worked and created a truly wonderful world, a work still in progress because you continue to put the finishing touches on salvation. May we accept your invitation to be part of this work so that your "kindom" shall come upon this earth. Amen.

The Holy Land (Middle East) is a place of defining and transforming crises. Current events in that part of the world cause us to ask whether Jesus, who once walked upon that land, continues to be present in the midst of seemingly endless conflict and senseless war.

Our journey takes us not away or around crises and conflicts but through the bewildering chaos that seems to overwhelm our daily lives. And we are not always prepared for crises when they come. Whether it be like the great flood in Noah's time or Christ's coming while we work in the field or grind at the office mill, the crisis brought on by his arrival can be occasion for danger or opportunity, for joy or sorrow, for joyful laughter or gnashing of teeth.

Our capacity and willingness to be aware and to prepare makes a great difference in the meaning and significance of Christ's coming in our life. A visit from a teacher for a dedicated and well-prepared student occasions joy and celebration. The one who takes school work less seriously or as a painful experience would receive the visit with fear and anxiety or even apathy.

Many were the crisis moments in my life when I felt that the Holy Spirit had visited me; God's coming was a moment of joy and hope. Through those visits I know that God can write straight even on crooked lines. God can place the song of the rainbow within my heart even in the midst of despair and sorrow. Living in this *holy land* means that we live in uncertainty as well as expectation. We live always in God's time, which defines our anticipation of the future and our life in the present.

PRAYER: O God of infinite wisdom and great mercy, may the crises of our lives provide us with days and years full of meaning and a meaningful journey. Amen.

The *holy land* journey takes us to places of expectation. I remember being deeply impressed by the greatness of Abraham Lincoln. I dreamed of visiting the places in his life: his birthplace, the schools, the churches that nourished his spirit. And I thought, *What if in my visit to one of these places, the good man himself opened the door, invited me to come in, and offered to have conversation with me?* In this conversation he himself, not just a fleeting, illusory image, would reflect on his life events and the values, vision, and views that shaped his decisions—all the important things that I could only read about in the biography. My interpretation of his life and the history of this country would change drastically as I viewed the information no longer through the eyes of an author but through the lens of personal relationship.

The Christ who came in a specific time and place promised to come to us in the specific contexts of our lives. We meet him in the most unlikely places and at times when we least expect him to come. Who knows what door might open to reveal the Christ standing there ready to welcome us. So the Gospel writer advises us to stay awake and be alert. Be aware and be prepared.

Christ comes to us by the wayside and by the mountainside, among the tombs and in the midst of busy marketplaces, inside temples and on top of hills—often initially as a stranger but not for long. We meet him in person when we respond to his call to help make this world a loving place, to invest our time and energy and resources to help tame the world's savagery, to help establish the loving reign of God, and to share Christ's love and compassion for all of God's people.

PRAYER: We greet the future, O God, expecting your Spirit to break open the possibilities of love, compassion, justice, and peace in every situation and in every relationship. Help us to prepare and be ready. Amen.

Our tour of the *holy land* of mystery takes us on a route that we have traveled before as we anticipate Jesus' birth. Around the world people begin to focus on the journey of Joseph and Mary to Bethlehem. But it is not yet time for us to go to Bethlehem. We have another route to take.

Matthew 24:36-44 offers us the words of Jesus concerning the coming of the Son of Man. In some circles the events described are called the rapture. Best-selling books appear on fiction and nonfiction shelves, and all offer theories or descriptions of this Second Coming of the Christ. Some Christians spend much time in efforts to anticipate which world leader or world event will trigger this day of judgment. The speculation is nothing new; Christians in the first century saw Nero as the Antichrist who would trigger the apocalypse. Such speculation seems based on our human need for certainty and for predictability.

Against this need for certainty, Jesus simply invites us to live in preparedness. "The Son of Man is coming at an unexpected hour," he says. Earlier he states, "But about that day and hour no one knows, neither the angels of heaven, nor the Son. . . ." We live in a time between and a time undefined. To live without the certainty of answers and timetables means that we live without answers, only questions: When? Where? Why? Even deeper than these lies the question of whether I am serving God in love in all ways. Do I love my neighbors as I love myself? Is my life open to the surprises of grace?

Be ready. Be prepared. The Christ is coming at an unexpected hour. As we anticipate the celebration of Jesus' birth, we celebrate the grace of one moment in history. This other visit calls for a more revolutionary sense of anticipation. Jesus bids us live in the mystery of time and in the certainty of God's reign. Live in readiness!

PRAYER: O God, these places of holy mystery reveal Christ's presence with us as we travel from the womb to the tomb. May we be aware of Christ's arrival and be prepared. Amen.

FIRST SUNDAY OF ADVENT

The journey continues. No longer a tourist but a citizen, I find myself the unfinished work of God's creation and redemption. I was born in a fishing and farming village north of Manila in 1944. The intensity of the world war touched the life of our village in profoundly devastating ways. My family took refuge within the walls of a church in hopes that both the building and faith in God would provide protection and keep the members safe in the midst of the raging battle between the Japanese forces and the American army that sides with the Filipino guerrillas.

My mother gave birth to me in front of the altar of the church. My father, the pastor of this Methodist congregation, took this as a sign that God intended that I be dedicated to the work of pastoral ministry. He impressed that thought upon my mind as far back as I can remember.

My journey to the *holy land* took me through the restless and rebellious years of my youth, through the many crises and crossroads that ultimately led me to meet the Christ at a youth camp. There I came face-to-face with the profound meaning of God's redemptive design for my life. And God continues the finishing touches of God's salvation work every day I live.

As though a great painter has taken the blank canvas of my life to paint a magnificent picture, each day unfolds a variety of colors, some dark and some light, the blending of which seems to be a creation of beauty for which I am genuinely thankful. I hope that at the end of the day, when the painter is ready to put away the brush and end the task, that the last strokes will be exclamation points of amusement and amazement, of smiles and laughter, of thanksgiving and celebration.

PRAYER: O God, may we, catching a glimpse of your grace and the quietest hint of your presence, offer ourselves to the task of placing the finishing touches on the salvation work through Jesus Christ in the lives of those we meet in our journey. Amen.

The Way and Practice of Peace

December 3–9, 2007 • *Pamela D. Couture*[‡]

MONDAY, DECEMBER 3 • **Read Psalm 72:1-7, 18-19**

The modern world commonly associates monarchy with wealth, inherited privilege, custom and ritual—though usually at some distance from those political processes that actually make a difference in the lives of people. Not so in the Hebrew Scriptures where the king has a direct relationship with the people. The people look to him for fair judgment, protection, and sustenance in hard times. The expectations people have of the Jewish king are like, in the modern world, the expectations some United Methodist Africans have of their bishops. At dawn supplicants line up at the door of the bishop's house, asking for food, shelter, or healing. After addressing individual needs, the bishop may attend to projects that support the common good of the area. The needs of the suffering are always before him. Regardless of human frailty, the ideal of the one who can use the power of a leadership role to dispense justice, mercy, care for the poor, and deliverance of the needy inspires humility and awe.

The ideal of the king in the Hebrew Scriptures offers one of the finest visions of leadership: the leader is one who always keeps in mind the balance of power in the community, shoring up the power of those who are poor and vulnerable and curbing the power of those who have accrued power and use it in oppressive ways. The good and wise leader uses the power of office to care for the needs of each person in the community, to promote the common good, and to empower others for voice and participation.

PRAYER: God of kings and queens, guide the exercise of our responsibility in the various leadership roles in our lives, that we may be just and merciful. Amen.

[‡]Vice president for Academic Affairs and Dean, Saint Paul School of Theology; Kansas City, Missouri.

Read this passage again aloud. Breathe in and out with each phrase. Pray its cadence. Then focus on the meaning of the words—the beauty of the royal image. Jesse's royal lineage is remembered for its reach toward goodness; a new king will grow from its stock. This king will embody the most important virtues for leadership—wisdom, understanding, counsel, might, knowledge, and the fear of the Lord. His personal qualities will be beckoned forth by the Spirit of the Lord that rests upon him. He will not be fooled by appearances or tempted by deceit. This king will adjudicate conflicts, aware both of those who make themselves easily known and those who are hidden in the byways. This king will judge with the poor and the meek in mind.

Hurricane Katrina created a rare moment in the national life of the United States. The general public saw the poor and the meek—those who are normally hidden. Two years hence, many people from Louisiana and Mississippi know Katrina not as an event of the past but as a reality shaping their present. People have felt the effect of human judgments. The actions of various leaders may or may not have been generally helpful.

Where have those most affected by this disaster found leadership that approximates the measure of virtue of the messianic king for whose coming we now prepare? They have found it in those who take seriously their discipleship, in those who have responded "unofficially" with gifts of hope—food, shelter, and love. Let us call to mind the sights of the poor and the meek whose image may have receded. Let us meditate on the goodness of the messianic king we seek. Let us also seek to imitate the messianic king—the Christ—we have found. Let us disciple ourselves to Christ's wisdom, understanding, counsel, might, knowledge and the fear of the Lord.

PRAYER: Spirit of the Lord, bring to our view those who get ready attention and those who live in obscurity. Create us for wisdom that guides us to follow in Christ's ways. Amen.

WEDNESDAY, DECEMBER 5 • Read Isaiah 11:6-10

The king's exercise of virtue yields righteousness that seeks one aim: peace. "They will not hurt or destroy on all my holy mountain; for the earth will be full of the knowledge of the LORD as the waters cover the sea." In God's peace, power and vulnerability lie together. This peace does not ignore conflict or difference; rather, in this peace the vulnerability in power and the power of vulnerability become companions. Neither threatens the other; instead, the friendship of power and vulnerability transforms expected hostilities into deep, deep peace. When we read these ancient words, we can feel it: This peace is what God means for our lives.

When we translate this passage from ancient to contemporary human images, however, our feelings may change. Can we really imagine antagonists who lie down together? The grand dragon of the Ku Klux Klan and the African American baby; the CEO of the multinational fruit company and the farmworker; the leader of the religious right and the transgendered person; the leader of the religious left and an official of the Bush administration; the Palestinian and the Jew, the Japanese and the Korean, the Tutsi and the Hutu; the urban, suburban, and rural children of our countries sitting beside one another in the same school. Even desiring this peace threatens us. To seek this peace we would need to give up the hostility and self-righteousness that defines us. Is discipling ourselves to the messianic king not a call to seek the peace that he holds out before us, to work actively for this peace even when it means giving up our fears? Of whom are we most afraid?

PRAYER: Spirit of the Lord, disciple us in the ways that lead to your holy mountain. We pray now for our enemies, whom we name in our hearts. We pray for ourselves, that we may transform our hostilities and fears into an openness to your possibilities. Where there seems to be no way, help us find the way to your holy mountain. Amen.

"Repent, for the kingdom of heaven is at hand." In Advent and Lent the traditional purple color of altar vestments and clergy stoles reminds us these are seasons of preparation, repentance, and reshaping our lives. Some congregations have changed their Advent colors to a warmer, more inviting blue. How might this blue recall the meaning of repentance in Advent? God does not offer the opportunity for repentance to make us feel despondent about ourselves but to help us find new ways of living toward God's purposes—and in so doing, to feel and be reconciled, centered and whole. The opportunity for self-examination is a gift!

In Isaiah, God promises the peace of the holy mountain in elegant imagery; in Matthew, John the Baptist announces the nearness of the reign of God, where such peace is the rule rather than the exception. Repentance may have to do with remembering those we would rather forget. Sometimes, our conflicts with ourselves and our conflicts with persons with whom we have immediate relationships seem the most intractable. We find emotional ways to flee, to forget, to ignore our own participation in those conflicts. Other times, our social conflicts between persons of poverty and wealth, of different genders, races, sexual orientations, and of theological and faith divisions call us to examine the ways we rectify social conflict. Repentance means focusing in a sustained way on what, with God's help, we can change in ourselves rather than what we want to change in others. It also calls us to learn ways to engage constructively, rather than to flee from conflict. Have we remembered those whom we want to forget? Toward whom do we need to turn?

PRAYER: God, show me the face of those persons I would rather forget; show me the ways that I can live differently, toward your peace. Amen.

FRIDAY, DECEMBER 7 • Read Matthew 3:3

Matthew's reference to Isaiah 40:3 connects the end of Israel's exile with the coming of Jesus. In Isaiah the people have turned toward God; their time of penance is over, and God extends comfort for their suffering. John the Baptist's speech in Matthew joins the acts of human repentance with God's comfort. The deep connection between these actions shapes the ritual action of baptism that people are about to receive. In this action God's grace—understood in Wesleyan theology as prevenient (before we are aware of it), convicting (bringing us to God), justifying (forgiving and accepting), and sanctifying (helping us to live a renewed life)—presents itself fully.

In both our personal and social relationships, human beings tend to live as if we need to earn God's grace. How hard it is to live from a sense that as we turn toward God, God's comfort is immediately available! We experience that comfort when human beings extend it in a range of relationships, especially when we are unsure: when the family member we have neglected is glad to see us, when the colleague we have offended receives us rather than holding a grudge; when the stranger we have stereotyped explains our mistake rather than dismisses us. We experience God's forgiveness in all these actions, and we disciple ourselves to Christ when we extend comfort and patience where hostility is expected. These are the small acts of nonviolence and reconciliation that prepare us for the coming of the Prince of Peace.

PRAYER: Comforting God, we give thanks for the way you extend your surprising comfort through the scriptures, through other human beings, and even, at times, through us. Amen.

"John the Baptist dressed in camel's hair and ate locusts and wild honey." We hear these vivid and strange details as part of the Advent story so frequently that they are easily domesticated. But they do not simply add drama to the story. They speak to the heart of John the Baptist's prophetic religiosity. John eats and dresses simply, disdaining the feasts and pomp and circumstance of the Saduccees, Pharisees, and Roman elite. In so doing, he challenges their reliance on reputation, status, public piety, wealth, and political power—those aspects of human existence that so easily become idolatrous. (See Warren Carter, *Matthew and the Margins: A Sociopolitical and Religious Reading*, Orbis Books, 2000).

Most of us struggle with our sympathies with John the Baptist and his followers and our complicity in the contemporary equivalent of the power structures John challenges. Very little separates our realistic concerns for our livelihood from our idolatrous attachment to particular ways of eating and dressing that communicate status, reputation, and power. We easily forget that all that we have and are depends upon God's grace rather than on what we have personally earned. The dividing line between our gratitude for what we have and our excitement about what is superfluous is less clear during the holiday shopping season.

On one hand, we have genuine Advent desires to express our love for family, friends, and strangers in material gift-giving at Christmas. On the other hand, we know that our need for material gift-giving and receiving may not be motivated so much by a religious impulse as by the persuasiveness of advertisers and economic power brokers. Persons who have chosen voluntary poverty after the fashion of John the Baptist, including historical figures such as Francis of Assisi, John Wesley, and Dorothy Day, remind us that a godly life depends not on attachment to material possessions but on gratitude for what we have and our willingness to share with others.

PRAYER: **For our daily bread and for all that we have, we give thanks to you, O God. Amen.**

SECOND SUNDAY OF ADVENT

Some Christians assume that the scriptures of "former days"—the Hebrew Scriptures—are a testimony to be transcended. Not so. God's hope for harmony in Romans is born of the same hope for peace that the Hebrew Scriptures depict; the Hebrew Scriptures are offered by God to encourage and strengthen God's people in this hope. Imagine a diptych: the first half contains the collage of images of deep peace that illustrate the Hebrew Scriptures and the second half portrays the way of Christ and Christ's disciples. A frame separates them, rendering them as distinct images of peace. Still, these parts have an organic connection with each other. Neither half dominates the other, but the revelation of peace of the first half inspired the imagination of Jesus of Nazareth, the Jewish rabbi who led the Christian way. Regardless of this intimate relationship, Jews and Christians often stand in need of reconciliation with each other for the sake of the peace to which their scriptures point.

This week's scriptures have reassured us that God seeks to bring people who are separated from one another into relationship. As we busily prepare for and celebrate the Christian traditions through which we glorify God, we have the opportunity to encounter and appreciate the ways that people of other faiths offer their witness. Finite people encounter only one aspect of God's wholeness. People of different faiths offer one another a window toward God that may help us understand ourselves and the revelation God has provided through our particular scriptures. May we gain sight and insight from one another, following the way to peace.

PRAYER: Holy God, transform our religious hostility into the way and practice of peace. Amen.

Slow Down

December 10–16, 2007 • Lesley Powell Cooper[‡]

MONDAY, DECEMBER 10 • Read Isaiah 35:1-2, 5-7

Rain. Nose-dripping, umbrella-flipping, gray-sky, dreary rain. It has been raining torrents for seven days. I sit here nursing a cold, wishing that the rain would stop, and longing for the blue-sky, warm days of summer.

My mind wanders, visiting summers past. Our first year here we planted forty trees. Summer came with its searing Alabama heat, unbearable to me and death to my baby trees. What I would have given for this rain then! My young trees must have felt like the desert in Isaiah. When it finally did rain, I imagined them slurping their gratitude for the life-giving water. Just like me.

Many times I too have felt parched by times of loneliness and grief; times when no one seemed to appreciate me; times when parenting was gut-wrenchingly difficult. I was cracked, parched, and dry—soul dry. I longed for the water to "gush forth in [my] wilderness" (NIV).

During those times, God's rain started with one drop (a smile from a grocery clerk). And then another (a phone call). And another (an answered prayer). Before I knew it, I found myself in a shower of God's life-giving water. I drank it in as my trees drank, with slurps of gratitude. My "burning sand" became a "pool." My "thirsty ground" bubbled with God's spring (NIV).

Living water. God's sustenance.

During these dark midwinter days of Advent, whether we rush from one activity to the next or nurse a cold at home, let us take time to remember the droughts in our lives and dance with joy because God gives us the grace-filled rain of divine love.

PRAYER: Lord, we thank you for Jesus' life-giving water. Fill us up so that we can overflow for others. Amen.

[‡]Spiritual formation group and retreat leader, author; mem'
United Methodist Church, Montgomery, Alabama.

I woke up crabby this morning. A restless night, troubled by worries about today's responsibilities, has left me feeling grouchy. I turn on the Christmas lights and try to read today's Advent meditation, but I worry about getting everything done. I have to set up tables at the nursing home for my handbell choir. The Christmas cards need to be mailed. Did I remember to pay the power bill? Tonight is the last rehearsal for the children's musical. I have to finish making the shepherds' costumes. Our Sunday school party starts at 7:00. I need to make a squash casserole. Can we go caroling before the party?

What is the matter with me? I give up on my quiet time when the dog reminds me that she wants to go for her morning walk. Grudgingly I snap on her leash, and we head outside. The wreath has fallen off our front door. I ignore it.

The frigid gray-sky day makes me feel crabbier than ever, but suddenly the sun peeks from behind a cloud. I am warmed by its glorious heat, and it bathes my face in light as it sparkles on the puddles. Oh, God, thank you! We walk hand-in-hand, God's sun and I. The tension in my chest begins to relax. No longer focused on myself, I notice muddy footprints marching across the street—children's boots. A neighbor waves as he straps his toddler into the car seat. My dog perks up too. This sun isn't just for me. We share the comfort of God's warmth—all of us!

Thirty minutes of walking with God, and I feel like a new person. Verses 4-7 promise that God will take care of us. Blind, crippled, deaf, mute, parched—even crabby! We all fall under God's promise. My grumpiness simply confirms my self-centered failure to believe in that promise.

God takes care of us. During the dark midwinter days of the Advent season filled with overwhelming responsibilities, let us take the time to be warmed by God's Son.

PRAYER: Thank you, Lord, for the change that takes place in us when we walk with you. May we reflect Christ's love to everyone we encounter today. Amen.

Storms interrupt our lives when we least expect them. Today's hurricane interrupted everything on my schedule. My mother, who lives at the beach, has been evacuated to our home. The television, which is usually turned off, bombards us with nonstop weather updates. Treetops sway back and forth with the wind. Battery and candle ready, we sit waiting for the storm to build and the electricity to go off. Waiting with the weather anchor.

Storm sitting is such a helpless activity. This day the storm is outside. Often, though, the storm rages inside me: the emotional storm of waiting in an emergency room, a grief storm after terrible loss. Storms make us feel helpless. We can do nothing but wait. As I sit here watching the trees dance, I realize that God is with me in this hurricane—as in all the storms of my life.

Instead of spinning my emotional wheels in frustration, perhaps I might consider this an opportunity to slow down. I settle into my chair and quietly observe. My mother knits in front of the television. She doesn't seem to be anxious about her house at the beach. My husband gratefully accepts this opportunity to stay home and read a book. He isn't anxious either. Our dog takes a nap, unconcerned about the storm raging outside.

Might the worst storm be the one inside me? Could it be that God is forcing me to slow down? Too often I rush around, attempting to complete everything on my "to-do" list, creating anxiety storms for myself. But today is different. Today I will sit and be still. Slow down. Be still. Listen. I read the words: "Happy are those whose help is the God of Jacob." God is taking care of me in the midst of the storms—mine and nature's.

During the season of Advent the potential for storms is great. It is especially important to slow down during the holidays so that the Lord, who "who keeps faith forever," can calm our storm, no matter its cause.

Be still. Listen.

PRAYER: Slow us down, Lord. Calm our storms with your stillness. Amen.

I arrive late to church, and the balcony where I usually sit is full. I find a seat downstairs. A deep sigh escapes my soul. I can be still now. Rest and quiet—just what I need after a hectic week.

Sitting in this different place, I realize that pain surrounds me. An elderly man, bent with arthritis, shares the pew with me. I remember his younger and more vital years. He sits alone now; the wife who accompanied him is no longer here.

Here is Becky. Shriveled and bald, she has been fighting cancer for nearly twenty years. Recently she learned that the cancer is winning. How much longer will she be with us, Lord?

David and Beth sit near the front. Only a few of us know the struggles they have had with their children. No, not teenage children—grown ones. Will their anguish ever end, Lord?

John sits three rows in front of me with the young woman who broke up his marriage. How can he bring her to church, Lord? Doesn't he have any empathy for his ex-wife and children who sit in the balcony?

Pain. Pain. Pain. I realize that I am crying—weeping for the pain of us all. The sermon, based on the story of blind Bartimaeus, highlights Jesus' question: "What do you want me to do for you?"

"What do *you* want?" the minister asks. I imagine the answers from those around me:

"I want to see my wife one more time . . . "

"I want to be healed . . . "

"I want my children to be well . . . "

"I want my husband/Daddy back . . . "

The psalmist promises that God supports the cause of the oppressed, offers healing, and sustains the orphan and widow. We sit here together in the presence of the Great Physician, sharing our pain with one another and with God. We find peace here. Peace from the hurry. Peace from our worries. Peace in the midst of pain. And we find healing in the peace.

PRAYER: Thank you, Lord, for quiet and for those who share our pain with us. Amen.

I was in labor five days with my first child. They didn't induce me. I just had to wait. Night and day for five days I had contractions. No sleep. No rest. Constant work. The doctor termed it false labor. False or real didn't matter to me! I had been waiting nine months. My baby was three weeks late. And my labor was very, very long.

Waiting is hard.

At 3:10 A.M. on the fifth day, I finally prayed a prayer of desperation: "God, you're gonna have to help me. I can't do this any more." I didn't ask for an end to the labor—only for God's help to deal with it. Eight minutes later our daughter was born. Eight minutes! After months and weeks and days of waiting, God answered my prayer in a way that I never expected—quickly. The long wait ended.

Many times in life God answers our prayers with the word *wait*. This is, for me, very difficult. I would rather hurry things up and do it my own way.

But God says, "Wait." Just like the "farmer waits for the land to yield its valuable crop" (NIV), I had to wait for my baby's birth. Growth comes in the waiting. Growth in the mother's womb. Growth in the farmer's field. Growth in me. Growth in you. God uses this time to grow us.

And so we wait.

And we learn patience.

And we trust, knowing that God will meet us at the point of our greatest need.

And we learn that waiting is really a gift, . . . because we find God in the waiting.

PRAYER: During this season of waiting for the birth of your son, Lord, lead us to the place of peace where we wait for you. Amen.

She was a spunky little lady. At eighty, she swam laps every day in the pool. She loved people and they loved her. An academic, she studied everything from Merton to Progoff. Her hearing impairment allowed her hearing aid to become a means of instantaneous centering. Finger to ear, she would switch the hearing aid off—and that, quite simply, was that. She then found herself alone with God.

I met her during the last year of her life. A Catholic nun, she graciously agreed to do spiritual direction with three other Protestant women and me. I drove four hours each month to meet with her in a room that became holy ground.

She died unexpectedly at the end of our year together, the victim of a logging truck accident. Her funeral celebrated a life lived right. As her casket left the chapel, we stood as one—rich, poor, black, white, Mexican, Catholic, Methodist, priest, nun, and lay—and spontaneously applauded. I could almost hear a voice saying, "Well done, good and faithful servant." She didn't preach, but the way she had lived her life spoke volumes about who she was and Whom she served.

When John's disciples ask, "Are you the one?" Jesus does not give a long, complicated answer or genealogical outline. He tells them what he has done. Jesus' actions reveal who he is.

Christians' behavior during Advent suggests that we not only believe but also follow Jesus' teaching. We give freely to Angel Trees and Salvation Army Santas. During this season of giving, many willingly share time and money with those who need it; the rest of the year it's more difficult.

Jesus detailed for John's disciples a lifetime of service. His message to us might be, "Go and do likewise—not just during Advent, but year-round." Actions really do speak louder than words—for my Catholic nun, for Jesus, and for us.

PRAYER: May the words of our mouths, the meditations of our hearts, and the conduct of our lives be acceptable in your sight, O Lord, our Rock and our Redeemer. Amen.

THIRD SUNDAY OF ADVENT

He isn't a bad man. As a matter of fact, he is one of the most generous people I know. A good father and husband, he lives a very moral life. He works hard, gives freely, and loves his friends. If you didn't know him, you would say he's a good Christian.

But he isn't a Christian. He isn't anything, for that matter. He was not raised in the church, and a painful encounter with an overzealous evangelist ensured that he will probably never be a Christian. Does he believe in God? I think so—but I'm not sure. Occasionally he asks about my faith. I tread lightly, not wanting to repeat the evangelist's mistake. But I *do* tell him.

Sometimes in life we are called to plant a seed. We can't water it or provide the sunshine. We may never get to see the seed grow. But we plant the seed anyway, trusting that God will grow it. In the case of my friend, I may be the only person who plants a seed of faith in him. I pray that I will get to see it grow. But the growing is not my responsibility—only the planting.

John the Baptist is in prison when he sends his disciples to Jesus. He faces the end of his ministry near the close of his life. The Jews believed that before the Messiah came, Elijah would return to herald his coming. Jesus hails John as the herald when he alludes to Malachi 3:1; 4:5, "I am sending before you my messenger." But John doesn't get to see the fulfillment of his prophecy. He never sees the cross. He plants seeds heralding the coming of the Messiah that God sent him to plant. That is all.

Seed planting. We are called to plant seeds whenever we can. Seeds of kindness. Seeds of belief-sharing. Seeds of invitation. We plant them with faith that God will grow them. Like John, we may never see them grow, but we plant them anyway. The growing is God's job.

PRAYER: Creator God, thank you for the seeds of faith that you have planted in us. Prepare us to plant for others. Amen.

A Long Wait for Christ's Coming

December 17–23, 2007 • Michael O'Laughlin[‡]

MONDAY, DECEMBER 17 • Read Romans 1:1–7

Many people can pinpoint a moment in their past when they felt Christ's presence in a decisive, new way. That moment divided life into a BC and an AD. For many of us, life seemed different after that one moment when Christ entered our story and dwelt with us in a clearer way. In the AD years that follow, we look ahead, increasing in maturity and walking in the light. But let us stop and look back for a moment. As part of this Advent period, let us return to that BC time—before Christ was present to us. The Advent readings remind us of a time before the gospel could be recognized clearly by us or by anyone. It was another era, a time of gestation, of hidden clues, of latent possibilities.

This week's readings call for spiritual hindsight into misty beginnings: when we look back at the BC part of our life or the life of God's people, we see that Christ was indeed always there. Although often unseen or unheralded, he was not silent. Paul's opening declaration in the letter to the Romans states that the gospel of Christ was spoken long before by the prophets. Paul sees God's continuity and even the face of Jesus in the scrolls left behind by the great preachers of Israel's past.

Let us try to link our AD back to an earlier BC period. Christ has not changed, and thus he was always with us. This is indeed part of God's way, to lie in gestation and in waiting. Thus Christ lay once as a baby in a manger, waiting in silence for a mission that lay many years in the future.

PRAYER: **Help me, God, to see that you were always with me. Help me to remember the unclear and uncertain feeling of not knowing and to see that even in my earliest beginnings, you were near to me. Amen.**

[‡]Roman Catholic theologian and spiritual director, editor and author; living in Carlisle, Massachusetts.

Paul loses no time laying out Jesus' messianic qualifications. We have heard the words that Paul employs so often that for us they may have lost their punch, but let us try to imagine how serious, even audacious, this passage might have sounded to Paul's first readers. "Christ," used here as part of the name of Jesus, means "anointed one"; thus it is itself a messianic title. Also, Jesus descends from David, a claim vividly developed in the Gospels. "Does not the Scripture say that the Christ will come from David's family?" (John 7:42, NIV). As a descendant of the great king, Jesus brings all of biblical history to a climax.

The qualifications continue, but let us pause over the somewhat insignificant word *born*. Paul states that in human terms Jesus is born from the Davidic line. Elsewhere Paul says that Jesus is "born of a woman, born under the law" (Gal. 4:4). Why is this interesting? For one thing, Paul only mentions the birth of Jesus in passing. How paradoxical that from this small beginning would flower the richest of Christian meditations: The birth of Jesus, the story of God's incarnation and appearance on the universal stage, eventually becomes the centerpiece of Christian faith and culture.

Jesus' birth is ever at the heart of Christianity, so today let us hear again Paul's simple affirmation: Jesus was a son of the house of David. To be born means to be human, and thus Christ is truly one of us. We need not imagine that Jesus was some strange superman or cosmic intruder. He was born among us; this simple truth is the touchstone of Christmas.

PRAYER: **Dear Jesus, help me to see you as a human being, and help me to see your birth as the beginning of God's work of reconciliation with the world. Help me to sense more deeply that the world awaits God's redemption and you, God's redeemer. Amen.**

Outside my window the landscape is studded with granite boulders. The first settlers of this area stacked some of these into walls and fences. Others, too big to move, remain where retreating glaciers deposited them eons ago. The ancient ice rounded and shaped the rocks it left behind.

The Book of Psalms is much like the rocks beyond my window. It is our common prayerbook, shared by Christians with another people of the book, the Jews. No collection of prayers has been more often used or more deeply plumbed than the rolling cadences of the psalms. Through countless repetitions and countless applications they have given expression to our highest exaltations and our deepest sorrows. Over time the Psalms have also been rounded and shaped, given new meaning and new applications. Like huge rocks, they will always be with us, but we can observe the marks time has made in their shaping and their interpretation.

The psalmist cries for God to come like a shepherd to gather and lead the flock to safety. Suffering has gone on too long, and the people beseech God to intervene and save them from their foes. Our reading focuses upon a figure at God's "right hand," and the people urge God to reach out to touch and strengthen this one. Probably the ancient Israelites refer to the king, who serves as a mediator between the people and God. In later centuries the figure of the king and the messiah merge, and, with the coming of Jesus, the psalms became charged with Christological significance. Just as the granite boulders around me were shaped over time, many psalms took on wholly new meaning and importance when later applied to Christ. They become the songbook of the true king and the true son of the Father, who here is found at God's right hand—touched, strengthened, and confirmed.

PRAYER: Lord, help me to grow and change. Like Christ, I also need to be strengthened and confirmed by your touch. Amen.

I remember reading books as a teenager that explained how the Old Testament revealed Christ with amazing, uncanny precision. Like evidence in a court case, these books seemingly laid out verses to convince young believers that everything about Jesus was miraculously foretold. I would learn later that these passages were called "proof texts."

Proof texts are most important at a certain stage of faith development. When Christianity itself was in its youth, proof texts were considered *prima facie* evidence in the debate over the Messiah. Christians combed the Hebrew Scriptures to find verses with messianic content, and in today's passage they struck pure gold, the finest proof text of all: "Behold, a virgin is with child. She will bear a son, and you shall call his name Emmanuel." Remarkably, the name means, "God is with us." Thus you have the whole doctrine of the Incarnation in one prophetic verse—not only is the Messiah born of a virgin, he is recognized as God. In those communities that used the Greek version of the Bible this verse was so effective that Jewish authorities stopped recognizing the validity of Greek translations. It is one reason Jews favor Hebrew to this day.

Emanu in Hebrew means "with us," and *El* is a name for God that is also a component in names like Michael or Daniel. No other word I know better sums up the core of Christian truth—Emmanuel means God is with *us*. Not just with me, because Christ has come to all of us and holds all of us together —saints and sinners, young and old, rich and poor—all in unity. Christ comes to us as a reconciler and a unifier. Christ unites all, making new and setting free.

PRAYER: **Together we are transformed.**
O come, O come, Emmanuel, and ransom captive Israel.
We pray for the unity of Christ and the transformation of his people. Amen.

We have called this passage a proof text. In proof texting, sometimes New Testament writers link verses to Christ that originally had quite different meanings. They use them to refer to Jesus because of a different historical understanding. The first Christians did not simply link Hebrew Scriptures to Christ; they swept numerous religious concepts and holidays into the Christian camp. December 25 originally celebrated the birth of a Roman deity, Sol Invictus, rather than the birthday of Jesus.

This does not invalidate our celebration of Christmas, nor does it mean that Christians disavow the Old Testament. However, to understand God's ways more deeply, it is valuable to recognize the original intention of the writers of ancient Israel and appreciate the early Christians' later reinterpretation. The present text, so full of Christological meaning, originally related a prophecy made by Isaiah to the unbelieving king Ahaz. This king feared several neighboring kingdoms and did not trust in God's protection. Isaiah tells Ahaz to ask God for a sign, and Ahaz refuses. At this point Isaiah utters his fateful words: "Then God himself will give you a sign." Isaiah looks around the room and picks out a pregnant woman, who may have been the king's wife. He predicts that before the child she is expecting can tell right from wrong, God will have humbled the two kingdoms that Ahaz fears so deeply. The symbolic name of the child will be Emmanuel, meaning that God is indeed with Israel.

Perhaps you, like Ahaz, have felt caught by fear. The threats of terrorism and disease make us wonder whether the earth can sustain life. We wonder whether world leaders will seek peace rather than war. In our times of fear Isaiah continues to remind us of Emmanuel. God is indeed with us!

PRAYER: **Dear God, help me to understand the scriptures and the history of salvation. Give me an open heart with which to explore your word. Amen.**

Of the first three Gospels, Mark is the oldest. The Gospels of both Matthew and Luke expand Mark's briefer narrative. Both sacred writers decided to include the story of Jesus' birth. Matthew and Luke present the birth from different perspectives and offer independent witness. The Gospel writers want to record this miracle while making it clear that Christ was born a real human being.

Matthew tells the story from Joseph's perspective. Later in the story, Joseph has disappeared and only Mary is mentioned. This, then, is the one place in our story where Joseph, the father of Jesus, takes the spotlight. We learn that Joseph is an upright man and one to whom God spoke through dreams, both here and again in the following chapter. Mary's pregnancy represents a moral dilemma; Joseph finds himself engaged to a tainted woman. He resolves to divorce her informally to spare her disgrace. At this point he receives a revelation that Mary is pregnant through God's Holy Spirit and that her son must be called Jesus, because he will save his people from their sins.

In that day dreams were understood to communicate God's purpose much more than today, yet it is still admirable that Joseph, just as much as Mary, believed in and accepted God's intervention in his life and his world.

Is Matthew merely being patriarchal in focusing on Joseph, or does he wish to bring out the propriety and goodwill of the father of Jesus? In hindsight, the story of Jesus would be much poorer without this brief account of Joseph. We would do well to consider the quiet witness of Joseph, for he shows us facets of God's grace.

PRAYER: Help me to understand through Joseph's example the importance of having and being a father. Help me see in all parents a reflection of your providence. Amen.

FOURTH SUNDAY OF ADVENT

In one of the great dramatic moments of the twentieth century, a black preacher stood on the steps of the Lincoln Memorial facing a sea of yearning faces and announced that he had a "dream." As part of that memorable speech, he intoned, "We hold these truths to be self-evident, that all men are created equal," quoting, as everyone knew, from Thomas Jefferson's Declaration of Independence. That day Martin Luther King Jr. gave new life to those hallowed words. By invoking them, he made the civil rights movement a part of the fundamental American desire for freedom and equality.

In fact, King enlarged Jefferson's meaning, for Jefferson had meant that white landowners in the colonies were equal to their English counterparts. However, Jefferson's words took on new meaning over time, and they assumed their true significance only when Dr. King spoke them that day.

The same is true of the Emmanuel prophecy. It had been first spoken centuries before and in a different context. Once taken up by the early church, it now forms the climax of the story of Jesus' birth in the Gospel of Matthew. In its new context the meaning of the familiar words expands—the Messiah has come, and we see with astonishment that God is born incarnate among us! Prophets and kings come as witnesses of the birth of this wondrous child. His name is a common one, but it is also enriched and infused with heightened significance—*Jeshua* means "Yahweh will save." As the angel tells Joseph in this passage, this must be his name because he will save his people from their sins. We form part of an even larger sea of people longing for freedom and fulfillment, so let the gospel ring out in the heavens and in our hearts.

Behold, a new day is born! The Lord God walks among us and will save us from all evil! May God truly dwell in our hearts and reform our lives. Let us rejoice at his coming!

PRAYER: O God, we rejoice at your coming among us. Amen.

Unwrap the Gift!

December 24–30, 2007 • Hazelyn McComas[‡]

MONDAY, DECEMBER 24 • Read Luke 2:1-20

How precious the Bible is, for it contains the stories of God's self-revelation to men and women of faith who went before us. Such encounters are holy and defy description. Thus all scripture is a telling beyond expression and a hearing beyond comprehension. So it helps to think of the Bible as a place—a place where God and persons meet. That pushes me, as I read it, to stand in the place and reexperience the presence of God in their time and in mine.

Today we read again the wonderful Christmas story of a baby in the manger, angels in the sky, a pondering mother, and worshiping shepherds. The Luke passage is so familiar that we find it hard to *really* hear it. So let's try to be *in* that place on the night we are reading about. Imagine Mary's weariness and Joseph's anxiety as they settle into the stable. Feel the pains of birth and the warmth of the animals' breath. Experience the joy and release of the baby's delivery. See Mary and Joseph resting on clean hay, holding the baby close, thanking God.

Or stand with the shepherds under a night sky. As it grows brighter and brighter and a sense of holiness overwhelms us, peace and new hope begin to grow in our hearts. We experience what they did that night—the holy divine made visible as a baby who is God's love incarnate! We cannot understand this mystery, but today we can kneel by the manger and allow the presence of God in Jesus to flood our souls.

SUGGESTION FOR REFLECTION: **Reread Luke 2:5-20. See it as a place. Be present on that night. Allow the word to speak to your heart, and give thanks.**

[‡]Adjunct faculty, Upper Room Academy for Spiritual Formation, study leader at regional and conference Schools of Christian Mission, lay Bible teacher; living in Milwaukee, Wisconsin.

The apt symbol of the evangelist John is the eagle, for throughout the Gospel his words soar. They climb ever higher, ever closer to the reality of the Mystery Who Is God. Some say that the eagle can fly so high because it is the only creature that can look directly at the sun and not be blinded. Fact or fiction, it is an appropriate symbol, for John looks at Jesus and sees God. Not being blinded he also sees the most truly human being he knows. God incarnate—the Word made flesh—dwelling among us.

John struggles with "expressing the inexpressible," as Paul says and tells us about the Word. It is in the beginning, present when "God created the heavens and the earth." The Word was there with God—but John feels that is not enough. The Word *was* God. Nothing was made without the Word. The Word was the channel for life and light for all of creation.

Dark as our world may seem at any moment—our moment is a good one to think about—the light and the life of God and the Word have never been and will never be overcome! The light shines in the darkness, and the darkness will never put it out.

That's a Christmas gift to cherish. Unwrap it this year and hold it close. Meditate on it; learn to trust it. Trusting the Word stretches us until the trust, by the grace of God, becomes a deeper and deeper love. The presence of God becomes more and more real in our lives. God's light begins to shine through us. May it be so for us this Christmas and ever after.

PRAYER: Holy Light, shine in my life today. Shine through me for others. Teach me to walk as light in darkness. May my praise become your joy. Amen.

What an ecstatic exclamation of praise for all the glimpses of God's glory made visible to us! Caught up in a paroxysm of praise, the psalmist stretches human words to their utmost limit in the attempt to encompass all that God has done in the act of creation. What words could possibly suffice to thank such a God?

Starting with the heights of heaven, angels, and all the heavenly host, the psalmist moves through sun and stars to fire, snow and wind, mountains, trees, animals and birds, all the way down to the monsters of the deep. Finally we come to men and women, old and young, all of whom are called to praise the name of the Holy One, who not only created but is ever present, sustaining life forever.

How appropriate to read this poem on the day after Christmas, when we are newly aware of the magnitude of God's love for us. God took our human limitations and came to earth as one of us, so that we could truly see and know, love and follow our God. Each Christmas the miracle of the Incarnation blows my mind! If the psalmist stretched to find words to thank God for the creation, how much more must we stretch to find adequate words of praise to our God for the new creation given in the life, death, and resurrection of Jesus our Lord? But even more precious than creation and the gospel events is the reality of God's presence with us every day of our lives and the action of the Holy Spirit through us as we answer the call to be disciples in our time.

Prayer: Holy One, may my life be praise. Make me who you know I am and who you long for me to be. Only then may I be your disciple in my world; do as you will through me. In Jesus' precious name. Amen.

So often scripture reminds us that we are part of a people—the people of God. God most often revealed the divine self in the life of the people in Old Testament times. They came to count on God's gracious deeds and favor.

When the psalmist and the prophets want to describe God, they often use the Hebrew word *hesed*. It has many translations and a broader meaning than any English word. It appears as steadfast love, loving-kindness, mercy, devotion, loyalty, and faithfulness. It is God's faithfulness to the covenant made with our ancestors at the foot of Mount Sinai. God has brought them out of slavery in Egypt and saved them. God invites them into a covenant relationship: "I will be your God. Will you be my people?" A grateful people accept the new relationship, and God has remained faithful ever since, meeting us with love and mercy. The prophets continually ask the people if they are keeping their part of the bargain. Micah 6:8 asks, "What does the LORD require of you but to do justice, to love kindness, and to walk humbly with your God?" How are we keeping this commitment?

Jesus spoke of the covenant relationship in different words, but they mean the same thing. Jesus said, "The kingdom of God has come near; repent, and believe the good news." What is the kingdom but the rule, the sovereignty, of God? Jesus asked his followers and asks us today to choose God and to shape our lives so that we live under God's rule in the midst of our world. We are covenant people, blessed by God's *hesed* and challenged to show *hesed* to all the world.

SUGGESTION FOR REFLECTION: How do I experience God's *hesed* in my life? How do I reflect *hesed* to others? Ask God to work through you today.

We long for God; we search for the holy, looking for the extra-ordinary. Yet God is all around us, and we see the holy in the ordinary when we learn to look with the eyes of God. Mechtild of Magdeburg, an early mystic, said, "The moment of my spiritual awakening was the day I saw, and knew I saw, all things in God and God in all things."

How easy it is for us to see the masks without seeing and praising the God who is behind them! Isaiah is clear about the difference when he says, "It was no messenger or angel but [God's] presence that saved them; . . . lifted them up and carried them." As we walk through our daily joys and sorrows, the presence of God becomes the most precious reality of our lives. God is always with us and never leaves us. God cries when we cry and holds us up when we falter. The holy Presence is our constant companion. God be praised!

In fact, God's name is God's promise. The Hebrew letters YHWH are a form of the verb "to be" and have traditionally been translated as "I AM THAT I AM." But Gerhard Von Rad, an Old Testament scholar, tells us that the scriptures never speak of God in the abstract but always in the relational. So the name is better translated as "I am here with you." "I am here with you" is the very name of our God!

The presence of God—God's *hesed* toward us—is unchanging and eternal. God is righteous and faithful to the covenant. In response, will we allow God to shape our lives after the life of Jesus?

PRAYER: O come, O come, Emmanuel, and remake us in your image. Amen.

Within several decades of Jesus' death and resurrection, the author of Hebrews addressed a group of Jewish-Christian believers. They were asking an age-old question, so beautifully stated in Psalm 8:3-5:

When I look at your heavens, the work of your fingers,
the moon and the stars that you have established;
what are human beings that you are mindful of them,
mortals ? that you care for them?
Yet you have made them a little lower than God,
and crowned them with glory and honor.

By faith and belief that God had come as Jesus, fully divine and fully human, the writer assures the Hebrews that they are now brothers and sisters of Christ. As Jesus shared our life with its joys and its sufferings, so we now share in Jesus' life. The wonderful implication of that is that we are truly children of God! We share God, our Parent! We are related! All of us are family!

The image of the pioneer of our salvation made perfect, mature, completely like us and completely like God through suffering, is a beacon before us in all the dark places of our life and our world. God knows us; God loves us; God suffers with us; God needs our hands, our wills, our voices to confront the suffering of the world—to make life better for all our sisters and brothers everywhere.

We are all children of God, and God intends good for us all. God is always with us in this work. Verse 18 assures us, "Because he himself was tested by what he suffered, he is able to help those who are being tested."

SUGGESTION FOR REFLECTION: **What suffering will God ask me to be present to today? Dare I trust God enough to do something about it? How might I rely on God's willingness to use me, and will I be subject to God's leading?**

God's plan to dwell among us involves someone's faithful willingness to do what God asks. In Luke's Gospel we see in Mary a woman of perfect faith: "Here am I, the servant of the Lord; let it be with me according to your word." In Matthew, we see in Joseph a righteous man who obeys God's commands exactly and immediately. Such perfect obedience is rare, even in scripture!

Joseph is not only righteous; he is kind. He is neither legalistic nor judgmental, as so many "righteous" people often are. When he discovers Mary's pregnancy, he wishes not to shame her as the law permits but to free her quietly from her bonds to him. When an angel of God comes to Joseph in a dream, Joseph abandons his plan and obeys the voice of God. He takes Mary as his wife and becomes part of the salvation story.

At God's command, Joseph gets up in the middle of the night and takes his family away from all they know into Egypt. They become exiles, refugees—surely not a role they would have chosen for themselves but one shared by millions of families in our world today! They act in trust and obedience to the divine voice. Years later, in God's time, Joseph gets up again and returns with his family to the land of Israel. God and he decide that Nazareth will be safer than Bethlehem, so there he goes.

Righteousness enables Joseph to be flexible, open to dreams, ready to hear a new or unlikely word from God, and courageous enough to obey it. What a model for us in our time! When we live according to this model, God can best use us today.

PRAYER: Holy One, give us obedient, loving, caring hearts so that, upheld by your presence, we may become your will in our world. In Jesus' precious name. Amen.

Sing a New Song

December 31, 2007 • Roland Rink[‡]

MONDAY, DECEMBER 31 • Read Ecclesiastes 3:1-13

As the clock ticks toward midnight, the song that is this old year rapidly begins to fade. The writer of Ecclesiastes senses and exposes the turmoil of our human condition. As we reflect on the past twelve months, life seems to have oscillated from one extreme to the other. In retrospect, it seems as if there really has been a time for everything and a season for every activity under heaven. We have planted, we have uprooted; we have wept, we have laughed; we have mourned, we have danced; we have been silent and we have spoken. We have been alive.

What have we gained from all the worry, anxiety, and busyness we have allowed ourselves to become enmeshed in over the past twelve months? Why have we not trusted God—the one who has made everything beautiful in its time, who has set eternity in the hearts of all humanity. We have not begun to fathom what God has accomplished during this past year. More often than not, we've simply been too busy, too tired, too distracted.

Yet, despite all the distractions of the world, our loving God has persisted with us! God waits patiently for us to remember that we are God's beloved children. As the world prepares to send expensive fireworks hurtling into the sky to mark the end of the old year, can we find it in our hearts to light a single candle on behalf of the refugee, the poor, the humble, the disenfranchised? As the clock ticks toward midnight, the song that is this old year thankfully begins to fade.

PRAYER: Loving God, we have not loved you with our whole heart. We have been distracted by too many things to hear your voice or sense your presence in the everyday. Forgive us we pray. Lord, help us to sing a new song. Amen.

[‡]Coordinator of Upper Room publishing on the African continent; living in Johannesburg, South Africa.

The Revised Common Lectionary‡ for 2007
Year C—Advent / Christmas Year A
(Disciplines Edition)

January 1–7
BAPTISM OF THE LORD
Isaiah 43:1-7
Psalm 29
Acts 8:14-17
Luke 3:15-17, 21-22

> **January 1**
> **New Year's Day**
> Ecclesiastes 3:1-13
> Psalm 8
> Revelation 21:1-6a
> Matthew 25:31-46

> **January 6**
> **EPIPHANY**
> Isaiah 60:1-6
> Psalm 72:1-7, 10-14
> Ephesians 3:1-12
> Matthew 2:1-12

January 8–14
Isaiah 62:1-5
Psalm 36:5-10
1 Corinthians 12:1-11
John 2:1-11

January 15–21
Nehemiah 8:1-3, 5-6, 8-10
Psalm 19
1 Corinthians 12:12-31a
Luke 4:14-21

---

‡Copyright © 1992 by the
Consultation on Common Texts
(CCT). All rights reserved. Reprinted
by permission.

January 22–28
Jeremiah 1:4-10
Psalm 71:1-6
1 Corinthians 13:1-13
Luke 4:21-30

January 29–February 4
Isaiah 6:1-13
Psalm 138
1 Corinthians 15:1-11
Luke 5:1-11

February 5–11
Jeremiah 17:5-10
Psalm 1
1 Corinthians 15:12-20
Luke 6:17-26

February 12–18
THE TRANSFIGURATION
Exodus 34:29-35
Psalm 99
2 Corinthians 3:12–4:2
Luke 9:28-43

February 19–25
FIRST SUNDAY IN LENT
Deuteronomy 26:1-11
Psalm 91:1-2, 9-16
Romans 10:8b-13
Luke 4:1-13

> **February 21**
> **ASH WEDNESDAY**
> Joel 2:1-2, 12-17
> (*or* Isaiah 58:1-12)
> Psalm 51:1-17
> 2 Corinthians 5:20b–6:10
> Matthew 6:1-6, 16-21

February 26–March 4
SECOND SUNDAY IN LENT
Genesis 15:1-12, 17-18
Psalm 27
Philippians 3:17–4:1
Luke 13:31-35
  (*or* Luke 9:28-36)

March 5–11
THIRD SUNDAY IN LENT
Isaiah 55:1-9
Psalm 63:1-8
1 Corinthians 10:1-13
Luke 13:1-9

March 12–18
FOURTH SUNDAY IN LENT
Joshua 5:9-12
Psalm 32
2 Corinthians 5:16-21
Luke 15:1-3, 11*b*-32

March 19–25
FIFTH SUNDAY IN LENT
Isaiah 43:16-21
Psalm 126
Philippians 3:4*b*-14
John 12:1-8

March 26–April 1
PALM/PASSION SUNDAY

  Liturgy of the Palms
  Luke 19:28-40
  Psalm 118:1-2, 19-29

  Liturgy of the Passion
  Isaiah 50:4-9*a*
  Psalm 31:9-16
  Philippians 2:5-11
  Luke 22:14–23:56
    (*or* Luke 23:1-49)

April 2–8
HOLY WEEK
  Monday
  Isaiah 42:1-9
  Psalm 36:5-11
  Hebrews 9:11-15
  John 12:1-11

Tuesday
Isaiah 49:1-7
Psalm 71:1-14
1 Corinthians 1:18-31
John 12:20-36

Wednesday
Isaiah 50:4-9*a*
Psalm 70
Hebrews 12:1-3
John 13:21-32

Maundy Thursday
Exodus 12:1-14
Psalm 116:1-2, 12-19
1 Corinthians 11:23-26
John 13:1-17, 31*b*-35

Good Friday
Isaiah 52:13–53:12
Psalm 22
Hebrews 10:16-25
John 18:1–19:42

Holy Saturday
Job 14:1–14
Psalm 31:1-4, 15-16
1 Peter 4:1-8
Matthew 27:57-66

April 8
Easter Sunday
Acts 10:34-43
  (*or* Isaiah 65:17-25)
Psalm 118:1-2, 14-24
1 Corinthians 15:19-26
John 20:1-18
  (*or* Luke 24:1-12)

April 9–15
Acts 5:27-32
Psalm 150
Revelation 1:4-8
John 20:19-31

April 16–22
Acts 9:1-20
Psalm 30
Revelation 5:11-14
John 21:1-19

April 23–29
Acts 9:36-43
Psalm 23
Revelation 7:9-17
John 10:22-30

April 30–May 6
Acts 11:1-18
Psalm 148
Revelation 21:1-6
John 13:31-35

May 7–13
Acts 16:9-15
Psalm 67
Revelation 21:10, 22–22:5
John 14:23-29
    (or John 5:1-9)

May 14–20
Acts 16:16-34
Psalm 97
Revelation 22:12-14, 16-17, 20-21
John 17:20-26

May 17
ASCENSION DAY
(These readings may be used Sunday, May 20.)
Acts 1:1-11
Psalm 47 (or Psalm 110)
Ephesians 1:15-23
Luke 24:44-53

May 21–27
PENTECOST
Acts 2:1-21
Psalm 104:24-34, 35b
Romans 8:14-17
John 14:8-17, (25-27)

May 28–June 3
TRINITY SUNDAY
Proverbs 8:1-4, 22-31
Psalm 8
Romans 5:1-5
John 16:12-15

June 4–10
1 Kings 17:8-24
Psalm 146
Galatians 1:11-24
Luke 7:11–17

June 11–17
1 Kings 21:1-21a
Psalm 5:1-8
Galatians 2:15-21
Luke 7:36–8:3

June 18–24
1 Kings 19:1-15a
Psalm 42
Galatians 3:23-29
Luke 8:26-39

June 25–July 1
2 Kings 2:1-2, 6-14
Psalm 77:1-2, 11-20
Galatians 5:1, 13-25
Luke 9:51-62

July 2–8
2 Kings 5:1-14
Psalm 30
Galatians 6:1-16
Luke 10:1-11, 16-20

July 9–15
Amos 7:7-17
Psalm 82
Colossians 1:1-14
Luke 10:25-37

July 16–22
Amos 8:1-12
Psalm 52
Colossians 1:15-28
Luke 10:38-42

July 23–29
Hosea 1:2-10
Psalm 85
Colossians 2:6-19
Luke 11:1-13

July 30–August 5
Hosea 11:1-11
Psalm 107:1-9, 43
Colossians 3:1-11
Luke 12:13-21

August 6–12
Isaiah 1:1, 10-20
Psalm 50:1-8, 22-23
Hebrews 11:1-3, 8-16
Luke 12:32-40

August 13–19
Isaiah 5:1-7
Psalm 80:1-2, 8-19
Hebrews 11:29–12:2
Luke 12:49-56

August 20–26
Jeremiah 1:4-10
Psalm 71:1-6
Hebrews 12:18-29
Luke 13:10-17

August 27–September 2
Jeremiah 2:4-13
Psalm 81:1, 10-16
Hebrews 13:1-8, 15-16
Luke 14:1, 7-14

September 3–9
Jeremiah 18:1-11
Psalm 139:1-6, 13-18
Philemon 1-21
Luke 14:25-33

September 10–16
Jeremiah 4:11-12, 22-28
Psalm 14
1 Timothy 1:12-17
Luke 15:1-10

September 17–23
Jeremiah 8:18–9:1
Psalm 79:1-9
1 Timothy 2:1-7
Luke 16:1-13

September 24–30
Jeremiah 32:1-3a, 6-15
Psalm 91:1-6, 14-16
1 Timothy 6:6-19
Luke 16:19-31

October 1–7
Lamentations 1:1-6
Psalm 137
2 Timothy 1:1-14
Luke 17:5-10

October 8–14
Jeremiah 29:1, 4-7
Psalm 66:1-12
2 Timothy 2:8-15
Luke 17:11-19

October 8
Thanksgiving Day, Canada
Deuteronomy 26:1-11
Psalm 100
Philippians 4:4-9
John 6:25-35

October 15–21
Jeremiah 31:27-34
Psalm 119:97-104
2 Timothy 3:14–4:5
Luke 18:1-8

October 22–28
Joel 2:23-32
Psalm 65
2 Timothy 4:6-8, 16-18
Luke 18:9-14

October 29–November 4
Habakkuk 1:1-4; 2:1-4
Psalm 119:137-144
2 Thessalonians 1:1-4, 11-12
Luke 19:1-10

November 1
ALL SAINTS DAY
(May be used Sunday, Nov. 4.)
Daniel 7:1-3, 15-18
Psalm 149 (*or* Psalm 150)
Ephesians 1:11-23
Luke 6:20-31

November 5–11
Haggai 1:15*b*–2:9
Psalm 145:1-5, 17-21
2 Thessalonians 2:1-5, 13-17
Luke 20:27-38

November 12–18
Isaiah 65:17-25
Isaiah 12 (*or* Psalm 118)
2 Thessalonians 3:6-13
Luke 21:5-19

November 19–25
REIGN OF CHRIST
Jeremiah 23:1-6
Luke 1:68-79
Colossians 1:11-20
Luke 23:33-43

> **November 22**
> **THANKSGIVING DAY (USA)**
> Deuteronomy 26:1-11
> Psalm 100
> Philippians 4:4-9
> John 6:25-35

November 26–December 2
FIRST SUNDAY OF ADVENT
Isaiah 2:1-5
Psalm 122
Romans 13:11-14
Matthew 24:36-44

December 3–9
SECOND SUNDAY OF ADVENT
Isaiah 11:1-10
Psalm 72:1-7, 18-19
Romans 15:4-13
Matthew 3:1-12

December 10–16
THIRD SUNDAY OF ADVENT
Isaiah 35:1-10
Psalm 146:5-10
(*or* Luke 1:47-55)
James 5:7-10
Matthew 11:2-11

December 17–23
FOURTH SUNDAY OF ADVENT
Isaiah 7:10-16
Psalm 80:1-7, 17-19
Romans 1:1-7
Matthew 1:18-25

December 24–30
FIRST SUNDAY AFTER
CHRISTMAS DAY
Isaiah 63:7-9
Psalm 148
Hebrews 2:10-18
Matthew 2:13-23

> **December 24**
> **CHRISTMAS EVE**
> Isaiah 9:2-7
> Psalm 96
> Titus 2:11-14
> Luke 2:1-20

> **December 25**
> **CHRISTMAS DAY**
> Isaiah 52:7-10
> Psalm 98
> Hebrews 1:1-12
> John 1:1-14

December 31–January 6
Jeremiah 31:7-14
Psalm 147:12-20
Ephesians 1:3-14
John 1:1-18